DOCUMENTING A PROVINCE:

THE ARCHIVES OF ONTARIO AT 100

CHRONIQUE D'UNE PROVINCE :

LE CENTENAIRE DES ARCHIVES PUBLIQUES DE L'ONTARIO

The Archives of Ontario proudly dedicates this commemorative anniversary book to Ontario's first Archivist – Alexander Fraser

Les Archives publiques de l'Ontario sont fières de dédier cet ouvrage au premier archiviste de l'Ontario, Alexander Fraser

DOCUMENTING A PROVINCE
THE ARCHIVES OF ONTARIO AT 100

CHRONIQUE D'UNE PROVINCE
LE CENTENAIRE DES
ARCHIVES PUBLIQUES DE L'ONTARIO

Printed and Bound by University of Toronto Press
Printed in Canada

Imprimé et relié par les Presses de l'Université de Toronto
Imprimé au Canada

ISBN 0-8020-8953-4

Canadian Cataloguing in Publication Data
Données de catalogage avant publication (Canada)

National Library of Canada Cataloguing in Publication

Documenting a province : the Archives of Ontario at 100 – Chronique d'une province :
le centenaire des Archives publiques de l'Ontario.

Text in English and French.
ISBN 0-8020-8953-4

1. Archives of Ontario. 2. Ontario – Archival resources.
3. Archival resources – Ontario – Toronto.   I. Archives of Ontario   II. Title: Chronique d'une province.

CD3645.065D63 2003   027.0713   C2003-906064-0E

Catalogage avant publication de la Bibliothèque nationale du Canada

Documenting a province : the Archives of Ontario at 100 – Chronique d'une province :
le centenaire des Archives publiques de l'Ontario.

Texte en anglais et en français.
ISBN 0-8020-8953-4

1. Archives publiques de l'Ontario. 2. Ontario – Fonds d'archives.
3. Fonds d'archives – Ontario – Toronto.   I. Archives publiques de l'Ontario
II. Titre: Chronique d'une province.

CD3645.O65D63 2003   027.0713   C2003-906064-0F

Contents

Table des matières

Foreword

Avant-propos

It is my great pleasure to present the Archives of Ontario's commemorative anniversary book.

Ontario is a province steeped in history and enriched by the many ancestries, cultures and beliefs that define its identity. Records gathered by the Archives of Ontario and represented in this book tell many stories of the people who have contributed to the development of our province as a democratic society.

The Archives has provided all Ontarians with a window into history starting with the appointment of Alexander Fraser as the first provincial archivist in 1903. Since then, the Archives of Ontario has been collecting close to three centuries worth of history, from the bold Upper Canada era to the vibrant times of 21st century Ontario.

As the Archives of Ontario celebrates its 100th anniversary, I would like to commend the work of the staff who, over several decades, have contributed to making the Archives the primary source of Ontario's documentary memory.

This commemorative book is a tribute to their work and a reminder that archives are the gift of one generation to another. They help us remember where we come from, who we are and the role each one of us plays in making Ontario's history.

Dalton McGuinty, MPP
Premier of Ontario

Je suis très heureux de présenter l'ouvrage commémoratif du centenaire des Archives publiques de l'Ontario.

L'Ontario est une province pétrie d'histoire, et rendue plus riche par les nombreuses origines, cultures et croyances qui définissent son identité. Les documents amassés par les Archives publiques de l'Ontario et représentés dans ce livre renferment nombre d'histoires de personnes qui ont contribué à faire de notre province une société démocratique.

Les Archives sont l'observatoire de notre évolution depuis 1903, date de nomination d'Alexander Fraser comme premier archiviste de la province. Depuis lors, les Archives publiques de l'Ontario font l'acquisition de documents qui témoignent de près de trois siècles d'histoire ontarienne, de la vigueur du Haut-Canada au dynamisme de l'Ontario du 21e siècle.

À l'occasion du centenaire des Archives publiques de l'Ontario, je tiens à faire l'éloge de leur personnel, qui contribue depuis plusieurs décennies à faire des Archives la source première de la mémoire documentaire de l'Ontario.

Cet ouvrage commémoratif se veut un hommage rendu au travail du personnel des Archives et un rappel que les archives sont le don d'une génération à une autre. Elles nous aident à nous rappeler d'où nous venons, qui nous sommes et comment chacun et chacune d'entre nous écrit l'histoire de l'Ontario.

Le premier ministre de l'Ontario,
Dalton McGuinty, député

Honour the Past – Imagine the Future

Pour honorer le passé et inventer l'avenir

For a hundred years the Archives of Ontario has been gathering and preserving the records that comprise the collective memory of our province. These records document our origins, highlight our evolving history, and provide essential evidence of the legitimacy of our government and of our rights as citizens. The Archives preserves these records for you because they represent our past, but more importantly, they are the foundation for our future. A society that ignores its documentary heritage, or impedes access to this heritage, denies itself a rich source of information, knowledge and experience. That is why archives are so vitally important. Knowledge is power, and in a free and democratic society this power belongs to the people.

In spite of the vital role we play in our society, it is true that few Ontarians are familiar with the Archives of Ontario, and many have never considered using the precious public legacy that the Archives safeguards. This is unfortunate. We may take our freedoms, our rights and our entitlements for granted – even assume that they will always be there. But history instructs us that we must not be complacent. The documents held by the Archives are the fundamental evidence of who we are and where we came from. In our private lives, we know how important it is to keep the right records to protect our possessions, our health and our personal history. Once lost, they may be gone forever. Public documents are no less important, and it is the mission of the Archives of Ontario to acquire and make available the critical government records that protect all the citizens of our province.

Public records are not the only ones worth keeping though, and while the Archives of Ontario is here for you, we also depend upon you. Browse through these pages and notice how many of the documents, photographs and paintings have come to the Archives from individuals, families and private societies and associations. Donations of personal and family papers, business records, and the accumulated holdings of architectural and photographic firms, for example, are essential components of our historical evolution. They complement our government records and help us to understand the amazing complexity of our lives. Private benefactors have been extremely generous to the Archives and we are all richer for it.

As the Archives of Ontario embarks on its second century, we hope to make everyone more aware of the wealth of our collections, and what these records mean to you. Researchers from all walks of life have already used our holdings to accomplish such diverse aims as: establishing a land claim, detecting a long-lost relative, decorating a period movie scene, or creating a character for a novel. One never knows where a bit of time spent at the Archives may lead! This publication is one way for us to connect with you, and share some of the millions of treasures that can be found in the Archives. In these pages you will see important government documents that mark symbolic moments in our history, and more humble records that trace the minutiae of daily life. We think that you will be surprised and delighted to discover the incredible range and diversity of our holdings, and we encourage you to learn more by visiting us. Make the Archives a part of your life – your life is what we are all about.

Miriam McTiernan
Archivist of Ontario

Depuis un siècle, les Archives publiques de l'Ontario réunissent et conservent des documents qui constituent la mémoire collective de notre province. Ces documents renseignent sur nos origines, éclairent notre histoire en devenir et témoignent du caractère légitime de notre gouvernement et de nos droits de citoyens. Les Archives conservent ces documents en notre nom, parce qu'ils représentent notre passé, et, ce qui est peut-être encore plus vital, parce qu'ils sont les fondements de notre avenir. Une société qui fait fi de son patrimoine documentaire ou qui en entrave l'accès se prive d'une riche source d'information, de connaissances et d'expérience. Voilà pourquoi les Archives sont d'une telle importance. Le savoir, c'est le pouvoir, et, dans une société libre et démocratique, ce pouvoir appartient à la population.

Malgré le rôle capital de l'établissement dans notre société, relativement peu de citoyens connaissent les Archives et un bon nombre n'ont jamais envisagé une utilisation quelconque du précieux patrimoine public qui s'y trouve. Il faut le déplorer. Nous tenons bien souvent pour acquis – et ce, pour toujours – nos droits et nos libertés. Or, l'histoire nous enseigne qu'il faut se garder de ce genre de présomption. Les documents conservés aux Archives sont la preuve fondamentale de notre identité et de nos origines. Dans notre vie personnelle, nous savons combien il est important de détenir les documents nécessaires à la sauvegarde de nos biens, de notre santé et de nos antécédents personnels. Une fois égarés, ils sont parfois irrémédiablement disparus. Les documents publics ne sont pas moins importants, et c'est la mission des Archives publiques de l'Ontario de réunir et de rendre accessibles les principaux documents gouvernementaux qui assurent la protection des citoyens de notre province.

Les documents publics ne sont pas les seuls dignes de préservation, toutefois; notre établissement est certes à votre service, mais il dépend aussi de votre apport. Il suffit de feuilleter ces pages, pour constater qu'une foule de documents, photographies et œuvres d'art ont été offerts aux Archives par des particuliers, familles, sociétés et associations privées. Les dons d'archives personnelles et familiales, de dossiers d'entreprise et de fonds cumulatifs de cabinets d'architectes et de photographes, par exemple, forment des volets essentiels de notre évolution au fil des ans. Ces compléments de nos documents gouvernementaux nous aident à comprendre l'étonnante complexité de nos vies. Les particuliers ont été extrêmement généreux à l'égard des Archives, ce qui est à notre avantage à tous.

À l'orée du deuxième siècle d'existence des

Archives publiques de l'Ontario, nous aspirons à faire mieux connaître à la population les richesses de nos collections et la signification de ces documents pour chacun d'entre nous. Des chercheurs de tous horizons ont déjà eu recours à nos collections à des fins aussi diverses que les suivantes : fonder une revendication foncière, retracer un lointain parent, meubler une scène de film d'époque, étoffer un personnage de roman. Qui sait à quoi peuvent mener quelques heures passées aux Archives! La présente publication est une façon pour nous de vous joindre et de vous inviter à partager quelques-uns des millions de trésors que renferment les Archives. En parcourant ces pages, vous apercevrez des documents gouvernementaux de marque, qui signalent des étapes symboliques de notre histoire, ainsi que des pièces plus modestes, qui font revivre les gestes du quotidien. À n'en pas douter, vous serez surpris et émerveillé face à l'éventail et à la diversité inimaginables de nos fonds, et nous vous encourageons à poursuivre l'exploration en nous rendant visite. Pourquoi ne pas intégrer les Archives à votre vie – après tout, c'est votre vie qui est notre raison d'être.

L'archiviste de l'Ontario,
Miriam McTiernan

Acknowledgements

Remerciements

The development of this commemorative anniversary book began in the spring 2002. Over the past year and a half, numerous staff at the Archives of Ontario contributed their knowledge, creativity and enthusiasm to develop and produce this publication. Through a remarkable team effort, they transformed a collage of words and images into a journey that not only highlights the Archives collection but documents our province as well.

I would like to recognize the following staff for their dedication to this project and their tireless efforts: Suzy Aston, Scott Barrie, Jayne Best, James Bowers, Stewart Boden, Christine Bourolias, Greg Brown, Lawrence Chapman, Ralph Coram, Michele Dale, Mark Epp, Sandra Ferguson, James Gorton, Owen Jenkins, Mary Ledwell, Serge Paquet, Gillian Reddyhoff, Anastasia Rodgers, Lisa Singer, Alysson Storey and Jim Suderman.

A special recognition and thanks to Curtis Fahey for his structural editing services and helping us to tell our story through one voice.

Finally, my sincere personal thanks to Peggy Mooney and Agatha Garcia-Wright whose dedication and leadership ensured that all aspects of this challenging and complex undertaking were completed in a timely and professional manner.

Miriam McTiernan
Archivist of Ontario

Notre ouvrage commémoratif a commencé à prendre forme au printemps 2002. Au cours de la dernière année et demie, de nombreux employés des Archives publiques de l'Ontario ont conjugué leurs connaissances, leur créativité et leur enthousiasme dans le but d'élaborer et de réaliser cette publication. Grâce à un remarquable travail d'équipe, ils et elles ont réussi à transformer une simple juxtaposition de mots et d'images en un périple exploratoire qui non seulement met en valeur notre collection, mais raconte superbement notre province.

Je tiens à souligner le dévouement et le labeur inlassable qu'ont investis dans le projet les employés dont le nom suit : Suzy Aston, Scott Barrie, Jayne Best, James Bowers, Stewart Boden, Christine Bourolias, Greg Brown, Lawrence Chapman, Ralph Coram, Michele Dale, Mark Epp, Sandra Ferguson, James Gorton, Owen Jenkins, Mary Ledwell, Serge Paquet, Gillian Reddyhoff,

Anastasia Rodgers, Lisa Singer, Alysson Storey et Jim Suderman.

Notre gratitude et des remerciements particulièrement sentis vont à Curtis Fahey, qui, par de précieux services d'édition de fond, nous a aidés à unifier le ton de nos commentaires et à en uniformiser la présentation.

Enfin, à titre personnel, je voudrais exprimer mes remerciements les plus sincères à Peggy Mooney et à Agatha Garcia-Wright, dont l'initiative et la diligence à chacune des étapes ont permis l'achèvement, dans les délais et de façon toute professionnelle, de cette tâche complexe et exigeante.

L'archiviste de l'Ontario,
Miriam McTiernan

Introduction

Introduction

The opening years of the twentieth century brimmed with historical importance. In 1903 alone, the Wright brothers made the first successful flight by powered airplane, Marconi completed his first two-way public wireless message between North America and England and the electrocardiograph was invented. Each of these innovations – and there were many more that year – would forever alter the shape of the world. And, in the midst of it all, the Archives of Ontario was created.

While this may seem to be a far-fetched leap, the connection between the establishment of the Archives and larger social trends is actually quite strong. In 1903 the province of Ontario was on the cusp of its own age of discovery, growth, and transformation. That year saw the discovery of one of the richest silver veins in the world in Cobalt, Ontario, which would open up the north to economic development. This event, along with others that followed, reshaped Ontario society in fundamental ways. The province was evolving, as were the lives of its inhabitants. In order to keep up with the ever-changing face of Ontario, and to profit and learn from each advancement and setback, the consequences of social and economic change needed to be documented and preserved. The future depended on it.

The Archives of Ontario's mandate is to document and safeguard the physical evidence of the province's historical development, but in fact its purpose goes far beyond that. In order to maintain a running narrative of Ontario's history for future generations, the Archives does not confine itself to collecting contemporary records, but rather delves deeply into the past. Its collections cover a wide range of subjects, including births, deaths, and marriages and property transactions; photographs and government documents reflecting the growth – and, in some cases, the shrinkage – of cities and towns; fine art, architectural, and cartographical records depicting the province's changing landscape over the course of the twentieth century; proceedings of important court cases; reports of government inquiries; and precious physical artifacts. Everything described and preserved at the Archives helps define how Ontario came to be and, more precisely, who was involved in directing its journey.

Given the importance of the Archives' role, it is astonishing that its existence was questioned, and even threatened, for an extended period of time. But so it was. When the Archives of Ontario was first established, it was not met with enthusiasm or cooperation from other branches of government or from historical societies. Despite the obstacles, however, the Archives persevered – and survived. It is a remarkable story.

The Archives of Ontario owes its creation to one man. Alexander Fraser (1860-1936) was twenty-six when he left Scotland and made his way to Canada. Settling in Toronto, he almost immediately became an active member of the community. He worked in and helped organize several groups that aimed to preserve his new country's culture and traditions, serving as president of both the Scottish-Canadian Association and the Gaelic Society of Canada. He was also the grand chief of the Sons of Scotland and played a leading role in the founding of Toronto's 48th Highlanders. When he was not collaborating with his fellow Scotsmen, he was working at the Toronto *Mail*, first as a reporter and later as a city editor. It was while he was with the *Mail* that Fraser became increasingly fascinated with Ontario and its history, an interest he would soon indulge by devoting a large portion of his time to preparing an impressive two-volume chronicle of the history of Ontario. As he made a name for himself as a writer and researcher and based on his involvement in the Scottish-Canadian community, Fraser attracted the attention of Premier[1] George Ross, who gave him the monumental task of setting up the provincial archives. In July 1903, the Government of Ontario passed an Order-in-Council appointing Alexander Fraser as the Archivist for the Province of Ontario.

Fraser had definite ideas about what should be preserved in the Archives, and how it should be done. Seeing government records as only partially reflecting the life and times of the people of Ontario, he took it upon himself to start collecting documents from schools and churches, as well as correspondence, manuscripts and other papers, which often were the only link to some of the earliest settlers. Also a fervent believer in narrative history, Fraser encouraged researchers to interview older members of communities and publish their stories so that memories of early Ontario would not be lost over time.

Fraser was fastidious both in the way he organized his office and in his acquisitions strategy. At the outset, after consulting several British and American archival publications, library associations, historical societies, and with faculty in the departments of history and economics at the University of Toronto, he formulated his plan. Within a year, Fraser had organized and completed a methodical survey of records in the various Ontario government departments by means of circulars addressed to each deputy minister requesting brief departmental histories and inventories of their holdings. His ultimate goal was to develop a network of agents made up of volunteers that would report on local archival materials.

Nevertheless, Fraser had to struggle every step of the way. Many people in local historical societies balked at the idea of collecting important historical documents and then shipping them to a central repository, which, they feared, would swallow up their own historical societies. Fraser also received only limited support from provincial authorities. The Archives had little influence within government and lacked the power to regulate the preservation of records. Fraser's requests that not a single piece of documentation be destroyed without sanction by the provincial archivist fell on deaf ears. Furthermore, he had no more than two staff members working for him,

---

1 The use of the title Premier or the title Prime Minister was a matter of personal choice by leaders of the Government of Ontario until 1972. In 1983, provincial legislation was enacted that permanently confirmed the title as "Premier". Throughout this publication, the title of Premier is used in reference to this position and former government leaders.

and it was not until 1914 that three clerks were added to help with incoming material. For the most part, Fraser worked unassisted in the collection of records. And, for the time being, his dream of a network of agents remained merely that.

Around 1922, to bolster his authority, Fraser started campaigning for a legislative act to establish protocol for the preservation of archival materials. He proposed the passing of a bill that would leave little or no room for interpretation as to the responsibilities of deputy ministers and branch heads in transferring records to the Archives. He felt that, after amassing hundreds of thousands of documents, the Archives had earned the right to be recognized as 'an Office of Record and a clearing house for Government papers.' The proposal was favourably received and in 1923 the Archives Act was passed. It stated that no government record was to be destroyed without the permission of the provincial archivist and all documents demanded by that person were to be turned over within twenty years of ceasing to be in 'current use.' The act still governs the Archives today. It has remained virtually unchanged ever since and is the oldest unrevised archives statute in Canada.

The Archives faced its most difficult period in the mid-thirties. In July 1934 Mitch Hepburn became the premier. Making good on its election promise to cut back drastically on government spending, the Hepburn government reduced considerably both the Archives' budget and the size of its staff. One cabinet minister felt that the Archives, with a budget of around $18,000, had a 'ridiculously expensive overhead.' On his advice, seven of the now 'large' staff of eleven were let go, including Fraser, who, with great reluctance, retired in January 1935. He died the following year.

The Archives faced its next major challenge in the 1950s and 1960s, when it became apparent that most government offices contained non-current records, which exceeded storage capacity and lengthened the time for information retrieval. George Spragge, Archivist of Ontario at the time, solicited Premier Leslie Frost's support to maintain the Archives' status as a separate department, essential to his plan for a systematic, government-wide records management program. Upon achieving this goal, Spragge set straight to work on preparing a proposal outlining the concept of a dormant records centre. Spragge's objective was to reduce the rate of record accumulation and increase the destruction of non-archival holdings, all the while retaining historically valuable records. However, because of some flaws in the planning, the project was almost shelved. The recently retired Premier Frost came to the Archives' aid once again and helped keep the plan alive, but it would take three more years before anything substantial was accomplished.

In that time a new provincial archivist, Donald McOuat, came into office and was quick to take up the cause. In 1965 an administrative structure was set up and the first Ontario government records schedule was approved for the Department of Labour. The following year, a records-storage facility opened in Cooksville to store non-active and semi-active records still in custody of government departments. With records management well established, the Archives of Ontario could now focus on improving its facilities and services, as well as acquiring additional items of historical significance – a selection of which can be seen in this book.

Since the development of the records management program, the Archives has continued to expand its collections and resources to meet customers' needs and provide expert care for its holdings. After reaching the milestone of one hundred years of service, the Archives can proudly proclaim itself to be an institution whose vital role is recognized by government and public alike. The years of hardship and controversy have resulted in strengthening the Archives' resolve to continue developing programs and services that will enhance the preservation and documentation of Ontario's rich and diverse heritage. At the opening of the twenty-first century, the Archives of Ontario still endures and maintains the bridge that connects our past, our present, and our future.

Le vingtième siècle s'est ouvert sur un cortège d'événements qui font date. Ainsi, pendant la seule année 1903, les frères Wright réussissent leur premier vol motorisé, Marconi inaugure la liaison transatlantique sans fil (Amérique du Nord-Angleterre), et l'électrocardiographe est mis au point. Chacune de ces innovations – sans parler de toutes les autres qui se succèdent cette même année – allait modifier à jamais la face de notre univers. C'est dans ce contexte que les Archives publiques de l'Ontario ont vu le jour.

Le rapprochement peut paraître outré – et pourtant, il existe un rapport réel et étroit entre l'établissement des Archives et les grands courants sociaux du temps. En 1903, la province de l'Ontario aborde pour sa part une ère d'exploration, de croissance et de transformation. Cette année-là en effet, on découvre à Cobalt (Ontario) un filon argentifère parmi les plus riches au monde, qui va lancer le développement économique dans le Nord. Cet événement et ceux qui vont suivre reconfigurent la société ontarienne sous des aspects fondamentaux. La province change, tout comme la vie de ses habitants. Or, pour se maintenir au diapason d'une réalité en mutation constante et pour tirer le meilleur parti de chaque avancée aussi bien que de chaque repli, il fallait consigner les effets du changement économique et social et conserver les documents correspondants. L'avenir était à ce prix.

Les Archives publiques de l'Ontario ont pour mandat de documenter l'évolution de la province au cours de son histoire et d'en conserver les preuves matérielles, mais, en fait, leur raison d'être transcende cet énoncé. Afin de tenir la chronique de la province pour la postérité, les Archives ne peuvent se contenter de colliger des documents contemporains, elles doivent remonter dans les profondeurs du passé. Les collections rassemblent les documents les plus divers, entre autres des registres de naissances, décès et mariages et des registres de transactions foncières; des documents photographiques et des documents gouvernementaux qui reflètent la croissance – et, parfois, le déclin – des villages et des villes; des documents cartographiques et architecturaux ainsi que des oeuvres d'art documentaire illustrant les métamorphoses du paysage ontarien durant le vingtième siècle; des transcriptions et procès-verbaux d'affaires judiciaires importantes; des rapports d'enquêtes publiques; enfin, de précieux artefacts. L'ensemble de ces pièces, décrites et conservées aux Archives, contribue à définir comment l'Ontario s'est constitué et, plus précisément, qui a présidé à l'orientation de ses destinées.

Vu l'importance du rôle des Archives, il est renversant qu'on ait si longtemps pu contester et dénier le bien-fondé de leur existence. C'est pourtant ce qui s'est passé. Au départ, l'institution des Archives publiques de l'Ontario n'a pas été accueillie avec bienveillance, ni par les instances gouvernementales ni par les sociétés d'histoire, qui n'étaient pas disposées à offrir leur collaboration. En dépit des obstacles, les Archives ont su persévérer – et survivre. Voilà la trame d'un récit remarquable.

Les Archives publiques de l'Ontario doivent leur instauration à un personnage unique, Alexander Fraser (1860-1936), venu d'Écosse au Canada à l'âge de vingt-six ans. À son arrivée à Toronto, Fraser ne tarde pas à prendre une part active à la vie de la collectivité. Il aide à mettre sur pied plusieurs groupes désireux de préserver la culture et les traditions de sa nouvelle patrie et au sein desquels il se dévoue, notamment à la présidence de la Scottish-Canadian Association et de la Gaelic Society of Canada. Devenu grand chef des Sons of Scotland, il tient un rôle de premier plan dans la fondation des 48th Highlanders de Toronto. Parallèlement à cette collaboration assidue avec des compatriotes écossais, il entre au service du *Mail* de Toronto, où il est d'abord journaliste, puis directeur de l'information. Durant sa carrière au *Mail*, Fraser se laisse gagner par une véritable fascination pour l'Ontario et son histoire, et il consacre une bonne portion de son temps à rédiger une imposante histoire en deux tomes de l'Ontario. Jouissant d'un certain renom en tant que journaliste, rédacteur et chercheur, de même que par ses activités dans la communauté canado-écossaise, Fraser se signale à l'attention du premier ministre George Ross, qui lui confie la tâche monumentale de créer des archives provinciales. En juillet 1903, le gouvernement de l'Ontario nomme par décret Alexander Fraser au titre d'archiviste pour la province de l'Ontario.

Fraser avait une idée arrêtée de ce qui est matériau d'archives et de la marche à suivre. À ses yeux, les documents gouvernementaux ne reflètent qu'en partie la vie des citoyens et de leur société; il prend donc l'initiative de rassembler des documents relatifs aux écoles et églises, outre des lettres, manuscrits et autres écrits représentant souvent les seules traces des pionniers qui nous soient parvenues. Fervent de la petite histoire, Fraser encourage les chercheurs à s'entretenir avec les aînés des collectivités et à publier leurs récits, pour empêcher que ne se perde irrémédiablement le souvenir de la colonie des débuts.

Fraser faisait preuve d'un soin méticuleux dans l'organisation de son bureau et de sa stratégie d'acquisition. Il commence par formuler son plan – non sans avoir consulté, tant du côté américain que britannique, une panoplie de publications archivistiques, des associations de bibliothécaires, des sociétés historiques et plusieurs professeurs d'histoire et d'économie de l'Université de Toronto. En moins d'une année, Fraser effectue la recension méthodique des fonds documentaires existants dans les divers ministères ontariens. Il procède au moyen de circulaires, demandant à chacun des sous-ministres de lui présenter un bref historique de son ministère et un répertoire de son fonds. Il ambitionne de former un réseau d'agents volontaires, qui rendraient périodiquement compte du matériel d'archives local.

Il reste que Fraser doit lutter à chaque étape. D'une part, les sociétés d'histoire locales boudent l'idée de réunir des documents historiques importants pour les expédier aussitôt à un dépôt central, lequel va, craignent-elles, engloutir sans vergogne leurs petits organismes. D'autre part, Fraser ne reçoit qu'un appui restreint des autorités provinciales. Les Archives ont peu de poids au sein du gouvernement et n'ont pas le pouvoir de réglementer la conservation des documents. Fraser avait demandé qu'aucun document ne soit détruit sans l'autorisation de l'archiviste provincial, ce qui n'avait pas trouvé le moindre écho. En tout et pour tout, son personnel ne compte que deux personnes, et ce n'est qu'en 1914 qu'on lui adjoint trois commis, comme préposés au matériel qu'il reçoit sans relâche. Fraser est seul responsable de la réunion des documents. Pendant un certain temps, le réseau d'agents de ses rêves devra demeurer à l'état de projet.

Vers 1922, pour asseoir son autorité, Fraser tente d'obtenir les bases d'un protocole de sauvegarde du matériel d'archives. Il propose l'adoption d'un projet de loi où seraient clairement édictées les obligations des sous-ministres et chefs de directions quant au transfert des documents aux Archives. Il est fermement convaincu que, après avoir rassemblé des centaines de milliers de documents, les Archives ont droit à une reconnaissance officielle, à titre de « Bureau des archives » et service central des documents publics. La proposition est reçue favorablement, et, en 1923, la Loi sur les archives publiques est adoptée. Il y est stipulé que nul document gouvernemental ne doit être détruit à l'insu de l'archiviste de la province et sans son assentiment, et que tout document requis par cette personne doit être confié à sa garde dans les vingt années suivant la date où il cesse d'être d'usage courant. Cette même Loi, qui régit encore les Archives de nos jours, n'a guère changé; c'est la plus ancienne des lois canadiennes sur les archives qui n'ont pas été révisées.

Au milieu des années trente, les Archives affrontent leur phase la plus critique. En juillet 1934, Mitch Hepburn devient premier ministre. Mettant en oeuvre sa promesse électorale, qui était de sabrer dans les dépenses publiques, le gouvernement Hepburn réduit considérablement le budget et l'effectif des Archives. Selon un de ses ministres, les Archives, dont le budget avoisinait un faramineux 18 000 $, présentaient des frais généraux exhorbitants. Sur sa recommandation, sept des onze membres du « nombreux » personnel sont licenciés, dont Fraser, qui, avec la plus grande

réticence, prend sa retraite en janvier 1935. Il s'éteindra l'année suivante.

Le second défi majeur que doivent relever les Archives survient pendant les années 1950 et 1960 : il est devenu évident que la plupart des bureaux du gouvernement conservent une masse de documents périmés, qui dépasse leur capacité d'entreposage et ralentit la recherche documentaire. George Spragge, alors archiviste de l'Ontario, prie le premier ministre Leslie Frost d'appuyer le maintien des Archives publiques comme service distinct, statut selon lui essentiel au programme qu'il envisage pour la gestion systématique des documents à l'échelle du gouvernement. Une fois sa demande agréée, Spragge formule un projet de centre des documents semi-actifs. Ce projet vise à réduire le rythme d'accumulation des dossiers tout en conservant les documents à valeur historique et en détruisant ceux qui en sont dépourvus. Mais, en raison d'obscures erreurs de planification, le projet passe à deux doigts de la mise au rancart. De nouveau, le premier ministre Frost, retraité de fraîche date, se porte à la rescousse et aide à sauvegarder le projet – dont la concrétisation n'en prendra pas moins trois autres années.

C'est alors que le nouvel archiviste provincial, Donald McOuat, entre en fonction et se rallie promptement à la cause. En 1965, on établit une structure administrative et on fait approuver, pour le ministère du Travail, un premier calendrier de conservation des documents du gouvernement de l'Ontario. L'année suivante, une installation ouvre ses portes à Cooksville, pour l'entreposage des documents semi-actifs et inactifs qui demeurent sous la garde des ministères. Une fois en place le système de gestion des documents, les Archives publiques de l'Ontario peuvent songer à améliorer leurs locaux et services, et à acquérir d'autres pièces à valeur historique – dont un certain nombre sont reproduites dans le présent ouvrage.

Depuis le lancement du programme de gestion des documents, les Archives n'ont pas cessé d'enrichir leurs collections et d'améliorer leurs ressources, de façon à répondre aux besoins de sa clientèle et à se conformer aux meilleures normes en matière de conservation. À ce stade mémorable de leurs cent années de service, les Archives sont à juste titre fières du rôle crucial qui leur est désormais reconnu, par la population comme par le gouvernement. Les années de luttes et de contreverses ont eu pour effet de renforcer leur détermination de continuer à développer les programmes et services les plus aptes à préserver et à documenter le patrimoine ontarien, d'une telle diversité dans sa profusion. En ce début du vingt et unième siècle, les Archives publiques de l'Ontario réaffirment leur mission et consolident le pont qu'elles jettent entre notre passé, notre présent et notre avenir

PART I

IMAGES OF OURSELVES

À NOTRE IMAGE

The first part of this book includes various kinds of material – documentary art, maps, and portraits – that can help us better understand past generations. Facts can certainly be found here in abundance – both documentary art and maps are replete with concrete details, from topographical data to information on the growth of the built environment – but alongside these facts are faces of people and glimpses of the society in which they lived. The illustrations are diverse, ranging from paintings of early Upper Canada to Toronto street scenes in the early twentieth century, from French regime maps of the North American continent to township plans in nineteenth-century rural Ontario, and from portraits of lieutenant-governors and Native people to amateur home movies.

In this section, too, is another type of material – government records. These records, of course, overflow with factual information, detailing land settlement, business partnerships, and births, marriages, and deaths, among many other things, but they also include revealing insights into the minds of individuals in the past, as well as into the fabric of their society. Here can be found, for example, documents relating to the Spanish flu epidemic of 1918-19, school examinations, and wills and estate files of the historic, such as Thomas Ridout, and the eccentric, such as Charles Vance Millar, whose will awarded his estate to the Toronto mother who gave birth to the greatest number of children over ten years.

Though many of these records may have been created for prosaic reasons – to document the landscape and the built environment, to chart population growth, and to oversee commercial relationships – all of them help to illuminate both the nature of the past and the lives of our ancestors. They also help to demonstrate the innumerable connections between past and present, between our ancestors and ourselves.

La première partie de cet ouvrage présente un matériel éclectique – art documentaire, cartographie, portrait –, susceptible de nous aider à mieux comprendre les générations passées. Les faits y occupent assurément une grande place. En cartographie comme en art documentaire, le détail concret foisonne, des précisions topographiques aux aléas de l'environnement bâti. Ces faits prennent pourtant visage, des protagonistes, scènes et anecdotes y viennent cristalliser des traits de société. Les illustrations sont diverses : depuis les tableaux des débuts du Haut-Canada aux scènes de rues torontoises au tournant du vingtième siècle; depuis les cartes du continent nord-américain issues du régime français aux plans de cantons ruraux du dix-neuvième siècle; depuis les portraits de lieutenants-gouverneurs et d'Autochtones aux films familiaux tournés par des amateurs.

Cette même section renferme également un autre type de matériel – les documents gouvernementaux. Nous voici certes au royaume du factuel, puisque ces actes répertorient entre autres des concessions de terres, sociétés de commerce, enregistrements de naissances, mariages et décès, mais ils nous dévoilent en outre le tour d'esprit des gens de l'époque et font entrevoir la trame de leur société. S'y retrouvent, par exemple, des documents relatifs à l'épidémie de grippe espagnole de 1918-1919, des examens scolaires, des testaments et dossiers de succession de personnages historiques, tels que Thomas Ridout, ou excentriques, tels que Charles Vance Millar, ce dernier léguant un avoir considérable à la Torontoise qui, dans les dix années suivantes, aurait donné naissance à la plus nombreuse progéniture.

Une foule de ces documents répondent à des nécessités pratiques – renseigner sur le paysage et l'environnement bâti, suivre la croissance démographique et surveiller les relations commerciales – mais tous, d'une façon ou d'une autre, mettent en lumière la nature du passé et la vie de nos aïeux. Ils contribuent aussi à faire ressortir les multiples liens entre présent et passé, entre nous-mêmes et nos ancêtres.

1

DOCUMENTARY ART

L'ART DOCUMENTAIRE

A Pic-nic at Sloat's Lake, near Sydenham, Township of Loughborough

1-1

The Archives of Ontario has approximately 4,000 documentary art records created by both amateur and professional artists. The collection contains oil paintings, drawings, watercolours, and prints, with material spanning the period from the 1790s into the twentieth century. Some of the artists are well known, including Thomas Burrowes, Caroline Armington, William Armstrong, C.W. Jefferys, George Reid, Elizabeth Simcoe, Captain Hervey Smyth, Robert Sproule, Owen Staples, Anne Langton, and Dorothy Stevens.

Paintings of Upper Canada/Ontario originated in the British military's need for topographical surveys. Many officers were trained in draughtsmanship and watercolour sketching at the Royal Military Academy in Woolwich, England, and the paintings they produced in Canada were important tools of military reconnaissance. Yet, while painting was part of an officer's work, it sometimes also became a diversionary pastime between duties. This was certainly true, for example, of Lieutenant Robert Pilkington of the Royal Engineers, stationed in the new colony of Upper Canada in the 1790s, who produced numerous sketches of different parts of the colony, from Georgian Bay to Lake Erie.

But not all artists in early Canada were military men. Before photography, sketching was a popular activity practised by many amateur artists who travelled abroad. Often, as in the case of Elizabeth Simcoe, wife of Lieutenant-Governor John Graves Simcoe and a friend of Lieutenant Pilkington, their sketches and watercolours were not intended for sale but rather were produced as souvenirs. Some of the early landscape painters in Upper Canada did become professionals, however, selling their paintings both locally and abroad. These artists painted features of the Canadian landscape, such as Niagara Falls, that were thought by many in Britain to be exotic and picturesque.

At first, watercolour was popular because it was a versatile medium and the artist could paint images in transparent washes or with a thicker application of opaque colour. But, over time, watercolours alone could not satisfy the growing demand for pictures of foreign lands. To this end, watercolour sketches were often transformed into prints through a variety of printing methods, including engraving, etching, woodcuts, and lithography. In order to make the prints more attractive, they were often tinted with watercolour. Landscape prints from early Canada are still collected today for their aesthetic qualities and their high level of topographical detail.

Early views of Upper Canada in the Archives of Ontario's documentary art records are the creations of artists who came here in search of adventure and new beginnings, and, as such, often display a certain naive optimism. Later works are more mature. Whether early or late, and whatever their strengths and weaknesses as works of art, however, these records are precious historical documents.

Au chapitre de l'art documentaire, les Archives publiques de l'Ontario possèdent quelque 4 000 oeuvres, émanant d'artistes amateurs aussi bien que professionnels. La collection renferme des peintures à l'huile et des aquarelles, des dessins et des gravures, et illustre une période qui s'étend des années 1790 jusqu'à la fin du vingtième siècle. Certains de ces artistes sont bien connus, ainsi Thomas Burrowes, Caroline Armington, William Armstrong, C. W. Jefferys,

George Reid, Elizabeth Simcoe, le capitaine Hervey Smyth, Robert Sproule, Owen Staples, Anne Langton et Dorothy Stevens.

Dans le Haut-Canada (l'Ontario des débuts), la peinture devait communément répondre aux besoins de l'armée britannique en matière de levés topographiques. Nombre d'officiers avaient été formés au dessin et au croquis à l'aquarelle à la Royal Military Academy de Woolwich, en Angleterre, et leurs peintures réalisées au Canada étaient en fait d'importants outils de reconnaissance militaire. Cependant, même si le dessin et la peinture faisaient partie des tâches d'un officier, ce dernier en venait parfois à s'y adonner comme passe-temps. C'était certainement le cas du lieutenant Robert Pilkington des Royal Engineers, en poste dans la nouvelle colonie du Haut-Canada dans les années 1790, qui est l'auteur de nombreux croquis décrivant différentes parties de la colonie, depuis la baie Georgienne jusqu'au lac Érié.

Mais tous les artistes des débuts de la colonie n'étaient pas des militaires. Avant l'invention de la photographie, le croquis était une activité courante pour de nombreux artistes amateurs qui voyageaient à l'étranger. Souventes fois, comme dans le cas d'Elizabeth Simcoe, épouse du lieutenant-gouverneur John Graves Simcoe et amie du lieutenant Pilkington, leurs croquis et aquarelles n'étaient pas destinés à la vente, mais constituaient plutôt des souvenirs. Certains des premiers paysagistes du Haut-Canada sont toutefois devenus des artistes professionnels, dont les œuvres se sont vendues au pays et à l'étranger. Ces artistes prenaient pour sujets des sites et phénomènes propres au Canada, par exemple les chutes Niagara, qui étaient considérés comme exotiques et pittoresques en Grande-Bretagne.

L'aquarelle s'est d'abord répandue en raison de sa polyvalence et de sa souplesse, l'artiste pouvant doter ses images de lavis transparents ou d'une couche plus épaisse de couleur opaque. Mais, bientôt, l'aquarelle n'a plus réussi à satisfaire une demande croissante pour les représentations de pays étrangers. C'est ce qui explique que les croquis à l'aquarelle aient souvent donné lieu à des estampes, aux procédés les plus variés : gravure, eau-forte, xylographie, taille-douce et lithographie. Afin de rehausser leur attrait, on teintait les gravures à l'aquarelle. Les collectionneurs recherchent toujours les estampes paysagistes des débuts du Canada, pour leur qualité esthétique et la minutie de leur détail topographique.

Les premières vues du Haut-Canada de la collection d'art documentaire des Archives sont le fait d'artistes qui venaient ici en quête d'aventure et d'un nouveau départ, et, à ce titre, manifestent volontiers un certain optimiste naïf. Les œuvres ultérieures font preuve d'une plus grande maturité. Quoi qu'il en soit et quelles que soient leurs forces et leurs faiblesses du point de vue artistique, ces pièces constituent des documents historiques précieux.

1-2 & 1-3: Elizabeth Posthuma Simcoe (1762-1850) has been called the 'First Lady of Upper Canada.' Born to a wealthy family in Aldwincle, England, Elizabeth was orphaned at birth and raised by her Aunt Margaret and her husband, Admiral Samuel Graves. As a child, she displayed considerable talent in painting and sketching, a hobby that she pursued constantly. At age sixteen she married John Graves Simcoe, the godson of Admiral Graves, and accompanied him to Upper Canada in 1792 when he took up his duties as the colony's first lieutenant-governor. Throughout her stay in Canada, Elizabeth Simcoe travelled extensively, recording her memories in her diaries and her many sketchbooks.

1-2 et 1-3 : Elizabeth Posthuma Simcoe (1762-1850), qu'on connaît aussi sous le titre de « première dame du Haut-Canada », était issue d'une famille aisée d'Aldwincle, en Angleterre. Orpheline de naissance, Elizabeth est élevée par sa tante Margaret et son mari, l'amiral Samuel Graves. Dès son enfance, elle se montre douée pour le croquis et la peinture, passe-temps auquel elle s'adonnera sa vie durant. À l'âge de 16 ans, elle épouse John Graves Simcoe, filleul de l'amiral Graves, et l'accompagne dans le Haut-Canada en 1792, lorsqu'il devient le premier lieutenant-gouverneur de la colonie. Pendant tout son séjour au Canada, Elizabeth Simcoe allait faire de nombreux voyages et fidèlement noter ses impressions dans un journal intime et de nombreux carnets de croquis.

1-2

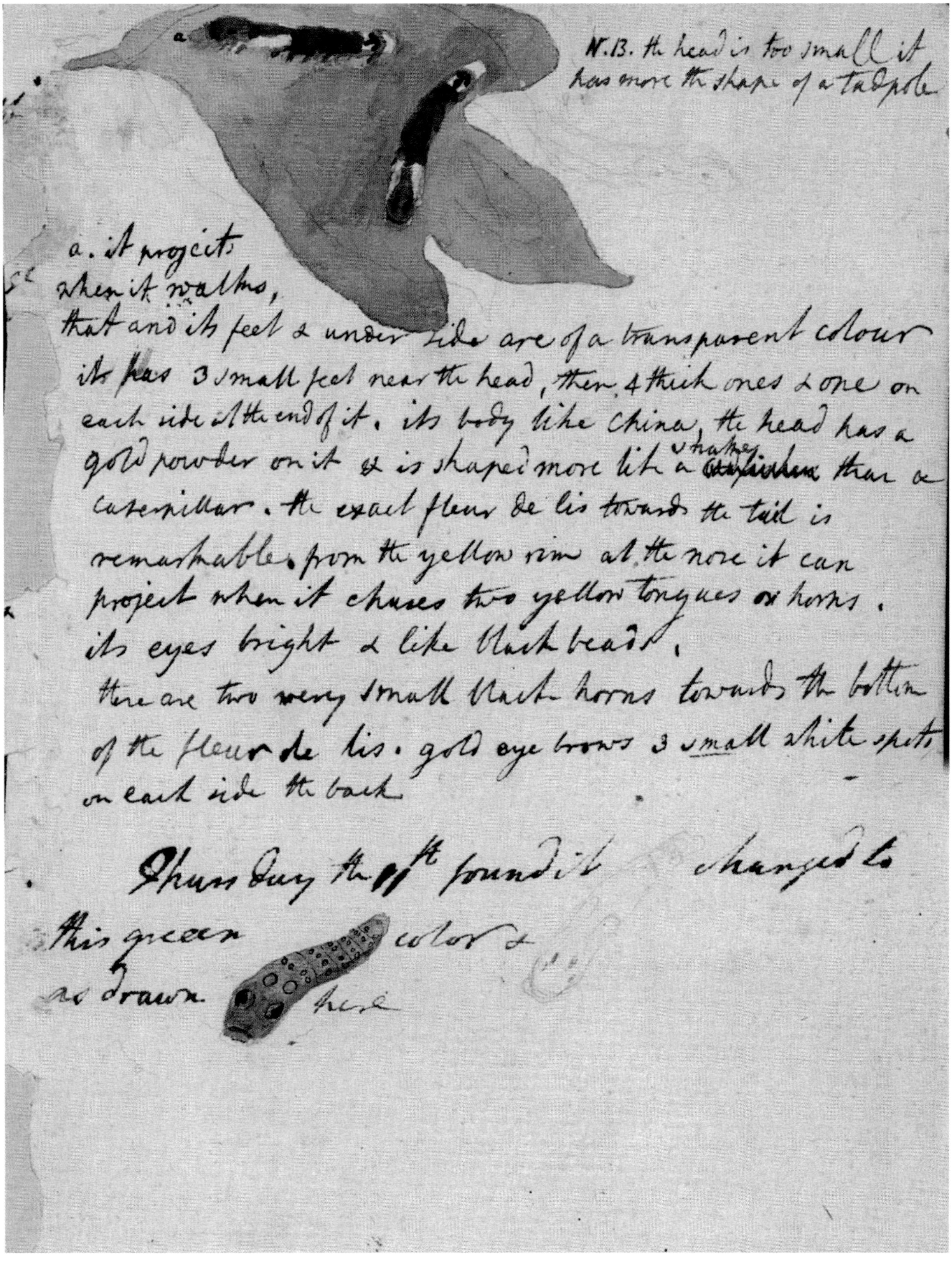

N.B. the head is too small it
has more the shape of a tadpole

a. it projects
when it walks,
that and its feet & under side are of a transparent colour
it has 3 small feet near the head, then 4 thick ones & one on
each side at the end of it. its body like china, the head has a
gold powder on it & is shaped more like a snake than a
caterpillar. the exact fleur de lis towards the tail is
remarkable, from the yellow rim at the nose it can
project when it chuses two yellow tongues or horns.
its eyes bright & like black beads.
there are two very small black horns towards the bottom
of the fleur de lis. gold eye brows 3 small white spots,
on each side the back

Thursday the 11th found it changed to
this green color &
as drawn here

1-3

Images of Ourselves / À notre image   9

1-4 & 1-5: [1-4] Simcoe had a keen eye and a lively curiosity about the inhabitants of her new home. Her sketches, such as this one showing a Native lodge, may have been done hurriedly, but they are invaluable records of a distant time.

[1-5] In her more finished works, Simcoe showed herself to be an accomplished artist. This painting evokes an era of pristine wilderness. The clouds moving across the sky, the virgin forest, and the wisps of campfire smoke crossing the calm lake are the romantic elements that make this scene of early days in Canada so charming to us today.

1-4 et 1-5 : [1-4] Elizabeth avait le sens de l'observation et une vive curiosité à l'égard des habitants de son nouveau pays. Ses croquis, dont celui-ci, où l'on voit une hutte autochtone, sont parfois ébauchés à la hâte, mais n'en demeurent pas moins de précieux documents sur une époque lointaine.

[1-5] Les œuvres plus travaillées d'Elizabeth révèlent un talent accompli. La peinture que nous voyons ici évoque une ère de nature sauvage, primitive. Dans cette scène des débuts de la colonie, les nuages barrant le ciel, la forêt vierge et la fumée d'un feu de camp s'échappant en traînées au-dessus des eaux calmes sont autant de touches romantiques qui font son charme pour nous.

1-4

1-5

1-6 & 1-7: Some scenes in Elizabeth Simcoe's sketchbooks are repeated many times over as the artist tried to capture not only the locale but also a particular moment in time – much as a photographer would do today. These sketches of Twenty Mile Creek are a good example. The same view was quickly painted again and again in order to capture the activity of the boaters and the sunlight that illuminated the scene.

In 1796, after five years in Canada, the Simcoes moved back to England, never to return again. Despite their short time in Upper Canada, both husband and wife left an indelible mark on the Canadian landscape, found in the names of places, towns, and rivers, as well as providing some of the first views of a young country.

1-6 et 1-7 : Certaines scènes des carnets d'Elizabeth reviennent fois après fois, l'artiste s'efforçant de rendre un même décor, à divers moments de la journée – à la façon d'un photographe d'aujourd'hui. Ces croquis de Twenty Mile Creek en sont un bon exemple. La même vue y est rapidement retouchée, afin de saisir le mouvement des bateliers et la course du soleil qui baigne la scène.

En 1796, cinq ans après leur arrivée au Canada, les Simcoe rentrent en Angleterre, pour ne jamais revenir. Malgré la brièveté de leur séjour dans le Haut-Canada, ils devaient tous deux laisser sur la toponymie canadienne une marque durable, à témoin de nombreux noms de lieux, de villes et de rivières, de même que certaines des premières représentations d'un pays en gestation.

1-6

1-7

1-8 & 1-9: [1-8] Captain Thomas Burrowes (1796-1866) came to Canada in 1815 and obtained a position on Colonel John By's staff to help build the Rideau Canal. During his employment as overseer of works for the canal (1826-35) and clerk of works at Bytown (1835-46), Burrowes used his artistic talents to record the construction of this challenging engineering project.

After the War of 1812, there was a perceived need for a safe bypass of the St Lawrence River between Montreal and Kingston in order to transport supplies from Lower to Upper Canada. The route chosen for this bypass followed the Ottawa River to the Rideau lakes and along the Cataraqui River to the Royal Navy base at Kingston on Lake Ontario.

[1-9] Construction of the Rideau Canal began in 1827 and was completed in 1832. Forty-seven locks at twenty-three lock stations linked 126 miles of waterway. The canal served as an active and busy route until the building of the deep-water canal locks around the rapids of the St Lawrence River in 1849. Its commercial heyday over, and no longer of military significance, the Rideau Canal now became one of Ontario's most popular tourist destinations, and it is still possible to see traces of the canal as Burrowes painted it well over one hundred years ago.

1-8 et 1-9 : [1-8] Le capitaine Thomas Burrowes (1796-1866) arrive au Canada en 1815 et joint les rangs des effectifs recrutés par le colonel John By en vue de l'aménagement du canal Rideau. Au cours de son mandat comme contremaître des chantiers du canal (1826-1835) et délégué du maître d'ouvrage à Bytown (1835-1846), Burrowes emploie ses dons artistiques à documenter la réalisation de cet ambitieux projet d'ingénierie.

La guerre de 1812 avait souligné l'importance de trouver une voie sûre pour contourner le Saint-Laurent entre Montréal et Kingston, aux fins du transport des fournitures et provisions du Bas-Canada vers le Haut-Canada. Le tracé arrêté pour ce faire emprunte l'Outaouais et passe par les lacs Rideau, avant de suivre la rivière Cataraqui jusqu'à la base de la Royal Navy à Kingston, sur le lac Ontario.

[1-9] La construction du canal Rideau débute en 1827, pour s'achever en 1832. Quarante-sept écluses aménagées dans vingt-trois postes d'éclusage ponctuent cette voie navigable, qui s'étend sur 126 milles. Le canal a été très fréquenté jusqu'en 1849, date où des écluses en eaux profondes permettant de contourner les rapides du Saint-Laurant sont aménagées. Sa grande époque révolue et son importance militaire étant chose du passé, le canal Rideau est devenu l'une des destinations touristiques les plus populaires de l'Ontario. Il est encore possible d'y examiner les vestiges de l'ouvrage tel que l'a dépeint Burrowes, il y a plus de cent ans.

1-8

1-9

1-10 & 1-11: Note the contrast between the sketch from 1829 and the later image from 1856. The earlier picture, with its many tree stumps and Spartan log cabins, shows that the engineers and canal builders are just barely keeping nature at bay. The later image, showing the completed canal locks, railway bridge, mill, and tidy little blockhouse, presents a vastly different scene – one in which nature is rather more tamed and subdued.

Burrowes lived at Kingston Mills for more than thirty years with his second wife, Margaret Morrison. They had one son and six daughters.

1-10 et 1-11 : Notons le contraste entre le croquis de 1829 et l'image postérieure de 1856. Le premier, où s'élèvent de frustes cabanes en rondins sur une aire parsemée de souches, atteste que les ingénieurs et les constructeurs du canal ont peine à tenir la nature en respect. Dans la deuxième image, où sont achevés les travaux – écluses, pont ferroviaire, moulin et pimpant petit fortin –, le tableau change du tout au tout : la nature s'y fait beaucoup plus discrète, domestiquée.

Burrowes a vécu à Kingston Mills pendant plus de trente ans avec sa seconde épouse, Margaret Morrison. Leur progéniture compte un fils et six filles.

1-10

1-11

1-12

1-13

1-12 & 1-13: [1-12] In the nineteenth century, one of North America's most popular tourist haunts was Niagara Falls. Although souvenir stands offering postcards did not yet exist, the desire to have a souvenir was just as strong as it is today. Many artists attempted to capture the beauty and grandeur of the Falls and some of their paintings included tiny human figures to contrast with the vastness of the natural scene. Others preferred to focus on Niagara Falls' pure sublimity.

[1-13] James Pattison Cockburn was a military man who studied under renowned watercolourist Paul Sandby at the Royal Military Academy in Woolwich, England. Cockburn created numerous paintings and drawings during his postings both in Europe and in North America.

1-12 et 1-13 : [1-12] Au dix-neuvième siècle, Niagara Falls était l'un des hauts lieux du tourisme nord-américain. Le kiosque de souvenirs et cartes postales n'existait pas encore, mais le désir de rapporter des souvenirs était tout aussi vif que de nos jours. Une pléthore d'artistes ont tenté de fixer sur papier ou sur toile la grandiose beauté des chutes, recourant parfois à de minuscules figures humaines pour faire valoir le gigantisme du phénomène. D'autres ont préféré se concentrer sur le pur sublime que dégagent les chutes.

[1-13] Le militaire James Pattison Cockburn avait été disciple de l'aquarelliste renommé Paul Sandby, à la Royal Military Academy de Woolwich, en Angleterre. Cockburn a réalisé de nombreux dessins et tableaux pendant ses affectations, tant en Europe qu'en Amérique du Nord.

1-14

1-14: William Armstrong was a trained artist and military engineer who immigrated to Canada in 1851. In his painting of Lake Superior's Thunder Cape, the artist has included a small manned boat set against the enormous geological feature, emphasizing man's insignificance beside nature's majesty. Indeed, it was common for painters of the period to exaggerate features of the landscape in order to increase the appeal and marketability of their paintings back home.

1-14 : William Armstrong, ingénieur militaire aussi peintre de formation, avait émigré au Canada en 1851. Dans sa peinture du cap Thunder, au lac Supérieur, l'artiste place en avant-plan de l'énorme falaise une frêle embarcation et ses occupants, faisant ressortir le peu d'importance de l'être humain en regard de la majestueuse nature. En fait, il était courant pour les peintres de l'époque d'hypertrophier certains éléments du paysage pour attirer l'attention et accroître la valeur marchande de leurs œuvres dans la mère patrie.

1-15 & 1-16: The paintings and drawings of Anne Langton (1804-93) vividly depict the country scenery and townscapes of the places she lived at and visited in Canada during the mid-nineteenth century. Langton's favoured locales for her sketching were the rural areas around Peterborough and Fenelon Falls and sites in the vicinity of Quebec City, Ottawa, and Toronto, where she lived for extended periods during her time in Canada.

The Archives holds a large collection of Langton's work spanning more than six decades. Included are more than seven hundred items documenting her life in Canada and her visits to the British Isles and the continent. Immigrating to Upper Canada in 1837 to join her brother, John, Langton sought to record, in words and images, her experiences and adventures in the New World.

1-15 et 1-16 : Les dessins et peintures d'Anne Langton (1804-1893) recréent avec bonheur les paysages champêtres et urbains des lieux qu'elle a habités ou visités au Canada, vers le milieu du dix-neuvième siècle. Les endroits privilégiés de l'artiste pour ses croquis étaient les campagnes avoisinant Peterborough et Fenelon Falls, de même que les environs de Québec, d'Ottawa et de Toronto, où elle a passé de longues périodes pendant ses séjours au Canada.

Les Archives conservent une vaste collection d'œuvres de Langton, qui s'échelonnent sur plus de six décennies. Au total, plus de sept cents œuvres et objets illustrent sa vie au Canada et ses visites sur le vieux continent et dans les îles Britanniques. Ayant émigré dans le Haut-Canada en 1837 pour y rejoindre son frère John, l'artiste s'est efforcée de décrire, par l'écrit et par l'image, ses expériences et aventures dans le Nouveau Monde.

1-15

1-16

1-17 to 1-20: [1-17] Particularly noteworthy are Langton's images of the frontier farmlands near Peterborough where she first came to live with her brother. From 1851 to 1855 John Langton was a representative in the Legislative Assembly. At Confederation in 1867 he was appointed auditor-general and three years later he became deputy minister of finance; he served in both capacities until he retired in 1878.

[1-18 to 1-20] These early images by Langton depict the rustic setting of her brother's farm, reflecting the hard work that was necessary to provide for shelter and settle the land. Such scenes of farmland, stump-laden clearings, log cabins, and mills were typical of early settlements in Upper Canada.

1-17 à 1-20 : [1-17] Particulièrement remarquables sont les images que brosse Langton des terres agricoles des environs de Peterborough – à la limite du peuplement –, où elle a d'abord vécu, chez son frère. De 1851 à 1855, John Langton a été député à l'Assemblée législative. À la Confédération, en 1867, il était nommé vérificateur général et, trois ans plus tard, il devenait sous-ministre des Finances; il a agi à ce double titre jusqu'à sa retraite, en 1878.

[1-18 à 1-20] Ces premières images de Langton dépeignent, dans le cadre rustique de la ferme de son frère, le dur labeur nécessaire pour se donner un abri, défricher et s'établir. Ces scènes de terres à débroussailler, de clairières hérissées de souches, de cabanes en rondins et de moulins rudimentaires étaient typiques des débuts de la colonisation dans le Haut-Canada.

1-17

1-18

1-19

1-20

1-21: Moose Factory was founded in 1673 to serve as the second trading post of the Hudson's Bay Company (HBC). It was also the first English settlement in what is now the province of Ontario. The post was captured by the French in 1686 but returned to the HBC in 1713. Moose Factory, with its long and interesting past, is historic and, even in 1854, was considered a suitable subject for lithographers' art.

1-21 : Moose Factory a été fondée en 1673, comme deuxième poste de traite de la Compagnie de la Baie d'Hudson (CBH). C'était aussi la première colonie anglaise dans le territoire qui constitue maintenant la province de l'Ontario. Le poste, conquis par les Français en 1686, devait revenir à la CBH en 1713. Moose Factory, riche d'un long et intéressant passé, est un lieu historique et, en 1854 déjà, était considérée comme un sujet digne d'être lithographié.

1-21

1-22 & 1-23: These streetscapes show two different sides of Toronto. On the right is the city of progress, high aspirations, and money, while the image on the left depicts a derelict building on Bathurst Street. The work of these artists reminds us that, while many things change on the surface, the essential nature of the city has changed hardly at all.

1-22 et 1-23 : Ces paysages urbains illustrent deux facettes bien différentes de Toronto. À droite se dresse la cité du progrès, de l'ambition et de la haute finance, tandis que l'image de gauche figure un bâtiment délabré de la rue Bathurst. Les œuvres de ces artistes nous rappellent que, malgré une foule de changements apparents, le caractère essentiel de la ville est resté, à peu de chose près, sensiblement le même.

1-22

1-23

CITATIONS

1-1: *A picnic at Sloat's Lake, near Sydenham in the Township of Loughborough*, 1861, Thomas Burrowes (1796-1866) (Thomas Burrowes fonds, C 1-0-0-0-94. I0002213)

1-2: *40 Mile Creek, 40 from Niagara, towards the head of Lake Ontario*[ca. 1794], Elizabeth Simcoe (1762-1850) (Simcoe Family fonds, F 47-11-1-0-123. I0006975)

1-3: Description, by drawing and words, of a caterpillar [ca. 1793], Elizabeth Simcoe (1762-1850) (Simcoe Family fonds, F 47-11-1-0-105. I0006957)

1-4 Indian Bark Lodge [ca. 1796], Elizabeth Simcoe (1762-1850) (Simcoe Family fonds, F 47-11-1-0-288. I0006358)

1-5: Site of Charlotteville at Longpoint, [ca. 1795], Elizabeth Simcoe (1762-1850) (Simcoe Family fonds, F 47-11-1-0-1-185. I0007037)

1-6: *20 Mile Creek*, [10 May 1794], Elizabeth Simcoe (1762-1850) (Simcoe Family fonds, F 47-13-1-0-1129. I0006981)

1-7: *20 Mile Creek*, [10 May 1794], Elizabeth Simcoe (1762-1850) (Simcoe Family fonds, F 47-11-1-0-130. I0006982)

1-8: *North entrance of the Rideau Canal from the Ottawa River, taken from the Royal Eng. Office, Bytown, 1845*, Thomas Burrowes (1796-1866) (Thomas Burrowes fonds, C 1-0-0-0-14. I0002132)

1-9: *Locks at the Isthmus, the last ascent to the summit water of Canal from Lake Ontario*, 1841, Thomas Burrowes (1796-1866) (Thomas Burrowes fonds, C 1-0-0-0-36. I0002155)

1-10: *Brewer's Lower Mill; view down the Cataraqui Creek and clearing made for the canal*, 1829, Thomas Burrowes (1796-1866) (Thomas Burrowes fonds, C 1-0-0-0-67. I0002186)

1-11: Lower Kingston Mills, with Grand Trunk Railway bridge, [1856], Thomas Burrowes (1796-1866) (Thomas Burrowes fonds, C 1-0-0-0-74. I0002193)

1-12: [Niagara Falls] American from the American side, 1873, Anne Langton (1804?-93) (John Langton Family fonds, F 1077-9-1-23-1. I0008476)

1-13: *Horseshoe Falls at Niagara, entrance to the cavern on the English side*, 1801, Col. James Pattison Cockburn (1779-1847) (drawn by T. Allom, sketched by Col. James Pattison Cockburn, engraved by R. Sands) (Documentary Art Collection, C 281-0-0-0-19. I0003079)

1-14: *Thunder Cape, w. side, Lake Superior*, 1867, William Armstrong (1822-1914) (William Armstrong fonds, C 333-0-0-3. I0003094)

1-15: View of Ottawa [ca. 1876], Anne Langton (1804?-93) (John Langton Family fonds, F 1077-9-1-25-4 I0008426)

1-16: View of Ottawa [ca. 1876], Anne Langton (1804?-93) (John Langton Family fonds, F 1077-9-1-24. I0008427)

1-17: *Blythe Farm* [ca. 1847]-59, Anne Langton (1804?-93) (John Langton Family fonds, F 1077-8-1-2-53. I0008417)

1-18: *Interior of John's House*, [1837-1838], Anne Langton (1804?-93) (John Langton Family fonds, F 1077-8-1-4-22. I0008045)

1-19: *End view of John's House* [1837-8], Anne Langton (1804?-93) (John Langton Family fonds, F 1077-8-1-4-19. I0008042)

1-20: *Mills near Peterboro* [ca. 1847]-59, Anne Langton (1804?-93) (John Langton Family fonds, F 1077-8-1-2-28B. I0008400)

1-21: *Moose Factory*, 1854, William Trask (artist), Ford and West, Lithographers (Documentary Art Collection, C 281-0-0-0-31. I0003085)

1-22: *Mud and brick house, Bathurst Street and Sheppard Avenue, Toronto*, 1927, Stewart C. Shaw (1896-1970) (Documentary Art Collection, C 281-0-0-0-103. I0003138)

1-23: *King Street, Toronto* [ca. 1910], Dorothy Stevens (1888-1966) (Documentary Art Collection, C 281-0-0-0-14. I0003088)

1-1 : *A picnic at Sloat's Lake, near Sydenham in the Township of Loughborough*, 1861, Thomas Burrowes (1796-1866) (Fonds Thomas Burrowes, C 1-0-0-0-94. I0002213)

1-2 : *40 Mile Creek, 40 from Niagara, towards the head of Lake Ontario* [vers 1794], Elizabeth Simcoe (1762-1850) (Fonds Famille Simcoe, F 47-11-1-0-123. I0006975)

1-3 : Description visuelle et écrite d'une chenille [vers 1793], Elizabeth Simcoe (1762-1850) (Fonds Famille Simcoe, F 47-11-1-0-105. I0006957)

1-4 : Hutte indienne en écorce [vers 1796], Elizabeth Simcoe (1762-1850) (Fonds Famille Simcoe, F 47-11-1-0-288. I0006358)

1-5 : Site de Charlotteville à Longpoint [vers 1795], Elizabeth Simcoe (1762-1850) (Fonds Famille Simcoe, F 47-11-1-0-1-185. I0007037)

1-6 : *20 Mile Creek* [10 mai 1794], Elizabeth Simcoe (1762-1850) (Fonds Famille Simcoe, F 47-11-1-0-129. I0006981)

1-7 : 20 Mile Creek [10 mai 1794], Elizabeth Simcoe (1762-1850) (Fonds Famille Simcoe, F 47-11-1-0-130. I0006982)

1-8 : *North entrance of the Rideau Canal from the Ottawa River, taken from the Royal Eng. Office, Bytown*, 1845, Thomas Burrowes (1796-1866) (Fonds Thomas Burrowes, C 1-0-0-0-14. I0002132)

1-9 : *Locks at the Isthmus, the last ascent to the summit water of Canal from Lake Ontario*, 1841, Thomas Burrowes (1796-1866) (Fonds Thomas Burrowes, C 11-0-0-0-36. I0002155)

1-10 : *Brewer's Lower Mill; view down the Cataraqui Creek and clearing made for the canal* 1829, Thomas Burrowes (1796-1866) (Fonds Thomas Burrowes, C 1-0-0-0-67. I0002186)

1-11 : Lower Kingston Mills, avec le viaduc du chemin de fer du Grand Tronc, 1856, Thomas Burrowes (1796-1866) (Fonds Thomas Burrowes, C 1-0-0-0-74. I0002193)

1-12 : [Les chutes Niagara] Vue du côté américain, 1873, Anne Langton (1804?-1893) (Fonds Famille John Langton, F 1077-9-1-23-1, I0008476)

1-13 : *Horseshoe Falls at Niagara, entrance to the cavern on the English side*, 1801, Col. James Pattison Cockburn (1779-1847) (dessin de T. Allom; croquis du col. James Pattison Cockburn; gravure de R. Sands) (Collection d'art documentaire, C 281-0-0-0-19. I0003079)

1-14 : *Thunder Cape, w. side, Lake Superior*, 1867, William Armstrong (1822-1914) (Fonds William Armstrong, C 333-0-0-03. I0003094)

1-15 : Vue d'Ottawa [vers 1876], Anne Langton (1804?-1893) (Fonds Famille John Langton, F 1077-9-1-25-4. I0008426)

1-16 : Vue d'Ottawa [vers 1876], Anne Langton (1804?-1893) (Fonds Famille John Langton, F 1077-9-1-24. I0008427)

1-17 : *Blythe Farm* [vers 1847]-1859, Anne Langton (1804?-1893) (Fonds Famille John Langton, F 1077-8-1-2-53. I0008417)

1-18 : *Interior of John's House* [1837-1838], Anne Langton (1804?-1893) (Fonds Famille John Langton, F 1077-8-1-4-22. I0008045)

1-19 : *End view of John's House* [1837-1838], Anne Langton (1804?-1893) (Fonds Famille John Langton, F 1077-8-1-4-19. I0008042)

1-20 : *Mills near Peterboro* [vers 1847]-1859, Anne Langton (1804?-1893) (Fonds Famille John Langton, F 1077-8-1-2-28B. I008400)

1-21 : *Moose Factory*, 1854, William Trask (artiste), Ford and West, lithographes (Collection d'art documentaire, C 281-0-0-0-31. I0003085)

1-22 : *Mud and brick house, Bathurst Street and Sheppard Avenue, Toronto*, 1927, Stewart C. Shaw (1896-1970) (Collection d'art documentaire, C 281-0-0-0-103. I0003138)

1-23 : *King Street, Toronto* [vers 1910], Dorothy Stevens (1888-1966) (Collection d'art documentaire, C 281-0-0-0-14. I0003088)

2

MAPS

LES DOCUMENTS CARTOGRAPHIQUES

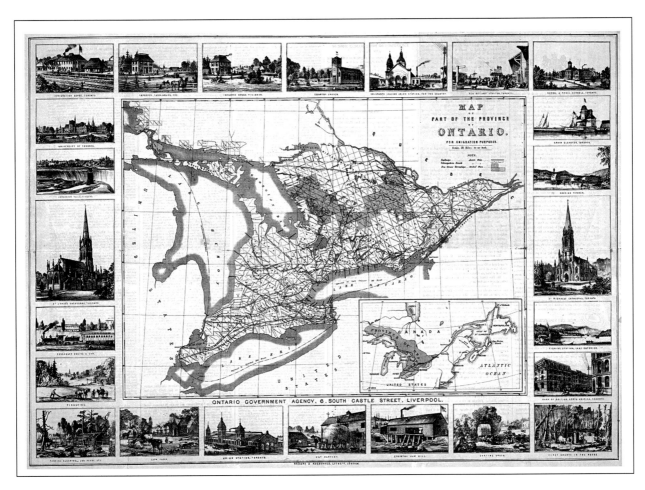

Few historical documents are as intriguing as maps. Glancing at an old map, one may start by seeking out a familiar place but then notice something else. Admiration of fine detail or vibrant colouring is soon followed by fascination with the shape and texture of a different world.

Since the mapmakers' art reflects the spirit of their age, a careful examination of an historical map can shed light on the assumptions and values of the past. For instance, the St Lawrence River was not the gateway to the riches of the Orient, but a sixteenth-century map clearly demonstrates that many Europeans of the time wished it were. Then, and for long afterwards, maps had a special ability to capture people's imagination; indeed, some saw their authority as even greater than that of the written word. It was therefore no accident that imperial nations of the past used maps to illustrate their might and reach; a map that showed an empire ruling from sea to sea was as effective as any other document, and perhaps more so, in declaring imperial power and grandeur.

Today, maps connect the present to the past in an immediate way, by including a family name on an old patent plan, for example, or, in the case of town street maps, indicating the first appearance of a certain street. The panoramic views of towns and cities created in the nineteenth century satisfy the natural human desire to see familiar surroundings documented in a map. Those artists knew that people took pride in their landmarks and were willing to pay for a map that displayed them.

Many of the 35,000 maps at the Archives of Ontario are exquisite, with elaborate cartouches, detailed borders, and bold inks. Yet there is more to them than their beauty, or their occasional flights of cartographic fancy, appealing as these are. The older maps – the earliest one in the Archives' collection dates to 1579 – reveal disputes between nations, lay claim to huge continents in the name of empire, and boast of progress and conquest. More modern ones (the most recent maps currently in the Archives' holdings date to 1999) indicate patterns of development and identify environmental trends. Even the most common road map of today can be absorbing, for, just as a map can mark the best way of reaching a destination, it can also show the place from which we came.

Rares sont les documents historiques aussi captivants que les cartes. En abordant une carte ancienne, on commence généralement par repérer un endroit connu, mais on a tôt fait de relever autre chose. L'admiration d'un détail méticuleux ou d'un brillant coloris débouche promptement sur la fascination qu'exercent la forme ou la texture d'un monde différent.

Puisque l'art du cartographe reflète l'esprit de son époque, l'examen attentif d'une carte ancienne peut permettre d'en dégager les croyances et valeurs. Par exemple, le Saint-Laurent s'est avéré ne pas être la route qui menait aux trésors de l'Orient, mais une carte du seizième siècle démontre clairement qu'un certain nombre d'Européens l'auraient bien souhaité. Les cartes avaient alors, comme longtemps par la suite, le don d'enflammer l'imagination; certains s'y fiaient même davantage qu'aux écrits. Ce n'est donc pas par hasard que les puissances coloniales d'antan avaient recours à des cartes pour illustrer leur suprématie et leur emprise; la carte d'un empire qui s'étendait d'un océan à l'autre était aussi sinon plus efficace que tout autre document pour témoigner du pouvoir d'un empire et de sa grandeur.

Aujourd'hui, les cartes établissent un lien direct entre passé et présent, par exemple lorsqu'on retrouve sur un vieux plan de concession l'inscription d'un nom de famille, ou encore, sur un plan de ville, la première apparition d'un certain nom de rue. Les vues panoramiques urbaines du dix-neuvième siècle répondent à notre désir naturel de voir des milieux familiers documentés par une carte. Comme le savaient pertinemment leurs auteurs, les gens sont fiers des atouts de leur collectivité et sont disposés à payer pour une carte qui les fait valoir.

Parmi les 35 000 cartes des Archives, il y en a d'exquises, aux cartouches ouvragés, aux bordures finement ornées et aux encres colorées. Pourtant, si charmantes qu'elles soient, elles nous apportent davantage que leur beauté ou des échappées occasionnelles de fantaisie cartographique. Les cartes historiques – la plus ancienne de la collection date de 1579 – parlent de conflits entre pays, de continents entiers revendiqués au nom d'un empire, de progrès et de conquêtes haut proclamés. Pour leur part, les cartes modernes (les plus récentes datent de 1999) retracent les schèmes de développement et les tendances environnementales. De nos jours, même la carte routière la plus banale a son intérêt : tout comme elle renseigne sur le moyen d'arriver là où nous allons, elle indique et rappelle le lieu d'où nous venons.

2-2

2-2: In 1570 Abraham Ortelius (1527-98), a rare book dealer in Antwerp, bound together a collection of maps that depicted the known world. Ortelius named the compilation *Theatrum Orbis Terrarum (Theatre of the World)* and thus was born the first modern atlas, which proved so popular that more than forty editions were published. The Archives has one of the maps from the atlas, entitled 'Americae sive novi orbis, nova descriptio' (New description of America or the New World), which originated in the 1579 Latin edition. This map was influenced by the travels of the explorer Jacques Cartier and shows the St Lawrence River extending across the continent to the Pacific Ocean. Despite this and many other inaccuracies, in the 1570s Ortelius's map was the most complete and detailed one of the western hemisphere.

2-2 : En 1570, Abraham Ortelius (1527-1598), marchand de livres rares d'Anvers, assemblait un recueil de cartes représentant le monde connu, sous le titre *Theatrum Orbis Terrarum* (Le Théâtre du Monde). C'est ainsi que voyait le jour le premier atlas moderne, qui a connu une faveur telle que plus de quarante éditions devaient se succéder. Les Archives possèdent une des cartes de cet atlas, intitulée *Americae sive novi orbis, nova descriptio* (Nouvelle description de l'Amérique ou du Nouveau Monde) et provenant de l'édition latine de 1579. Cette carte, qui tient compte des voyages de l'explorateur Jacques Cartier, montre un Saint-Laurent qui traverse le continent pour se jeter dans le Pacifique. Malgré cette méprise et bien d'autres, la carte d'Ortelius était la plus complète et la plus détaillée dont on ait disposé pour l'hémisphère occidental dans les années 1570.

2-3

2-3: Nicolas Sanson (1600-67) was reputed to be the best French mapmaker of the 1600s and is considered to be the founder of the French school of cartography. His work came to the attention of King Louis XIII, who was so impressed by Sanson's skill that he appointed him the *géographe ordinaire de roi* around 1630. This map by Sanson was one of the first to show the five Great Lakes in one map and was used as a model for other maps drawn by contemporaries, just as much of the information that Sanson used was extrapolated from maps created by other cartographers. This was a common practice and led to the perpetuation of many geographical errors in the maps of the seventeenth and eighteenth centuries.

2-3 : Nicolas Sanson (1600-1667) avait la réputation d'être le meilleur cartographe français des années 1600 et il est considéré comme le fondateur de l'école française de cartographie. Ses travaux avaient attiré l'attention de Louis XIII, qui, impressionné par le talent de Sanson, l'avait fait géographe ordinaire du roi vers 1630. Cette carte de Sanson était l'une des premières à représenter l'ensemble des cinq Grands Lacs et devait servir de modèle à d'autres cartes dressées par des contemporains, tout comme une bonne partie des données utilisées par Sanson avaient été tirées de cartes dessinées par d'autres cartographes. C'était là pratique courante et explique que se soient perpétuées une foule d'erreurs géographiques dans les cartes des dix-septième et dix-huitième siècles.

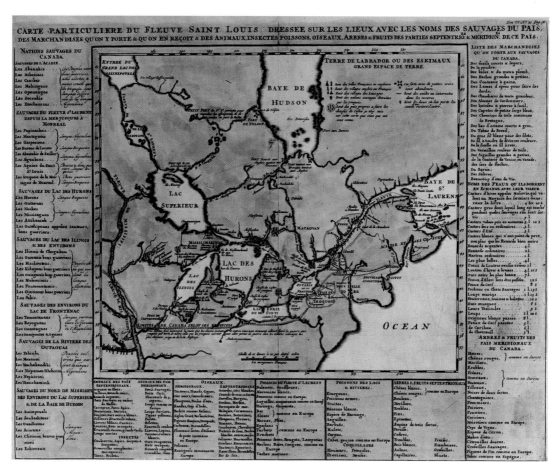

2-4

2-4: French cartographer Henri Abraham Châtelain (1684-1743) annotated many of his maps with extensive peripheral information about their subjects. On this well-known map, he listed various indigenous peoples, the flora and fauna of Canada, and the current prices for sundry merchandise traded between the New World and Europe. The map itself contains many idiosyncrasies, including its title, which refers to the 'Fleuve Saint Louis' even though the river on the map is labelled with the name by which it was more commonly known, the 'Fleuve de Missisipi.' The map also claims to show the best beaver trapping areas of New France, but Châtelain candidly notes in the legend that 'I only put in the [trapping areas] that I know about myself.'

2-4 : Le cartographe français Henri Abraham Châtelain (1684-1743) plaçait en annotation de ses cartes des détails poussés sur leurs sujets. Sur cette carte bien connue, il énumère les peuples autochtones, décrit la flore et la faune canadiennes et relève le prix courant de diverses marchandises échangées entre l'Europe et le Nouveau Monde. La carte même renferme de nombreuses idiosyncrasies, dont son titre de « Fleuve Saint Louis », bien que, sur la carte, ce cours d'eau porte le nom qui servait à le désigner le plus souvent, soit « Fleuve de Missisipi [sic] ». La carte prétend aussi indiquer les zones les plus propices pour piéger le castor en Nouvelle-France, mais, en légende, Châtelain note naïvement que « je n'indique que celles [zones de piégeage] que je connais personnellement. »

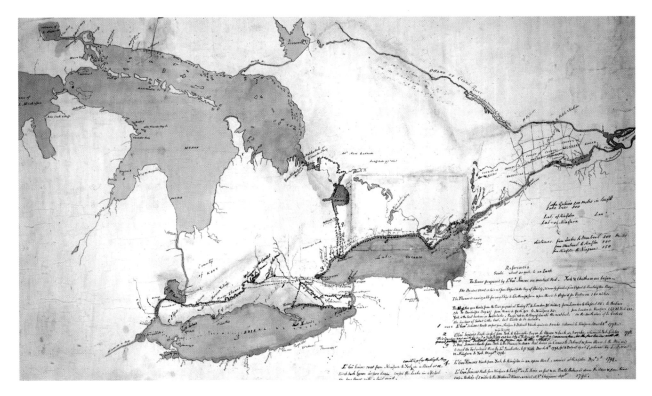

2-5

2-5: The Simcoe Family papers contain numerous manuscript maps that date primarily from 1792 to 1796, when Lieutenant-Governor John Graves Simcoe (1752-1806) and his wife, Elizabeth (1762-1850), lived in Upper Canada. Many of these maps are not signed but some have been attributed to Elizabeth Simcoe. This particular map is thought to be one of hers since it so closely resembles a map she drew on birch bark called 'Sketch of Upper Canada,' which was sent to the Prince Regent in early 1794. One of Lieutenant-Governor Simcoe's goals was to plan settlements and make arrangements for the defence of Upper Canada. This map tracks Simcoe's various trips around the colony, during which his vision took shape. It was most likely drawn over time; new information from each of his travels was gradually added to the map, as indicated by the different inks used. The bottom right corner of the map lists the trips taken by Simcoe.

2-5 : Les papiers de la famille Simcoe renferment de nombreuses cartes manuscrites datant surtout de 1792 à 1796, période du séjour dans le Haut-Canada du lieutenant-gouverneur John Graves Simcoe (1752-1806) et de sa femme Elizabeth (1762-1850). Beaucoup de ces cartes ne sont pas signées, mais certaines ont été attribuées à Elizabeth Simcoe. La carte que voici serait de sa main, vu son étroite parenté avec une autre, en croquis sur un morceau d'écorce de bouleau et intitulée « Sketch of Upper Canada », qui avait été envoyée au prince régent, au début de 1794. L'un des objectifs du lieutenant-gouverneur Simcoe était planifier le peuplement du Haut-Canada et de prendre des dispositions pour sa défense. Cette carte retrace divers voyages de Simcoe dans la colonie, au cours desquels ses projets avaient pris forme. Son exécution s'est probablement étalée sur une longue période; de nouveaux renseignements s'y étant graduellement ajoutés à chacun des voyages, ainsi que le suggère l'utilisation de plusieurs encres différentes. À l'angle inférieur droit de la carte, on trouve la liste des voyages effectués par Simcoe.

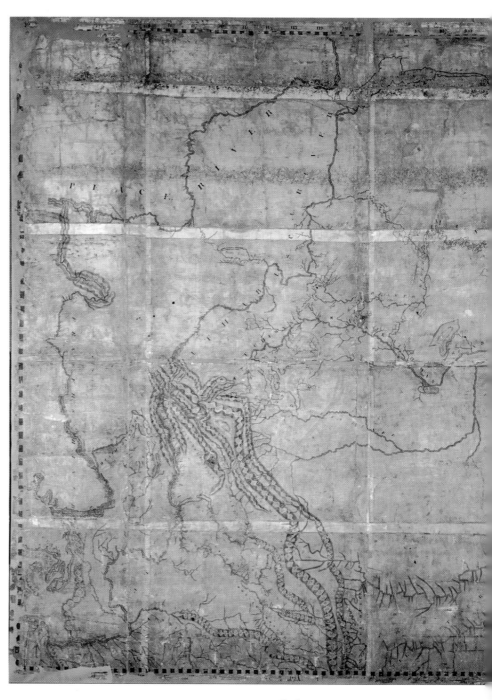

2-6

2-6: 'The Map of the North-West Territory of the Province of Canada,' by David Thompson (1770-1857), is one of the largest items in the Archives' collection and certainly among the most admired. Completed by Thompson in 1814, it is permanently on display in its own special climate-controlled case. Though he had limited tools and used a ship's sextant to take his readings, the map was so accurate that it remained the best depiction of the region for one hundred years. In 1905, the Archives acquired Thompson's masterpiece from the Department of Crown Lands.

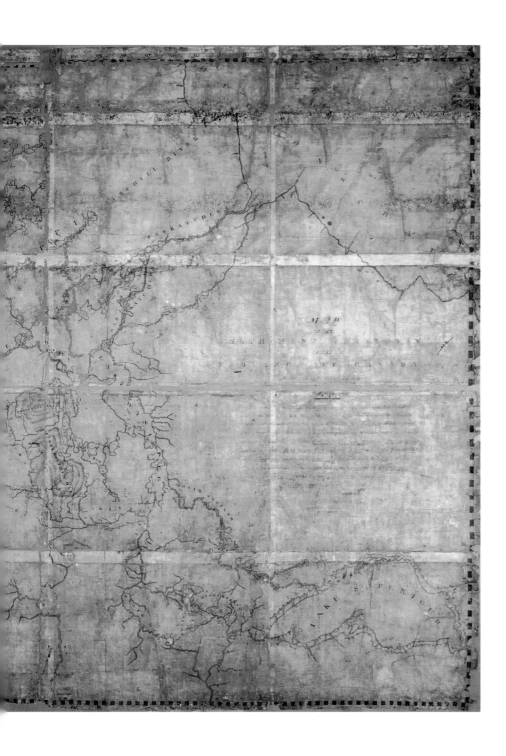

2-6 : « The Map of the North-West Territory of the Province of Canada », de David Thompson (1770-1857), est l'un des rares objets à format géant de la collection des Archives et elle compte très certainement parmi les plus admirés. Achevée par Thompson en 1814, elle est exposée en permanence dans une vitrine spéciale, climatisée. Bien que son auteur n'ait disposé que d'instruments primitifs et qu'il ait utilisé un sextant de marine pour effectuer ses lectures la carte était si précise qu'elle est demeurée la meilleure réprésentation de la région un siècle durant. En 1905, les Archives ont fait l'acquisition du chef-d'œuvre de Thompson, qui était en possession du ministère des Terres de la Couronne.

2-7: In addition to the David Thompson map, more than 5,000 patent plans from the Department of Crown Lands are included in the Archives' collection. These are some of the most heavily used records since a great deal of information may be gleaned from them. Originally, surveys of townships were conducted under the direction of the Surveyor General's Office. When a survey was completed and a plan prepared, an extra copy of each town or township plan was given to the Department of Crown Lands, which would record the name of each new patentee in the appropriate lot or portion of a lot and usually mark a 'D' in the spot for 'described.'

Until the late 1970s, the Ministry of Natural Resources used patent plans as quick reference tools to show the alienation of crown land. However, once this information was available in a computer database, the ministry no longer required the patent plans and they were transferred to the Archives. This particular patent plan of Machar Township illustrates how a record can have a long and useful life. The plan was created in 1876, has new notations until 14 April 1970, and, though it is no longer an active government record, is still in constant demand by researchers.

2-7 : Outre la carte de David Thompson, la collection des Archives comprend plus de 5 000 de concessions du ministère des Terres de la Couronne. Ces documents sont parmi les plus consultés, car on y trouve une mine de renseignements. À l'origine, on procédait au levé des cantons sous la direction de l'Arpenteur en chef. Une fois le levé effectué et le plan préparé, on remettait une copie de chaque plan de ville ou de canton au ministère des Terres de la Couronne, qui inscrivait le nom de chacun des nouveaux titulaires de terrains enregistrés dans le tracé correspondant à son lot ou à sa portion de lot, avec, dans l'espace prévu pour la « description », le « D » usuel.

Jusqu'à la fin des années 1970, le ministère des Richesses naturelles s'est servi des plans de concessions comme instruments de référence rapide concernant la cession des terres de la Couronne. Cependant, une fois ces renseignements stockés dans une base de données informatique, les plans ont cessé d'être utiles au ministère, qui les a versés aux Archives. Nous voyons ici un plan du canton de Machar, à témoin du fait qu'un document peut avoir une très longue vie utile. Dressé en 1876, le plan a reçu de nouvelles annotations jusqu'au 14 avril 1970 et, bien que ne faisant plus partie des documents publics actifs, il est toujours fréquemment consulté par les chercheurs.

2-7

2-8: Not all land transactions in Upper Canada were conducted through the Department of Crown Lands. Thomas Talbot obtained a grant of 5,000 acres of land from the crown in 1803 on the understanding that he would populate the lots with British settlers only (an understanding that he did not honour, since he would allow Americans to purchase land as well). Through his connections to highly placed government officials, including former Lieutenant-Governor Simcoe, Talbot was able to acquire a further 20,000 acres. He exercised close control over his domain, known as the Talbot Settlement, and appears to have disdained the usual procedures concerning land registration, pencilling in the names of his settlers on his own map and not bothering to inform the Surveyor General's Office.

Like other township surveys, the Talbot plans show survey grids and physical features, with coloured areas indicating crown (pink) and clergy (grey-green) reserves. This map of Yarmouth Township includes school reserves.

2-8 : Dans le Haut-Canada, toutes les transactions foncières ne passaient pas par le ministère des Terres de la Couronne. Ainsi, en 1803, Thomas Talbot avait obtenu la concession de 5 000 acres de terres de la Couronne; il s'engageait en contrepartie à peupler ses lots de colons exclusivement britanniques (engagement qu'il n'a pas tenu, puisqu'il permettait également à des Américains d'acheter des terres). En faisant jouer ses relations avec des éminences du régime, dont l'ex-lieutenant-gouverneur Simcoe, Talbot a par la suite réussi à acquérir 20 000 acres de plus. Il exerçait un étroit contrôle sur son domaine, connu sous le nom de Talbot Settlement (la colonie Talbot), et semble avoir fait peu de cas des formalités habituelles d'enregistrement foncier : il inscrivait le nom des colons au crayon sur sa propre carte, sans prendre la peine d'en informer le bureau de l'Arpenteur en chef.

À l'instar d'autres levés de cantons, les plans de Talbot comprennent des grilles de levés et l'indication des caractéristiques physiques, les zones colorées indiquant les réserves soit de la Couronne (en rose), soit du clergé (en gris-vert). Cette carte du canton Yarmouth englobe des réserves scolaires.

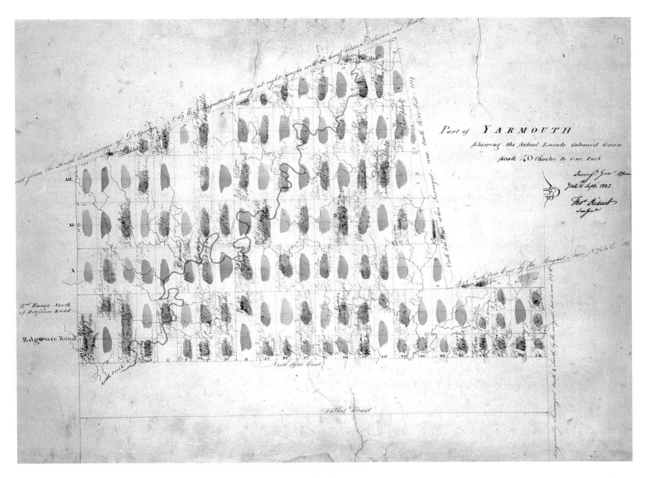

2-8

2-9: Settlement plans are often interesting and this one is an especially fine example. It shows the Elgin settlement (now the village of Buxton), the eventual home of many fugitive slaves who landed in Kent and Essex counties when they reached the end of the underground railway. The plan features the house of the Reverend William King, the leader of the Elgin settlement, and other key structures, including the church, schoolhouse, post office, mill, and shops. When the plan of this village was prepared, there were approximately 1,200 inhabitants and 250 families.

This drawing has many elements that set it apart from the usual township plan. The artist chose to draw the buildings and physical features as elevations and included small details such as smoke curling out of chimneys. These and other fine points give the map a human feel and help to offset the regularity of the grid pattern and lot size of the Elgin settlement.

2-9 : Les plans de villages sont souvent pleins d'intérêt, et celui-ci en est un bel exemple. Il s'agit de la colonie Elgin (aujourd'hui le village de Buxton), qui allait accueillir de nombreux esclaves fugitifs parmi ceux qui arrivaient au bout du chemin de fer clandestin, dans les cantons de Kent et d'Essex. Le plan indique la maison du révérend William King, chef de la colonie Elgin, ainsi que quelques-unes des principales constructions : église, école, bureau de poste, moulin et magasins. Lors de la préparation du plan de ce village, on y dénombrait quelque 1 200 habitants et 250 familles.

Ce dessin se distingue de l'habituel plan de canton par de nombreux éléments. Ainsi, l'artiste représente en élévation les bâtiments et caractéristiques physiques, en y apposant de menus ornements, tels que la fumée qui s'échappe en volutes des cheminées. Ces petites touches donnent un tour humain au document et compensent la froide géométrie du schéma de grille et de la répartition par lots de la concession.

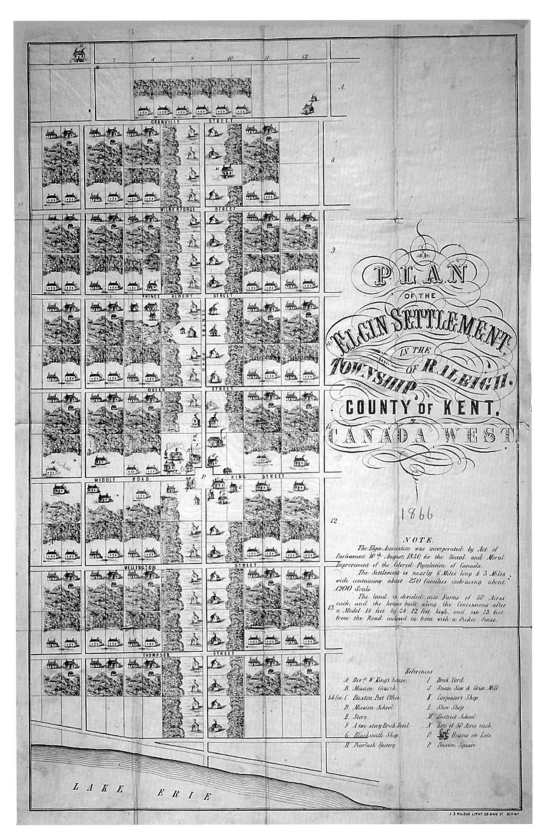

2-9

2-10: Panoramic maps were extremely popular all over North America in the latter part of the nineteenth century. Itinerant artists were kept busy travelling from town to town and creating somewhat fanciful drawings from the imagined vantage point of an oblique angle. These 'bird's eye views' were printed like modern-day posters and found a ready market. Consistent with the prevailing values of the time, the maps took great care to showcase all aspects of the subject town's commercial and industrial activity. Whatever errors there may have been in perspective mattered little to those whose primary interest was in promoting their town as one with great future growth potential. This panorama of Cobourg is typical of the genre, prominently featuring local businesses – at least those that had paid for the privilege!

2-10 : Les cartes panoramiques ont été extrêmement recherchées dans toute l'Amérique du Nord durant la dernière partie du dix-neuvième siècle. Des artistes ambulants s'affairaient, de petite ville en petite ville, à créer des dessins quelque peu fantaisistes, depuis un point d'observation imaginaire, en oblique. Ces « vues à vol d'oiseau » étaient imprimées, à la façon des affiches de nos jours, et trouvaient aussitôt preneurs. Dans le ton des valeurs dominantes de l'époque, les auteurs de cartes prenaient grand soin de mettre en valeur tous les aspects de l'activité industrielle et commerciale de la ville en cause. Les erreurs de perspective qui pouvaient se produire importaient peu aux intéressés, dont le premier souci était de promouvoir leur ville comme lieu d'un avenir exceptionnel. Ce panorama de Cobourg est représentatif du genre : les entreprises locales y sont en vedette – du moins celles qui en avaient fait les frais!

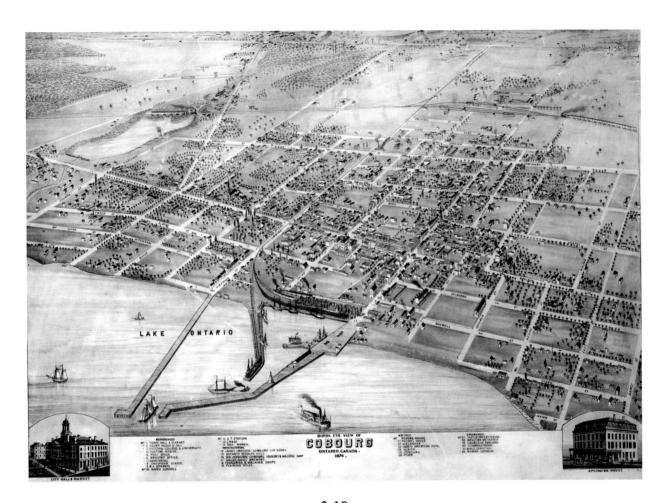

2-10

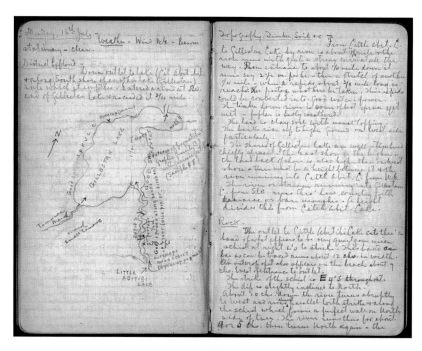

2-11

2-11: In December 1899 Premier George W. Ross instructed Director of Surveys George Fitzpatrick to explore the northern parts of the districts of Nipissing, Algoma, Thunder Bay, and Rainy River. The Department of Crown Lands appointed ten exploration parties to assess the potential mineral, forestry, and agricultural resources of these regions, which were then named New Ontario. The records that these parties produced were some of the first the Archives acquired.

Consisting of diaries, maps, and reports, the records provide a fascinating glimpse into the minds of the surveyors and geologists involved. As Fitzpatrick stated in his final report to the premier, he hoped that the surveys would 'spur on our sons to still greater achievements in the future. Assured that, under the blessing of the Almighty, if we are true to our best interests, throwing our energies into developing our province with all classes and nationalities standing firmly together, we shall build up a country second to none in this world ...'

2-11 : En décembre 1899, le premier ministre George W. Ross avait demandé au directeur des levés, George Fitzpatrick, de procéder à l'exploration des parties septentrionales des districts de Nipissing, Algoma, Thunder Bay et Rainy River. Le ministère des Terres de la Couronne a donc formé dix groupes d'exploration, afin d'évaluer les ressources sur les plans minéralogique, forestier et agricole de ces régions, qui devaient constituer le New Ontario (« Nouvel Ontario »). Les documents rédigés par ces groupes sont parmi les premiers acquis par les Archives.

Composés de cartes, rapports et journaux person-nels, ces documents donnent un aperçu fascinant du tour d'esprit de ces arpenteurs et géologues. Ainsi que Fitzpatrick le déclare dans son rapport final à l'intention du premier ministre, il entretient le vif espoir que les levés [traduction] « poussent nos fils à entreprendre un jour des projets d'une portée encore plus large. Dans la conviction que, forts de la bénédiction du Tout-Puissant et si nous restons fidèles à nos intérêts les plus nobles, investissant nos énergies dans le développement de notre province, toute classes et nationalités résolument solidaires, nous bâtirons un pays qui ne le cédera à aucun autre au monde… »

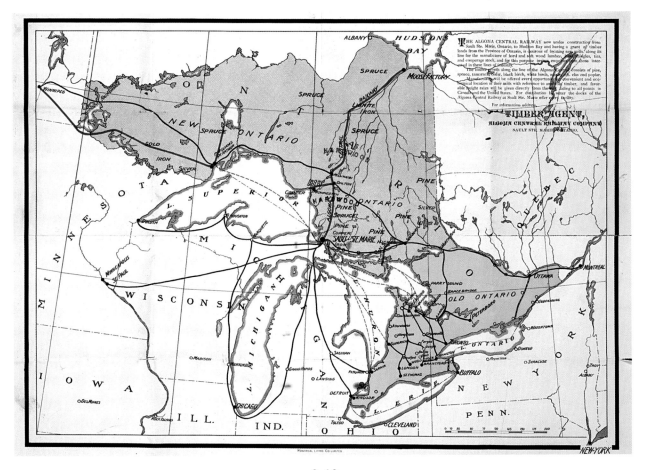

2-12

2-12: As the only practical form of transportation through the rugged Canadian Shield, railways spurred the development of New Ontario and shaped its development. The Algoma Central Railway was intended to promote the development of agriculture in the north. Its American owner, Francis Hector Clergue, promised the government that he would settle 10,000 people along its length, and, as a result, the railway was granted vast reserves of land. However, Clergue's endeavour never succeeded in spite of maps such as this one, designed as propaganda to lure settlers to the region.

2-12 : Seul moyen de transport pratique dans ces immenses contrées désertiques du Bouclier canadien, le chemin de fer a servi de levier et d'aiguillon au développement du « Nouvel Ontario », qu'il a façonné. L'Algoma Central Railway devait promouvoir les progrès de l'agriculture dans le Nord. Son propriétaire américain, Francis Hector Clergue, avait promis au gouvernement d'établir 10 000 colons sur son parcours; en conséquence, la société avait obtenu la concession de vastes réserves foncières. Cependant, le projet de Clergue ne devait jamais se concrétiser, malgré l'existence de cartes telles que celle-ci, conçues comme moyen de publicité et visant à attirer des colons dans la région.

2-13 & 2-14: Maps are often used to illustrate graphically the information contained in a statement or report; in fact, maps are extremely useful tools for quickly communicating complex data. The map below is an example of one compiled in 1882 by Dr P.H. Bryce, secretary to the Provincial Board of Health. In order to show patterns and trends in disease in Ontario, Bryce divided the province into ten districts based on differences in geographical formation and weather conditions. A map indicating the prevalence of disease in the various districts was issued on a weekly basis and text and tables included on the maps discussed the changes from week to week. Bryce's maps not only show the incidence and varieties of disease over a two-year period in Ontario but also reveal the increasing role of the government in public-health initiatives.

2-13 et 2-14 : Les cartes sont souvent l'illustration visuelle des renseignements qui figurent dans une déclaration ou un rapport; en fait, les cartes sont des outils extrêmement utiles pour condenser des données complexes et les communiquer rapidement. La carte ci-dessous a été établie en 1882, par le Dr P. H. Bryce, secrétaire du Conseil provincial de la santé de l'Ontario. Afin de représenter le tableau et les tendances de la morbidité en Ontario, Bryce avait divisé la province en dix districts, en fonction des différences géographiques et des conditions climatiques. On publiait toutes les semaines une carte qui faisait le bilan de la morbidité prévalente dans les divers districts, avec un exposé assorti de tableaux des changements survenus depuis la semaine précédente. Non seulement les cartes de Bryce indiquent l'incidence et l'éventail des maladies présentes en Ontario sur une période de deux ans, mais elles attestent également le rôle croissant que joue le gouvernement en matière de santé publique.

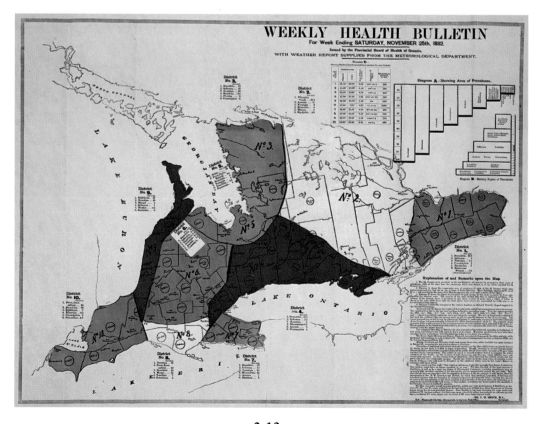

2-13

EXPLANATION OF THE MAP

—ISSUED BY—
The Provincial Board of Health,
—ILLUSTRATING THE—
WEEKLY PREVALENCE OF DISEASE
THROUGHOUT THE PROVINCE.

The information from which these reports are deduced is received from correspondents in various places situated in some one of the ten districts into which the Province is divided.

The Province has been divided for purposes of comparison into ten districts, the comparisons being based upon differences in geological formation, and meteorological conditions due to (a) difference in height above sea-level, (b) difference in prevailing winds, (c) difference in rain and snow-fall, (d) difference in forest areas. These divisions are due to the fact that relations more or less intimate are assumed to exist between the prevalence of certain diseases, and the predominance of one or more of these conditions.

The comparison of diseases in any district being dependent upon the number of cases reported by physicians as occurring in their own practice, it follows that the degree of correctness will be in proportion to the number and accuracy of reports received from any district. It is felt, however, that the number of reporters from the various districts is large enough to make the reports sufficiently accurate for Provincial comparison.

To make these reports more complete, the meteorological condition of the various districts is also appended to the map, the Dominion Weather Service having kindly consented to supply the Board with weekly reports.

As will be seen, the average height above the sea-level of any district is deduced from the heights of the various localities of such districts as are given on the map.

The names of the diseases which are given in the printed spaces are arranged in the order of prevalence, the one of which there is the greatest number of cases being placed first, the next greatest placed second, etc., etc.

Opposite each disease is placed its percentage value as compared with the total number of cases of all diseases reported from any district.

Explanation of diagrams—In the horizontal line opposite the number representing each district will be found the various weather conditions in their respective vertical columns. Thus comparisons can readily be made. Under the diagram representing the prevalence of disease are to be seen vertical columns with the left-hand vertical divided into ten parts, each equivalent to 10 %. This division is intended to represent the area of prevalence of any disease. Thus, where any one of the diseases prevalent in any one area is found, in all the others it will be equal to 100%, and so on for the other numbers below *ten*.

The breadth of the columns in diagram B is intended to represent the degree of prevalence of the six prevailing diseases. Thus, the disease with the highest degree of prevalence has a breadth of 6-8 in., and equals 100. Again, each in the decreasing order of prevalence is narrower by 1-8 in. Thus, the sixth in order of prevalence is only 1-8 in. in breadth.

DR. P. H. BRYCE, M.A.,
Secretary.

2-14

2-15 to 2-18: Another example of the many purposes for which maps are used are fire-insurance plans. In the nineteenth and early twentieth centuries, buildings in Canadian towns and cities were commonly constructed of wood. Thus, when a fire started it spread quickly, resulting in the devastation of many communities. Fire-insurance companies were established to respond to this problem and they had specialized plans prepared to help determine insurance rates for their clients. These large-scale maps indicated the heights and property lines of individual buildings, showed the proximity of fire halls, and noted potentially hazardous businesses. For instance, two downtown bakeries and their large ovens are clearly indicated on this plan of Rat Portage (now the town of Kenora).

Though fire-insurance plans have long outlived their original purpose, they continue to be prized highly for the details they contain, particularly by those interested in local history, architectural researchers, and environmental investigators. In addition to this plan for Rat Portage, the Archives holds fire-insurance and special-survey plans for nearly five hundred other communities in the province.

2-15 à 2-18 : Le plan d'assurance-incendie est un autre exemple des objectifs multiples auxquels répondent les cartes. Au dix-neuvième siècle et au début vingtième, les bâtiments des villes canadiennes étaient très souvent construits en bois. Lorsqu'un incendie se déclarait, il se propageait donc très rapidement, avec des effets dévastateurs pour les malheureuses collectivités. Pour parer à cette situation, des sociétés d'assurance-incendie ont été établies et ont fait dresser des plans spéciaux, leur permettant de déterminer les tarifs. Ces cartes, à grande échelle, indiquaient la hauteur et les limites de propriété de chaque bâtiment ainsi que sa distance du poste de pompiers, et signalaient les établissements pouvant être dangereux. Par exemple, deux boulangeries-pâtisseries du centre-ville, avec leurs grands fours, sont clairement marquées sur ce plan de Portage du rat (l'actuelle ville de Kenora).

Les plans d'assurance-incendie ne servent plus à leurs fins initiales depuis longtemps, mais ils ont toujours une grande valeur, en raison des détails qu'ils contiennent, particulièrement pour ceux qui s'intéressent à la petite histoire, les chercheurs en architecture et les enquêteurs en matière environnementale. Outre ce plan dressé pour Portage du rat, les Archives conservent des plans d'assurance-incendie et des levés spéciaux à l'égard de quelque cinq cents autres collectivités de la province.

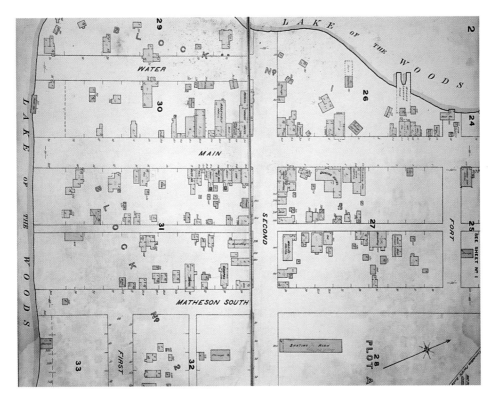

2-15

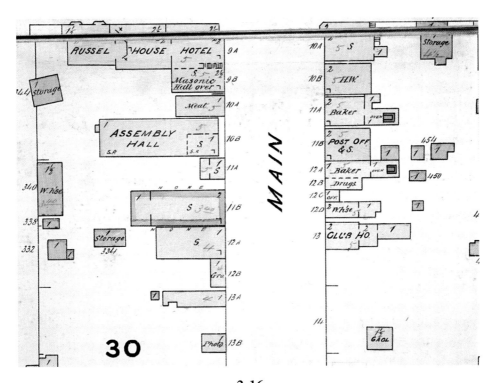

2-16

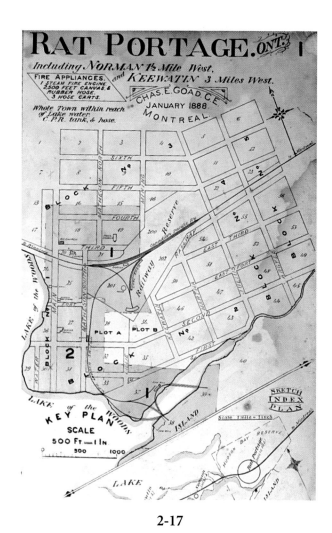

2-17

2-18

2-19

THE CARTOUCHE

2-19: As well as being ornate and attractive, maps are historical documents containing information on contemporary beliefs and values. For example, the decorative elements on maps can be highly symbolic. Cartouches, which commonly appear on maps, are enclosed areas that contain such details as the title, the cartographer's name, the date of publication, the dedication, and other related facts. Cartouches range from plain to highly ornamental and can reveal much about the intended audience for the map or even about the mapmaker who drew it.

Thomas Kitchin (1718-84), a prolific engraver and hydrographer to King George III of England, created lovely cartouches for his maps that were intended to reflect the landscape of the area on the map. This cartouche, unusual for its time, evokes a sense of the solitiude and majesty of the wilderness at the lake's shoreline.

LE CARTOUCHE

2-19 : En plus d'être ornementées et attrayantes, les cartes sont des documents historiques qui renseignent sur les croyances et valeurs de l'époque. Prenons par exemple les éléments décoratifs des cartes, à valeur fréquemment symbolique. Les cartouches, d'usage courant, y sont des encadrés renfermant des détails tels que titre, nom du cartographe, date de publication, dédicace et autres faits connexes. Les cartouches vont du plus sobre au très orné, et peuvent éclairer considérablement sur le public visé ou même sur le cartographe.

Thomas Kitchin (1718-1784), prolifique graveur et hydrographe de George III d'Angleterre, créait pour ses cartes de délicieux cartouches, censés refléter le paysage de la région décrite par la carte. Ce cartouche, inhabituel pour l'époque, est évocateur de la majesté de ces grands espaces désertiques et inexplorés, sur la rive du lac.

2-20

2-20: This cartouche from a hand-drawn map in the Archives' collection is an interesting anomaly. Maps drawn for military purposes were often dull and businesslike; however, on this one, the brightly coloured cartouche dominates the map. It may simply have been a whim of the mapmaker, a navy lieutenant, or reflected his ardent pursuit of the gentlemanly art of watercolour painting.

2-20 : Cet autre cartouche, tiré d'une carte dessinée à la main de la collection des Archives, présente une touche inédite fort intéressante. Les cartes à fins militaires étaient souvent ternes et purement factuelles; or, dans celle-ci, les couleurs brillantes du cartouche dominent. Nous devons peut-être cette anomalie à un simple caprice du cartographe, qui était lieutenant de marine, ou encore à sa ferveur pour le noble art de l'aquarelle.

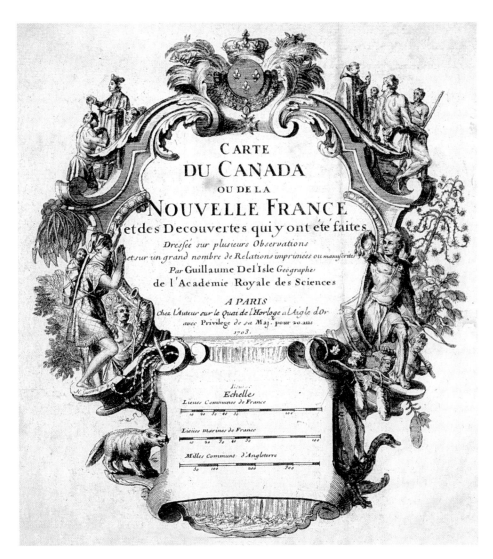

2-21

2-21: This cartouche is a typical example of its kind, found on a map of New France and drawn at a time when boundaries were disputed by rival empires. At the top of the cartouche are the crest and crown of France, clearly indicating the authority under which the map was issued. Clerics are shown baptizing and teaching Natives and there are additional depictions of other aboriginal people waiting for redemption. At the bottom, animals and vegetation illustrate the bounty of the New World, ripe for exploitation.

2-21 : Voici un cartouche exemplaire du genre, tiré d'une carte de la Nouvelle-France et conçu à une époque où les frontières étaient sources de conflit pour des empires rivaux. Dans le haut du cartouche apparaissent l'emblème et la couronne de la France, nette indication de l'autorité destinataire de la carte. On y distingue des religieux qui évangélisent les Autochtones et les baptisent; ailleurs, d'autres Autochtones sont en attente du salut. Dans le bas, des végétaux et des animaux figurent la corne d'abondance du Nouveau Monde, mûr pour sa mise en valeur.

2-1: *Map of Part of the Province of Ontario for Immigration Purposes*, 1877, Maclure and McDonald, lithographers (RG 11, Series R, A-14)

2-2: *Americae Sive Novi Orbis. Nova Descriptio*, 1579, Abraham Ortelius (B-46)

2-3: Le Canada ou Nouvelle France &c. Tirée de diverses Relations des François, Anglois, Hollandois, &c., Nicolas Sanson [ca. 1660] (C-78)

2-4: Carte particulière du Fleuve Saint Louis *dressée* sur les lieux avec les noms du sauvages des païs, *des* marchandises qu'on y porte & qu'on en reçoit & des animaux, insectes, poissons, oiseaux, arbres & fruits des parties septentrionales et meridionales de ce païs, 1719, Henri Châtelain (Miscellaneous Map Collection, C 279-0-0-0-10)

2-5: [Sketch map of Upper Canada showing the routes Lt.-Gov. Simcoe took on journeys between March 1793 and September 1795], [1795]. Attributed to Elizabeth Simcoe (Simcoe family fonds, F 47-5-1-0-37. I0004757)

2-6: *Map of the North-West Territory of the Province of Canada* by David Thompson, 1814 (David Thompson fonds, F 443, R-C(U), AO 1541)

2-7: Patent Plan of Machar Township, Parry Sound District, 1876 (Crown Lands, Patent Plans, RG 1-100, 243)

2-8: Yarmouth Township, 1823, Thomas Ridout (Talbot fonds, F 501-1-0-0-44)

2-9: *Plan of the Elgin Settlement in the Township of Raleigh, County of Kent, Canada West*, 1866, J.S. Wilson, lithographer (Miscellaneous Map Collection, C 279-0-0-0-3. I0004737)

2-10: *Bird's eye view of Cobourg, Ontario, Canada*, 1874 [H. Brosius] (Town and City Plans, C 295-1-34-0-1)

2-11: Geological notes taken by R.W. Coulthard on exploration north of Abitibi Lakes and Abitibi River, 1900 (Exploration parties of northern Ontario - Party No. 1, RG 1-411-1-8)

2-12: Map of Ontario Showing the Algoma Central Railway [ca. 1900], Algoma Central Railway Company (A-4)

2-13: *Weekly Health Bulletin*, 25 Nov. 1882, Dr P.H. Bryce (Abraham Groves Collection, C 303-1-0-0-8)

2-14: Explanation of the map issued by the Provincial Board of Health illustrating the weekly prevalence of disease throughout the province, Dr P.H. Bryce, 1882 (RG 62, Series B-4; Scrapbook vol. 464; MS 565, item 13)

2-15: Rat Portage, Fire Insurance Plan, 1888, Underwriters' Survey Bureau (Fire Insurance Plan Collection, C 234-1-317-1)

2-16: Rat Portage, Fire Insurance Plan, 1888, Underwriters' Survey Bureau (Fire Insurance Plan Collection, C 234-1-317-1), detail

2-17: Rat Portage, Fire Insurance Plan, 1888, Underwriters' Survey Bureau (Fire Insurance Plan Collection, C 234-1-317-1), detail

2-18: Rat Portage, Fire Insurance Plan, 1888, Underwriters' Survey Bureau (Fire Insurance Plan Collection, C 234-1-317-1), detail

2-19: *Lake Ontario to the Mouth of the River St Lawrence* [1772?], detail, Thomas Kitchin (C-87)

2-20: *Plan of Different Channels Leading from Kingston to Lake Ontario with the Rocks, Shoals, Soundings etc.*, [1796?], detail, Joseph Bouchette (H, Acc. 11459)

2-21: *Carte du Canada, ou de la Nouvelle France, et des Découvertes qui y ont été faites.* 1703, detail, Guillaume Del'Isle (B-46)

2-1 : *Map of Part of the Province of Ontario for Immigration Purposes*, 1877, Maclure and McDonald, lithographes (RG 11, série R, A-14)

2-2 : *Americae Sive Novi Orbis. Nova Descriptio*, 1579, Abraham Ortelius (B-46)

2-3 : Le Canada ou Nouvelle France, &c. Tirée de diverses Relations des François, Anglois, Hollandois, &c., Nicolas Sanson [vers 1660] (C-78)

2-4 : Carte particulière du Fleuve Saint Louis dressée sur les lieux avec les noms des sauvages du païs, des marchandises qu'on y porte & qu'on en reçoit & des animaux, insectes, poissons, oiseaux, arbres & fruits des parties septentrionales et méridionales de ce païs, 1719, Henri Châtelain (Collection de cartes diverses, C 279-0-0-0-10)

2-5 : [Croquis cartographique du Haut-Canada, indiquant le trajet suivi par le lieutenant-gouverneur Simcoe lors des voyages qu'il a effectués entre mars 1793 et septembre 1795] [1795]. Attribué à Elizabeth Simcoe (Fonds Famille Simcoe, F 47-5-1-0-37. I0004757)

2-6 : *Map of the North-West Territory of the Province of Canada*, par David Thompson, 1814 (Fonds David Thompson, F 443, R-C(U), AO 1541)

2-7 : Plan de concession du canton de Machar, district de Parry Sound, 1876 (Terres de la Couronne, plans de concessions, RG 1-100, 243)

2-8 : Canton de Yarmouth, 1823, Thomas Ridout (Fonds Talbot, F 501-1-0-0-44)

2-9 : *Plan of the Elgin Settlement in the Township of Raleigh, County of Kent, Canada West*, 1866, J. S. Wilson, lithographe (Collection de cartes diverses, C 279-0-0-0-3. I0004737)

2-10 : *Bird's eye view of Cobourg, Ontario, Canada*, 1874 [H. Brosius] (Plans de villes, C 295-1-34-0-1)

2-11 : Notes d'ordre géologique prises par R. W. Coulthard, lors d'une excursion au nord des lacs Abitibi et de la rivière Abitibi, 1900 (Groupes d'exploration du Nord de l'Ontario Groupe no 1, RG 1-411-1-8)

2-12 : Carte de l'Ontario, indiquant le tracé du chemin de fer Algoma Central [vers 1900], Algoma Central Railway Company (A-4)

2-13 : *Weekly Health Bulletin*, 25 nov. 1882, Dr P. H. Bryce (Collection Abraham Groves, C 303-1-0-0-8)

2-14 : Commentaire de la carte publiée par le Conseil provincial de la santé, comme bilan de la prévalence hebdomadaire de la morbidité dans la province, Dr P. H. Bryce, 1882 (RG 62, série B-4; Spicilège, vol. 464; MS 565, article 13)

2-15 : Portage du Rat, plan d'assurance-incendie, 1888, Underwriters' Survey Bureau (Collection des plans d'assurance-incendie, C 234-1-317-1)

2-16 : Portage du Rat, plan d'assurance-incendie, 1888, Underwriters' Survey Bureau (Collection des plans d'assurance-incendie, C 234-1-317-1), détail

2-17 : Portage du Rat, plan d'assurance-incendie, 1888, Underwriters' Survey Bureau (Collection des plans d'assurance-incendie, C 234-1-317-1), détail

2-18 : Portage du Rat, plan d'assurance-incendie, 1888, Underwriters' Survey Bureau (Collection des plans d'assurance-incendie, C 234-1-317-1), détail

2-19 : *Lake Ontario to the Mouth of the River St Lawrence* [1772?], détail, Thomas Kitchin (C-87)

2-20 : *Plan of the Different Channels Leading from Kingston to Lake Ontario with the Rocks, Shoals, Soundings etc.* [1796?], détail, Joseph Bouchette (H, Acc. 11459)

2-21 : *Carte du Canada, ou de la Nouvelle France, et des Découvertes qui y ont été faites*, 1703, détail, Guillaume Del'Isle (B-46)

3

PORTRAITS

LES PORTRAITS

3-1

Portraits touch our imaginations more than any other type of archival record. We may be able to catch a glimpse of ourselves in the portrait of an ancestor, and, even if the face in the portrait is unrelated to us, that face may communicate a variety of messages – about the personal character of the individual portrayed, the social class to which he or she belonged, and the kind of society of which they were a part.

The portrait collection at the Archives of Ontario amounts to hundreds of thousands of items and consists of sketches, paintings and photographs. Many of these works are by well-known artists, such as Elizabeth Simcoe and Anne Langton, and portray equally well-known subjects, such as Chief Justice John Beverley Robinson and Lieutenant-Governor John Colborne. All, however – regardless of the artist and the subject – contain a wealth of information. Surrounding the people portrayed are the trap-pings of their lives, including their clothes, objects that signify their roles or professions, and many other hints about their positions in the social hierarchy. This kind of information helps us to locate the sitter in time and place. It also helps us to understand – particularly in the case of formal portraits – how the subject wanted to be perceived. In short, portraits open a window both into the inner lives of people of the past and into the world that shaped them – and that they helped to shape.

Today, society is much less formal, with studio oil portraits and daguerreotypes replaced by snapshots, home movies, and videos. Yet these media, like the portraits of the past, speak to the human need to leave a record of ourselves that transcends the mundane details included in textual records. They will no doubt be as precious to our descendants as the portraits of our ancestors are to us, and for the same reasons.

Le portrait frappe notre imagination mieux que tout autre type de document d'archives. Nous saisissons parfois un reflet de nous-même dans le portrait d'un ancêtre, ou encore, même si le personnage n'est pas un parent, sa physionomie peut laisser transparaître des indices – de la personnalité du sujet, du rang social qu'il occupe et du type de société dont il fait partie.

La collection des Archives publiques de l'Ontario comprend des centaines de milliers de portraits, sous forme de croquis, peintures et photographies. Nous devons une partie de ces œuvres à des artistes bien connus, tels qu'Elizabeth Simcoe et Anne Langton, devant qui posent des sujets également bien connus, dont le juge en chef John Beverley Robinson et le lieutenant-gouverneur John Colborne. Toutes, cependant – peu importent l'artiste et le sujet – renferment une mine de renseignements. Les modèles sont campés dans un décor où les accessoires et vêtements nous éclairent sur leur quotidien, et des objets emblématiques sur leur rôle ou profession, tout en servant d'indices de leur position dans l'échelle sociale. Ces types de renseignements nous aident à situer le sujet dans l'espace et dans le temps, et aussi à comprendre – en particulier dans le cas de portraits « posés » ou de commande – l'aspect sous lequel le sujet désirait être perçu. En bref, les portraits font entrevoir ce qu'était la vie privée des gens de l'époque de même que l'univers qui les a façonnés – et qu'ils ont contribué à modeler.

De nos jours, dans une société beaucoup moins

formaliste, le portrait à l'huile en atelier et le daguerréotype ont cédé le pas à l'instantané, au film familial et à la vidéo. Pourtant, ces types de portraits, tout comme ceux du passé, répondent au besoin chez l'être humain de laisser une trace de soi qui transcende l'impersonnalité des documents textuels. Ils seront, sans aucun doute, aussi précieux pour nos descendants que les portraits de nos ancêtres le sont pour nous, et pour les mêmes raisons.

3-2

3-3

3-2 & 3-3: Elizabeth Simcoe's drawing of this Native chief is one of the earliest portraits in the Archives' collection. Although it is a simple sketch, she seems to have captured her subject's essence.

Anne Langton's sketch, for its part, is at once accom-plished and highly stylized. Langton received formal training in miniature painting in Paris, which may have influenced both her choice of subject matter and her style.

3-2 et 3-3 : Le portrait de ce chef autochtones, dessiné par Elizabeth Simcoe, est l'un des tout premiers de la collection des Archives. Dans ce croquis très simple, l'artiste semble avoir capté l'essence de son person-nage.

Le croquis d'Anne Langton, par ailleurs, est à la fois accompli et fortement stylisé. Langton avait été formée à l'art de la miniature à Paris, ce qui peut avoir influé tant sur son choix de sujets que sur son style.

3-4

3-4: In this pencil sketch, one of the few self-portraits in the Archives' documentary art collection, Anne Langton depicts her entire family, including herself. The careful use of frames and borders is typical of many of Langton's sketch portraits, but the intricate designs are particularly remarkable.

3-4 : Dans ce croquis à la mine de plomb, Anne Langton représente tous les membres de sa famille, elle-même comprise; on y voit donc l'un des rares autoportraits de la collection d'art documentaire des Archives. Le soin apporté aux cadres et bordures caractérise une foule de portraits signés par l'artiste, mais les fioritures du décor sont particulièrement frappantes ici.

3-5

3-5: Anne's portrait of her father, Thomas, and her brother, John, was painted approximately two years before Thomas died in 1838. This miniature portrait is painted in watercolour on a thin sheet of ivory, measuring only 9 cm x 15.5 cm. The ivory adds a translucent effect to the painting and the colours seem more vivid as a result.

3-5 : Le portrait, peint par Anne, de son frère John et de son père, Thomas, précède d'environ deux ans le décès de ce dernier, en 1838. Ce portrait miniature, à l'aquarelle sur une fine pellicule d'ivoire, ne mesure que 9 cm x 15,5 cm. L'ivoire confère un aspect translucide à la peinture, et les couleurs en semblent plus vives.

3-6

3-7

3-6 & 3-7: These two Upper Canadian worthies look remarkably alike, related through power if not through family. Sir John Colborne (1778-1863) served as the lieutenant-governor of Upper Canada from 1828 to 1836, while Sir John Beverley Robinson (1791-1863) was appointed the chief justice of Upper Canada in 1829 and was a member of the 'family compact,' the colony's ruling oligarchy.

3-6 et 3-7 : Ces deux notables du Haut-Canada dégagent une remarquable parenté, de par les liens du pouvoir sinon du sang. Sir John Colborne (1778-1863) a été lieutenant-gouverneur du Haut-Canada de 1828 à 1836, tandis que Sir John Beverley Robinson (1791-1863), nommé juge en chef du Haut-Canada en 1829, était membre du « family compact », l'oligarchie qui régnait alors sur la colonie.

3-8 to 3-10: The Denisons were one of Ontario's most illustrious military families. Men from several generations of Denisons were decorated military officers who then went on to have notable civilian careers. Colonel George T. Denison (1783-1853) initiated this proud tradition of military service by rising to fame during the War of 1812. His son, Colonel George T. Denison II (1816-73), had a distinguished military career of his own, and his son, Lieutenant-Colonel George T. Denison III (1839-1925), was active in the military for almost fifty years in addition to serving as a lawyer, historian, and public servant.

[3-9 to 3-10] This rare double gold locket contains daguerreotypes of Lieutenant-Colonel George T. Denison III paired with his wife Mary Anne. A third daguerreotype of Denison's father, George T. Denison II, is featured opposite clippings of his hair.

3-8 à 3-10 : Les Denison comptaient parmi les familles de militaires les plus illustres de l'Ontario. Depuis plusieurs générations, les hommes étaient des officiers qui, après s'être distingués comme militaires, poursuivaient des carrières remarquables dans la vie civile. Le colonel George T. Denison (1783-1853) avait amorcé cette fière tradition en se faisant un nom pendant la guerre de 1812. Son fils, le colonel George T. Denison II (1816-1873), avait lui-même connu une honorable carrière militaire, tandis que le fils de ce dernier, le lieutenant-colonel George T. Denison III (1839-1925), avait été militaire pendant près de cinquante ans, parallèlement à une carrière d'avocat, d'historien et de fonctionnaire.

[3-9 et 3-10] Ce rare médaillon en or est double : il arbore le daguerréotype du lieutenant-colonel George T. Denison III en pendant à celui de son épouse, Mary Anne. Un troisième daguerréotype représente le père du premier, George T. Denison II, avec une mèche de cheveux.

3-8

3-9

3-10

3-11

3-12

3-11 to 3-14: Hudson's Bay Company trader Bernard Rogan Ross took the photographs featured on this page and the next. While serving as chief trader of Rupert's House, Ross often experienced long stretches of isolation, and, to alleviate the boredom, he developed a keen interest in the emerging science of photography. His photographs are some of the oldest albumen prints held by the Archives. The albumen photographic process uses thin paper coated with albumen (egg-white protein) to act as the base medium for the image.

3-11 à 3-14 : C'est Bernard Rogan Ross, négociant de la Compagnie de la Baie d'Hudson, qui a pris les photographies illustrant cette page et la page de droite. Pendant son mandat de facteur en chef de Rupert House, Ross devait souvent passer de longues périodes dans l'isolement et, pour chasser l'ennui, avait commencé à s'intéresser à la technique nouvelle de la photographie. Ses images sont au nombre des plus anciens albuminotypes conservés aux Archives. Selon ce procédé, on enduisait le papier d'une couche d'albumine (protéine de blanc d'œuf), ce qui le rendait photosensible.

3-13

3-14

Within the illustration:
1847
A Chief of the
Sioux Tribe.

A. Potawatama.
Chief.

3-15

3-15: This brightly coloured portrait is of particular interest for its documentary value. It illustrates the clothing worn by Native people and their other adornments, including face paint.

3-15 : Ce portrait aux couleurs éclatantes revêt une valeur documentaire toute particulière. Il renseigne sur les vêtements portés par les Autochtones, leurs parures et leur usage de la peinture faciale.

3-16

3-16: The daguerreotype, patented in 1839 by Louis Daguerre, produces a mirror-like image. Because of this, the daguerreotype has been called a 'mirror with a memory.' This example of the daguerreotype features an unidentified child of the Cameron family, a prominent Toronto family active in politics, medicine, and law in the nineteenth century.

3-16 : La daguerréotypie, brevetée en 1839 par Louis Daguerre, produit une image en miroir. C'est pour cette raison qu'on a qualifié le daguerréotype de « miroir à mémoire ». Ce spécimen représente un enfant non identifié de la famille Cameron, de la haute société de Toronto au dix-neuvième siècle, qui a laissé sa marque en politique, en médecine et en droit.

3-17

3-17: In this daguerreotype showing members of the Cameron family, we can see the image deterioration that has occurred because of exposure to light and less than ideal storage conditions. Daguerreotypes were usually housed in elaborate casings consistent with their status as sentimental treasures.

3-17 : Dans ce daguerréotype, représentant des membres de la famille Cameron, on peut constater la détérioration picturale causée par l'exposition à la lumière et de mauvaises conditions de conservation. Les daguerréotypes étaient habituellement placés dans des cadres ouvrés, dont le raffinement correspondait à la valeur sentimentale.

3-18

3-18: Sir Matthew Crooks Cameron was active in politics, elected to positions in both city and federal government, and was made a judge in 1878. The Archives holds textual records of the Cameron family, including family correspondence and a rare parchment document of investiture for Sir Matthew's knighthood.

3-18 : Sir Matthew Crooks Cameron s'était illustré en politique et avait été élu à divers offices municipaux et fédéraux, avant de devenir juge en 1878. Les Archives possèdent des documents écrits de la famille Cameron, dont une partie de la correspondance familiale et un parchemin des plus rares, se rapportant à l'élévation à la pairie de Sir Matthew.

3-19

3-19: Ambrotypes, developed by Frederick Scott Archer in 1848, are thin, under-exposed negatives placed in front of a dark background to make the images appear positive. Embellishments such as hand colouring were used to give the photographs more life-like qualities. An excellent example of the process is seen in this portrait of an unidentified woman who has benefited from a liberal application of 'rouge' on her cheeks.

3-19 : L'ambrotypie, procédé mis au point par Frederick Scott Archer en 1848, consiste à placer sur fond obscur un négatif de verre mince, sous-exposé, pour faire apparaître une image à effet positif. On retouchait souvent les portraits, par exemple en les colorant à la main, pour les faire plus ressemblants. On voit ici un excellent spécimen du procédé dans ce portrait d'une femme non identifiée, dont on a généreusement rosi les joues au « fard ».

3-20

3-20: Another example of the ambrotype process is this typical family portrait, set at Niagara Falls. Today, it is not possible to take photographs quite so close to the Falls.

3-20 : Ce portrait de famille typique, pris à Niagara Falls, est un autre exemple d'ambrotype. Il est de nos jours impossible de se rapprocher autant des chutes pour prendre des photos.

3-21 to 3-23: Alvin D. McCurdy (1916-90) donated the photographs featured on this page. McCurdy was a carpenter and historian with a keen interest in the history of Black settlers in Ontario. Over the course of his life, he amassed an enormous collection of textual records documenting the many aspects of Black settlement and life in Ontario, including Black organizations, churches, and schools, and including as well oral histories and more than 3,000 photographs.

These photographs are tintypes. Introduced by Adolphe Alexandre Martin in 1853, tintypes brought portrait photography to the population at large since tintypes were affordable, rugged, and easily transportable.

3-21 à 3-23 : Alvin D. McCurdy (1916-1990) a fait don des photographies reproduites sur cette page. McCurdy, un menuisier amateur d'histoire, s'intéressait vivement à la chronique des Noirs devenus colons en Ontario. Tout au long de sa vie, il a ajouté à une vaste collection de documents écrits, portant sur maintes facettes de l'établissement et de la vie des Noirs en Ontario – organisations, églises et écoles – aussi bien que de récits oraux et de plus de 3 000 photographies.

Ces photographies sont des ferrotypes. Mise au point par Adolphe Alexandre Martin en 1853, la ferrotypie mettait le portrait photographique à la portée de tous et chacun, puisque le matériel était peu cher, robuste et facile à transporter.

3-21

3-22

3-23

3-24 to 3-27: Cartes-de-visite, or small visiting card portraits, were a popular choice for portraits beginning in the mid-1850s. André Adolphe Eugène Disdéri patented a method in 1854 whereby a number of portraits could be photographed on a single plate, thereby reducing the costs of production. Photographic prints were mounted on cards of varying sizes, including cartes-de-visite, which were about 6 x 9 cm. Cartes-de-visite of celebrities became popular and were traded and treasured much like today's sports cards. They were also used as calling cards or as a means of communication similar to postcards and photographers often advertised their services on the back of the cartes.

[3-24 to 3-27] These photographs are a sampling of the portrait photographs found in the Rugg-O'Connor family collection. The Rugg and O'Connor families, who were related by marriage, lived in Toronto in the late nineteenth and early twentieth centuries. William O'Connor ran a small photography business and took many pictures of his own family. The photograph of William O'Connor is of particular interest since it displays the cyanotype or blue-print process. This makes it rare, since the cyanotype process was not traditionally used for portraiture, and it is one of the few cyanotypes held by the Archives. Also of note is the hand-coloured carte-de-visite of the young child. It was common to embellish cartes-de-visite to enhance their appeal.

3-24 à 3-27 : Les cartes de visite ont été un format populaire pour les portraits, et ce à partir du milieu des années 1850. En 1854, André Adolphe Eugène Disdéri a fait breveter un procédé qui permettait la prise de plusieurs photographies par plaque, ce qui abaissait considérablement le prix de revient. Les photographies étaient montées sur des cartes de diverses dimensions, incluant celles d'une carte de visite (6 cm par 9 cm). Les « cartes de visite » de célébrités étaient très demandées : elles donnaient lieu à des échanges et à des collections, comme c'est le cas aujourd'hui pour les cartes sportives. Les photographes annonçaient souvent leurs services au verso. Les « cartes de visite » étaient bon marché, rendant ainsi le portrait photographique accessible au plus grand nombre.

[3-24 à 3-27] Ces images sont representatives des portraits photographiques de la collection des familles Rugg et O'Connor. Ces deux familles, parentes par alliance, ont vécu à Toronto à la fin du dix-neuvième siècle et au début du vingtième. William O'Connor dirigeait une petite entreprise de photographie et a beaucoup pris sa famille en photos. La photographie de William O'Connor est d'un intérêt particulier, car c'est un cyanotype ou image bleue. Or, on ne faisait généralement pas appel à la cyanotype pour le portrait; nous avons là un des rares cyanotypes conserves aux Archives. On notera également le portrait du jeune enfant, en carte de visite coloriée à la main. Il était courant d'embellir les cartes de visite, pour rehausse leur attrait.

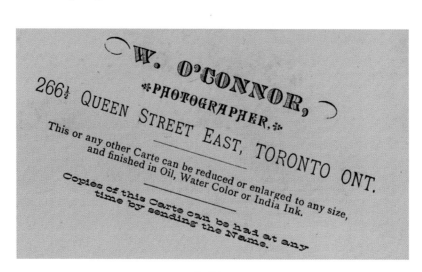

3-24a

3-24b

3-25

3-26

3-27

3-28

3-28: The cabinet card was the larger successor to the carte-de-visite. This cabinet card depicts John Sandfield Macdonald, the first premier of Ontario. Before the proliferation of photography, most people would have had no idea what well-known people looked like, including their premiers. Photographs like this cabinet card would have helped Ontarians put faces to the names of their government leaders.

3-28 : La photographie dite « cabinet card » en format « anglais », un peu plus grande que la carte de visite, a succédé à celle-ci. Ce spécimen représente John Sandfield Macdonald, qui a inauguré la fonction de premier ministre de l'Ontario. Avant que la photographie ne devienne courante, la plupart des gens n'avaient aucune idée des traits des personnages connus, leur premier ministre compris. Des photographies telles que cette « cabinet card » ont sans doute aidé les Ontariens à mettre un visage sur le nom de leurs dirigeants.

3-29

3-29: The albums of the Heward family are outstanding examples of nineteenth-century photograph albums. Featuring both cartes-de-visite and cabinet cards of family members, these albums also included pictures of celebrities. Apparently, pictures of the British royal family were as highly collectable in the nineteenth century as they are now.

3-29 : Les recueils de la famille Heward sont des exemples remarquables de l'album photographique du dix-neuvième siècle. Cartes de visite et « cabinet cards » de membres de la famille s'y côtoient, et l'on y trouve aussi des photos de célébrités. Selon toutes apparences, les photographies de la famille royale britannique étaient des objets de collection aussi recherchés au dix-neuvième siècle qu'aujourd'hui.

3-30   3-31

3-30 & 3-31: These two photographs of members of the Heward family, Mabel Heward (above) and Gussie Miller (right), demonstrate the importance of fashion and milieu in early-portrait photography. Researchers such as fashion historians, set designers, and filmmakers have found the Archives' portrait photographs a valuable resource.

3-30 et 3-31 : Ces photographies de deux membres de la famille Heward, Mabel Heward (ci-dessus) et Gussie Miller (à droite), démontrent l'importance de la mode et du milieu dans la photographie de portrait des débuts. La collection de portraits photographiques des Archives demeure une source de documentation précieuse pour les chercheurs, historiens de la mode, décorateurs et cinéastes.

3-32

3-32: By the end of the 1920s, movie cameras were being marketed widely. Seen as the best way to capture children's early years, weddings, and family vacations, filmmaking quickly became popular among the public.

The Archives of Ontario has amateur film collections, or 'home movies,' of the Irwin and McLaughlin families of Whitby and Oshawa. The films represent family subjects and range in date from 1925 to 1967. Both Norman Irwin and Ewart McLaughlin composed and edited descriptive intertitles into their silent films. Although the Irwins and McLaughlins were financially well-off in comparison to most Ontarians in the 1930s, their films make for fascinating social history in addition to being a rich record of family life.

3-32 : À la fin des années 1920, la caméra cinématographique s'est largement répandue. Considéré comme étant le meilleur moyen de se remémorer les mariages, les premières années des enfants et les vacances en famille, le tournage de films à caractère personnel a rapidement connu la vogue auprès du public.

Les Archives publiques de l'Ontario possèdent des collections de films amateurs ou « personnels » des familles Irwin et McLaughlin, de Whitby et Oshawa. Les films portent sur des sujets familiaux, et ils s'échelonnent entre 1925 et 1967. Norman Irwin et Ewart McLaughlin ont tous deux inséré des intertitres entre les séquences de leurs films muets. Il est vrai que ces deux familles étaient financièrement à l'aise relativement à la plupart des Ontariens dans les années 1930; mais leurs films contribuent à une fascinante histoire de la société du temps, en plus de constituer un document inestimable sur la vie familiale.

3-1: Children playing at Big Trout Lake, January 1956, John Macfie (John Macfie fonds, C 330-13-0-0-172. I000499)

3-2: *Canise or Great Sail, Chippewa Chief*, 16 July [ca. 1796], Elizabeth Simcoe (1762-1850) (Simcoe Family fonds, F 47-11-1-0-284. I0006355)

3-3: *Margaret Gregson* [ca. 1821-37], Anne Langton (1804?-93) (John Langton Family fonds, F 1077-7-3-2-4. I0008326)

3-4: Langton family portrait, 1815, Anne Langton (1804?- 93) (John Langton Family fonds, F 1077-9-4-2. I0008504)

3-5: Thomas Langton and son, John [ca. 1833-6], Anne Langton (1804?-93) (John Langton Family fonds, F 1077-7-1-0-8. I0008575)

3-6: Sir John Colborne (1778-1863) [ca. 1800], engraver unknown (Ontario Legislative Library print collection, RG 49-33-0-0-17. I0009120)

3-7: *Sir John Beverley Robinson, Chief Justice, Upper Canada* [ca. 1840], Hoppner Meyer (Documentary Art Collection, C 281-0-0-0-143. I0003072)

3-8: Closed locket [ca. 1865] (George T. Denison fonds, F 1009)

3-9: George T. Denison III and his wife Mary Anne [ca. 1865] (George T. Denison fonds, F 1009)

3-10: George T. Denison II and a lock of his hair [ca. 1865] (George T. Denison fonds, F 1009)

3-11: *Red Stocking's wife, Cree*, Rupert's House [ca. 1869], Bernard Rogan Ross (Captain Traill Smith photograph collection, F 2179-1-0-0-20. I0005058)

3-12: *Pewotaoh's wife and daughter* [ca. 1869], Bernard Rogan Ross (Captain Traill Smith photograph collection, F 2179-1-0-0-18. I0005112)

3-13: *Mulchetney Steerman Winnebago Indian, Rupert's House* [ca. 1869], Bernard Rogan Ross (Captain Traill Smith photograph collection, F 2179-1-0-0-7. I0005101)

3-14: *Pee-coo-ta-oh and son* [ca. 1869], Bernard Rogan Ross (Captain Traill Smith photograph collection, F 2179-1-0-0-10. I0005104)

3-15: *A Chief of the Sioux Tribe and a Pottawatama Chief*, 1847, unknown artist (Documentary Art Collection, C 281-0-0-0-57. I0003089)

3-16: Young child from the Cameron family [ca. 1865] (Cameron Family fonds, F 2142)

3-17: Woman and two children from the Cameron family [ca. 1865] (Cameron Family fonds, F 2142)

3-18: Matthew Crooks Cameron [ca. 1875] (Cameron Family fonds, F 2142)

3-19: Unidentified woman [ca. 1870] (C 166. I0010268)

3-20: Family group at Table Rock, Niagara Falls [ca. 1870] (Acc. 6760 S 4279. I0010269)

3-21: Unidentified woman, [ca. 1875] (Alvin D. McCurdy fonds, F 2076-16-3-4)

3-22: Unidentified woman, [ca. 1875] (Alvin D. McCurdy fonds, F 2076-16-3-4)

3-23: Young sailors, [ca. 1875] (Alvin D. McCurdy fonds, F 2076-16-3-4)

3-24 a: Back of photograph of Mrs William O'Connor [ca. 1880], William O'Connor (Rugg-O'Connor Family fonds, C 167-1-0-0-57)

3-24 b: Mrs William O'Connor [ca. 1880], William O'Connor (Rugg-O'Connor Family fonds, C 167-1-0-0-57)

3-25: William O'Connor, [ca. 1880], William O'Connor (Rugg-O'Connor Family fonds, C 167-1-0-0-142)

3-26: William O'Connor and his children [ca. 1880], William O'Connor (Rugg-O'Connor Family fonds, C 167-1-0-0-146)

3-27: Coloured carte-de-visite of an unidentified child [ca. 1880], William O'Connor (Rugg-O'Connor Family fonds, C 167-0-0-0-153)

3-28: John Sandfield Macdonald [ca. 1880] (Records of the Attorney General, RG 4. I0005342)

3-29: Album page featuring H.R.H. the Prince of Wales, H.R.H. the Princess of Wales, and the Queen. Mrs Marsh [ca. 1885] (Heward Family fonds, C 35, Album 4, 10)

3-30: Mabel Heward [ca. 1880] (Heward Family Fonds, C 35, Album 6, 1)

3-31: Gussie Miller, 9 May 1880 (Heward Family fonds, C 35, Album 6, 26)

3-32: Colour section of 16-mm. home movie showing fourteen-month-old Billy Irwin, who is crying because he has been deprived of his apple (Norman Irwin fonds, C 92-1-0-37)

3-1 : Enfants au jeu, au lac Big Trout, janvier 1956, John Macfie (Fonds John Macfie, C 330-13-0-0-172. I000499)

3-2 : *Canise or Great Sail, Chippewa Chief*, 16 juillet [vers 1796], Elizabeth Simcoe (1762-1850) (Fonds Famille Simcoe, F 47-11-1-0-284. I0006355)

3-3 : Margaret Gregson [vers 1821-1837], Anne Langton (1804-1883) (Fonds Famille John Langton, F 1077-7-3-2-4. I0008326)

3-4 : Portrait de la famille Langton, 1815, Anne Langton (1804?-1893) (Fonds Famille John Langton, F 1077-9-4-2. I0008504)

3-5 : Thomas Langton et son fils John [vers 1833-1836], Anne Langton (1804?-1893) (Fonds Famille John Langton, F 1077-7-1-0-8. I0008575)

3-6 : Sir John Colborne (1778-1863) [vers 1800], graveur inconnu (Collection de gravures de la Bibliothèque de l'Assemblée législative de l'Ontario, RG 49-33-0-0-17. I0009120)

3-7 : *Sir John Beverley Robinson, Chief Justice, Upper Canada* [vers 1840], Hoppner Meyer (Collection d'art documentaire, C 281-0-0-143. I0003072)

3-8 : Médaillon fermé [vers 1865] (Fonds George T. Denison, F 1009)

3-9 : George T. Denison III et son épouse Mary Anne [vers 1865] (Fonds George T. Denison, F 1009)

3-10 : George T. Denison II et mèche de cheveu [vers 1865] (Fonds George T. Denison, F 1009)

3-11 : *Red Stocking's wife, Cree*, Rupert's House [vers 1869], Bernard Rogan Ross (Collection de photographies Capitaine Traill Smith, F 2179-1-0-0-20. I0005058)

3-12 : *Pewotaoh's wife and daughter* [vers 1869], Bernard Rogan Ross (Collection de photographies Capitaine Traill Smith, F 2179-1-0-0-18. I0005112)

3-13 : *Mulchetney Steerman Winnebago Indian, Rupert's House* [vers 1869], Bernard Rogan Ross (Collection de photographies Capitaine Traill Smith, F 2179-1-0-0-7. I0005101)

3-14 : *Pee-coo-ta-oh and son* [vers 1869], Bernard Rogan Ross (Collection de photographies Capitaine Traill Smith, F 2179-1-0-0-10. I0005104)

3-15 : *A Chief of the Sioux Tribe and a Pottawatama Chief*, 1847, artiste inconnu (Collection d'art documentaire, C 281-0-0-0-57. I0003091)

3-16 : Jeune enfant de la famille Cameron [vers 1865] (Fonds Famille Cameron, F 2142)

3-17 : Une femme et deux enfants de la famille Cameron [vers 1865] (Fonds Famille Cameron, F 2142)

3-18 : Matthew Crooks Cameron [vers 1875] (Fonds Famille Cameron, F 2142)

3-19 : Femme non identifiée [vers 1870] (C 166.I0010268)

3-20 : Portrait de famille à Table Rock, Niagara Falls [vers 1870] (Acc. 6760 S 4279. I0010269)

3-21 : Femme non identifiée [vers 1875] (Fonds Alvin D. McCurdy, F 2076-16-3-4)

3-22 : Femme non identifiée [vers 1875] (Fonds Alvin D. McCurdy, F 2076-16-3-4)

3-23 : Jeunes matelots [vers 1875] (Fonds Alvin D. McCurdy, F 2076-16-3-4)

3-24 a : Dos d'une photographie de Mme William O'Connor [vers 1880], William O'Connor (Fonds Famille Rugg-O'Connor, C 167-1-0-0-57)

3-24 b : Mme William O'Connor [vers 1880], William O'Connor (Fonds Famille Rugg-O'Connor, C 167-1-0-0-57)

3-25 : William O'Connor [vers 1880], William O'Connor (Fonds Famille Rugg-O'Connor, C 167-1-0-0-142)

3-26 : William O'Connor et ses enfants [vers 1880], William O'Connor (Fonds Famille Rugg-O'Connor, C 167-1-0-0-146)

3-27 : Carte de visite en couleur d'un enfant non identifié [vers 1880], William O'Connor (Fonds Famille Rugg-O'Connor, C 167-0-0-0-153)

3-28 : John Sandfield Macdonald [vers 1880] (Dosiers du procureur général, RG 4. I0005342)

3-29 : Page d'album où apparaissent SAR le prince de Galles, SAR la princesse de Galles et la reine. Mme Marsh [vers 1885] (Fonds Famille Heward, C 35, Album 4, 10)

3-30 : Mabel Heward [vers 1880] (Fonds Famille Heward, C 35, Album 6, 1)

3-31 : Gussie Miller, 9 mai 1880 (Fonds Famille Heward, C 35, Album 6, 26)

3-32 : Segment en couleur d'un film familial 16 mm; Billy Irwin, âgé de 14 mois, pleure parce qu'on lui a enlevé sa pomme (Fonds Norman Irwin, C 92-1-0-37)

4

DOCUMENTING LIVES

LES DOCUMENTS BIOGRAPHIQUES

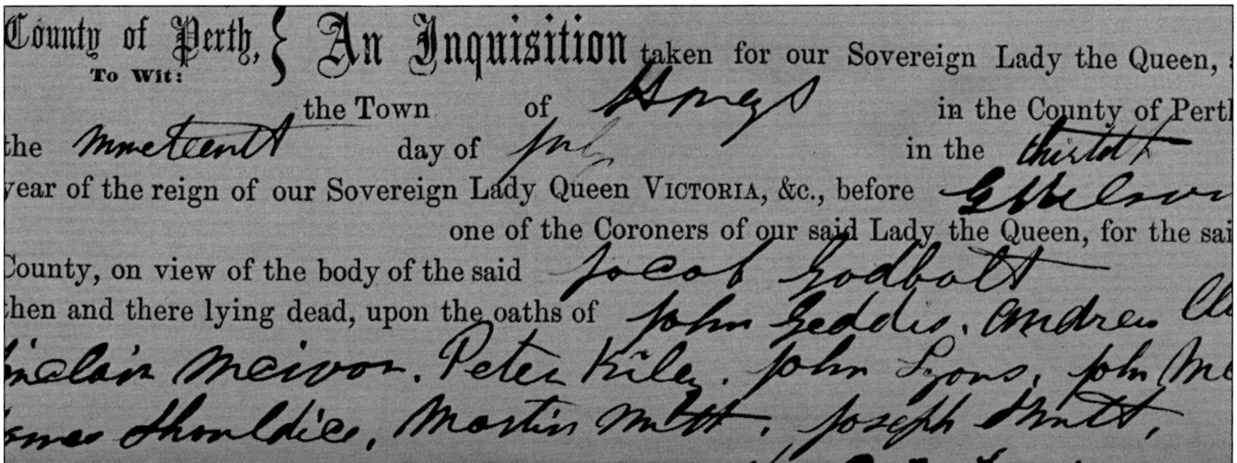

The Archives of Ontario has a varied collection of government records that bear directly upon the daily lives of our ancestors, records that include land settlement and ownership documents, court proceedings, business-partnerships agreements, and registrations of births, marriages, and deaths. The collection is enormous, consisting of hundreds of microfilm volumes of vital statistics records and tens of thousands of feet of property, court, and business records.

The most requested records of all are the registrations of birth, marriages, and deaths. The Upper Canada Marriage Act of 1831 required the clergy of most denominations to report marriages annually to a district clerk of the peace. Subsequently, the Census Act of 1847 required clergy to report baptisms, marriages, and burials quarterly to county clerks of the peace, who were then to forward the information to a newly created Board of Registration and Statistics. Civil registration began in 1869 with the passage of An Act to Provide for the Registration of Births, Marriages and Deaths, known since 1908 as the Vital Statistics Act, and with the creation under that act of the Office of the Registrar General. The latter's function was to record all births, deaths, and marriages as well as stillbirths, adoptions, and adult-name changes.

Vital statistics records are frequently put to use in the making of public policy. For example, statistical interpretation of these records identifies patterns in the movement of population from rural to urban areas, information that in turn enables the government to make informed choices concerning the distribution of funds for schools, public works, and health facilities. But the records do not remain at the Office of the Registrar General indefinitely. Because of their great genealogical and historical value, the records are transferred – at varying periods of time - to the Archives of Ontario. Birth records are transferred annually to the Archives ninety-five years after registration, marriage records eighty years after registration, and death records seventy years after registration. Microfilming of the records takes at least one year.

Besides vital statistics registrations, the Archives holds other government records documenting a person's history. The records of the local surrogate courts, beginning in 1793, contain wills and estate files listing the deceased's next-of-kin and inventories of property. Ontario's Supreme Court was given the power to grant divorces in 1931; the Archives holds divorce files from that year to 1978 and will annually acquire the series when the files become thirty years old. It holds as well thousands of court records from 1788 on, including those for the Courts of General Sessions of the Peace, which acted as the local municipal government until 1841.

The Archives also preserves an extensive collection of property records from when the land still belonged to the crown. These include settlers' petitions for crown land, warrants and fiats awarding settlement rights, grants to those serving in the militia or military, and sale and patent records awarding private ownership. These records are complemented by land-registry records documenting private land transactions and ownership. Researchers visiting the archives can consult historical land-registry records on microfilm, including instrument copybooks, abstract registers, and alphabetical indexes, some beginning as early as 1795.

For well over a century, Ontarians have been incorporating companies and registering partnerships, sole proprietorships, and business names and styles. Registration information about mostly defunct corporations can be found in the Archives' holdings of charter books, corporation files, and provincial-secretary records. The Archives also holds thousands of expired declarations of partnerships and sole proprietorships, dating to 1855. Many of these records are available on self-service microfiche or microfilm.

The Archives' collection of vital statistics records, along with the records concerning land settlement and ownership, court proceedings, and business partnerships, permits a researcher not only to piece together a family history but also to develop a fuller appreciation and understanding of the historical development of Ontario.

Les Archives publiques de l'Ontario possèdent une collection diversifiée de documents gouvernementaux qui se rattachent directement à la vie quotidienne de nos ancêtres : titres de concession et de propriété, comptes rendus d'instances judiciaires, contrats d'association d'affaires et enregistrements de naissances, mariages et décès. La collection est gigantesque; elle renferme des centaines de volumes de microfilms, reproduisant des documents d'état civil, ainsi que – sur des dizaines de milliers de pieds – des titres de propriété et des dossiers de sociétés et de greffes judiciaires.

Les documents les plus demandés de tous sont les enregistrements de naissances, de mariages et de décès. La loi de 1831 sur le mariage dans le Haut-Canada exigeait du clergé de la plupart des religions la remise annuelle d'un rapport sur les mariages célébrés au greffier de la paix du district. Par la suite et selon la loi de 1847 sur le recensement, le clergé sera tenu de présenter un relevé trimestriel des mariages, baptêmes et enterrements au greffier de la paix du comté, lequel devra ensuite transmettre ces données à la commission nouvellement formée pour l'enregistrement des statistiques de l'état civil. L'enregistrement des actes de l'état civil débute en 1869, à l'adoption de la loi sur l'enregistrement des naissances, mariages et décès (loi qui, en 1908, prend le nom de loi sur les statistiques de l'état civil). Cette loi instaure également un bureau du registraire général

de l'état civil, qui a pour rôle de consigner officiellement l'ensemble des naissances, mariages et décès, de même que les mortinaissances, adoptions et changements de nom à l'âge adulte.

Les documents de l'état civil sont souvent mis à contribution lors de l'élaboration des politiques publiques. En effet, l'interprétation statistique permet d'en dégager des schémas démographiques, notamment les déplacements de population des zones rurales aux centres urbains, données grâce auxquelles le gouvernement peut faire des choix éclairés quant à la répartition des fonds destinés aux établissements scolaires, aux établissements de santé et aux travaux publics. Mais les documents ne restent pas indéfiniment au Bureau du registraire général de l'état civil. En raison de leur grande valeur historique et généalogique, ces pièces sont périodiquement versées aux Archives publiques de l'Ontario. Les enregistrements de l'état civil passent annuellement aux Archives : au bout de quatre-vingt-quinze ans pour les naissances, de quatre-vingts ans pour les mariages et de soixante-dix ans pour les décès. Pour le microfilmage des pièces, il faut compter au moins une année.

Outre les enregistrements de l'état civil, les Archives conservent d'autres actes publics qui peuvent documenter la vie d'une personne. Les registres des tribunaux de successions et tutelles, qui remontent à 1793, renferment des testaments et des dossiers de succession où figurent l'inventaire des biens du défunt et la liste de ses proches parents. La Cour suprême de l'Ontario s'est vu conférer le pouvoir de prononcer des divorces en 1931; les Archives conservent des dossiers de divorces à compter de cette année-là jusqu'en 1978, et recevront annuellement les dossiers postérieurs dès leurs trente ans d'existence. On y retrouve encore des milliers de dossiers judiciaires dont les premiers datent de 1788, notamment ceux des cours des sessions générales de la paix, qui ont fait office d'administrations municipales jusqu'en 1841.

On peut par ailleurs consulter aux Archives une importante collection de titres de propriétés, du temps où les terres appartenaient encore à la Couronne. Ces titres comprennent des demandes de concession présentées par des colons, des décisions octroyant des droits d'établissement et des certificats de concession à ceux qui avaient servi dans la milice ou dans l'armée, ainsi que des lettres patentes et actes de vente conférant un titre de propriété privée. Ces pièces ont pour compléments des enregistrements fonciers qui renseignent sur les titres de propriété et les transactions foncières privées. Les chercheurs peuvent consulter sur microfilm les enregistrements fonciers historiques, y compris actes instrumentaires, résumés de transactions et index alphabétiques, dont certains remontent aussi loin que 1795.

Depuis plus d'un siècle les Ontariens enregistrent des actes et contrats d'association et de constitution en société, d'entreprises à propriétaire unique ou d'autres types et des raisons sociales. Les données relatives à l'enregistrement des sociétés, surtout de celles qui sont dissoules, se retrouvent dans le fonds des registres de chartes de compagnies, dans les dossiers de corporations et dans les registres du Secrétaire de la province. Les Archives sont aussi dépositaires de milliers de déclarations périmées relatives à des sociétés et entreprises individuelles, dont certaines remontent à 1855. Un bon nombre de ces documents sont disponibles sur microfilms ou sur microfiches en libre service.

La collection de documents gouvernementaux des Archives, qu'il s'agisse des documents de l'état civil ou de ceux qui se rapportent à la propriété et aux concessions de terres, aux instances judiciaires et aux associations d'affaires, permettent aux chercheurs non seulement de reconstituer la généalogie et l'histoire d'une famille, mais aussi de mieux comprendre et apprécier l'évolution de l'Ontario depuis ses origines.

4-1

4-1: John Sandfield Macdonald was Ontario's first premier, representing a coalition government of liberals and conservatives from 1867 to 1871. In 1869 his government was responsible for passing An Act to Provide for the Registration of Births, Marriages and Deaths and he can therefore be considered the father of Ontario's civil registration of vital statistics.

4-1 : De 1867 à 1871, John Sandfield Macdonald a inauguré les fonctions de premier ministre de l'Ontario, à la tête d'un gouvernement de coalition formé de libéraux et de conservateurs. Le gouvernement de Macdonald ayant adopté en 1869 une loi sur l'enregistrement des naissances, des mariages et des décès, son chef peut donc être considéré comme le père des statistiques de l'état civil en Ontario.

BIRTH

4-2-a & b: This is the birth registration for Gladys Louise Smith, born on 8 April 1892 to parents living in a small house on University Avenue in Toronto. Gladys would grow up to be one of the world's most celebrated movie stars during the days of silent pictures: Mary Pickford.

NAISSANCES

4-2-a et b : Voici l'enregistrement de la naissance de Gladys Louise Smith, née le 8 avril 1892; sa famille vivait dans une petite maison de l'avenue University, à Toronto. Gladys allait devenir l'une des célébrités mondiales du cinéma muet : Mary Pickford.

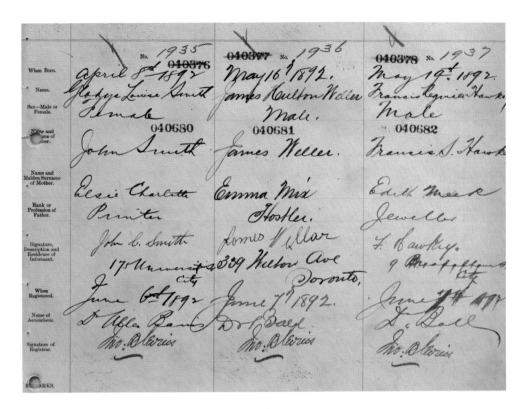

4-2a

4-2b

MARRIAGE

4-3: This document is one of the earliest marriage registrations held by the Archives. The volume in which it is found begins with this statement: 'Marriage Register for the Western District of the Province of Upper Canada, pursuant to An Act of the Legislature of said Province passed in the thirty third year of King George the Third, entitled, An Act to confirm and make valid certain Marriages heretofore contracted in the Country now comprized within the Province of Upper Canada, and to provide for the future solemnization of Marriage within the same.'

The document registers the marriage of Gregor McGregor, a lieutenant-colonel of the Kent Battalion of the militia. He declared that he married Susan Robert on 12 August 1776 in Detroit. Under the Quebec Act of 1774, Detroit in 1776 was part of the province of Quebec, and McGregor would have been there to help protect British interests in Detroit during the American Revolution. Gregor and Susan had had five children by the time this document was created in 1796, and he lists their names and birth dates too. They were still living in Detroit, which by 1796 had become part of Kent County in the Western District of Upper Canada, but the British were just about to transfer the city to the control of the United States (under the terms of the Treaty of Paris of 1783 and Jay's Treaty of 1794).

MARIAGES

4-3 : Ce document est l'un des premiers enregistrements de mariages conservés aux Archives. Le volume dans lequel on l'a découvert s'ouvre sur l'intitulé suivant : [traduction] « Registre des mariages du district occidental de la province du Haut-Canada, en vertu d'une loi de l'Assemblée législative de ladite province, adoptée pendant la trente-troisième année du règne de George III, sous le titre de "loi confirmant et validant certains mariages contractés jusqu'ici dans le territoire qui fait maintenant partie de la province du Haut-Canada et sanctionnant la célébration des mariages à venir dans ledit territoire" ».

Le document atteste le mariage de Gregor McGregor, lieutenant-colonel du bataillon Kent de la milice. L'intéressé déclare avoir épousé Susan Robert le 12 août 1776, à Détroit. Aux termes de l'Acte de Québec (1774), Détroit faisait partie de la province de Québec en 1776, et McGregor s'y trouvait sans doute pour la protection des intérêts britanniques pendant la révolution américaine. En 1796, au moment de la rédaction de ce document, Gregor et Susan avaient cinq enfants, dont les noms et dates de naissance sont énumérés. La famille vivait encore à Détroit, ville qui, en 1796, avait été annexée au comté de Kent, dans le district occidental du Haut-Canada, mais que les Britanniques s'apprêtaient à faire passer sous la gouverne des États-Unis (selon la prescription du Traité de Paris (1783) et du Traité Jay (1794)).

I Gregor McGregor, of the County of Kent, in the Western District, and Province of Upper Canada, Esquire, Lieutenant Colonel of the Kent Battalion of Militia, do solemnly swear in the presence of Almighty God, — that I did publicly intermarry with Susan Robert, of the same place, in the Town of Detroit, on the twelfth day of August, in the year of our Lord, One thousand, seven hundred and seventy six, and that there is now living issue of the said Marriage.

James, born on the 16th of May. 1779. —
Anne, born on the 1st day of April. 1781. —
Susan, born on the 4th of October, 1785. —
Catherine, born on the 2nd May. 1789. —
John, born on the 2nd February. 1792. —

Sworn before me, at Detroit in
the County aforesaid, this 1st day
of May. 1796. as the Law directs. —
\} signed/ Gregor McGregor. —

(L.S.) signed/ Thos. Smith. Justice Peace. W.D.

4-3

DEATH

4-4-a: The 1918 record of death for the district of Temiskaming tells part of the tragic story of the Spanish influenza pandemic of 1918-19. The Spanish flu killed some 21 million people, including 50,000 Canadians. It was spread in Canada by soldiers returning from the First World War, and in Ontario it reached even the most remote communities. This image shows the physician's portion of two facing pages in the death record for Timmins on 31 December 1918. Every one of the six persons shown died from influenza.

DÉCÈS

4-4-a : Le registre des décès du district de Temiskaming pour 1918 documente certains aspects de la pandémie de grippe espagnole survenue en 1918-1919. La maladie devait emporter quelque 21 millions de personnes, dont 50 000 Canadiens. Propagée au Canada par des soldats à leur retour de la Première Guerre mondiale, la maladie était parvenue jusque dans les villages les plus reculés de l'Ontario. Cette image reproduit la section réservée au médecin de deux pages contiguës, en date du 31 décembre 1918, dans le registre des décès de Timmins. Chacune des six personnes nommées ici est morte de cette maladie.

	Physician's Return of Death	Physician's Return of Death	Physician's Return of Death
Surname of Deceased.	Vaillancourt	Shea	Cruickshanks
Christian Name.	Irene	Andrew	Ian Frank
Date of Death.	Dec,Ist 1918	Nov,2nd,1918	Nov,25th,1918
DISEASE CAUSING DEATH.	Influenza	Influenza	Influenza
Duration.	Ten days	One week	66 hours
Immediate Cause of Death.	Toxaemia	Pneumonia	Cardia Failure
Duration.	twodays	3 days	Immediate
Physician's Name.	J A McInnis M D	Dr J A McInnis	H L Minthorn M D
Address.	Timmins,Ont.	Timmins Ont	Timmins,Ont
Date of Return.	Dec,2nd,1918	Nov,4th,1918	Nov,27th,1918
Remarks.			

I hereby certify the foregoing to be the true and correct entries of all Deaths returned to me for the quarter ending Dec,3Ist 19 18 Given under my hand this 3Ist day of Dec, A.D. 18 Division Registrar of Timmins,Ont

20 M—6—17.

4-4a

4-4b

	Physician's Return of Death	Physician's Return of Death	Physician's Return of Death
Surname of Deceased.	Senek	Kinnari	Salmi
Christian Name.	Ed	Alfred	Alex
Date of Death.	Oct 22nd,1918	Oct 26th,1918	Oct,23rd,1918
DISEASE CAUSING DEATH.	Influenza	Influenza	Influenza
Duration.	I week	IO days	2 days
Immediate Cause of Death.	Pneumonia	Pneumonia	Pneumonia
Duration.	four days	4 days	2 days
Physician's Name.	H H Moore M D	H H Moore M D	H H Moore M D
Address.	Timmins Ont	Timmins Ont	Timmins Ont
Date of Return.	Dec,IOth 1918	Dec,IOth 1918	Dec,IOth 1918
Remarks.			

I hereby certify the foregoing to be the true and correct entries of all Deaths returned to me for the quarter ending Dec,31st, 1918
Given under my hand, this 3Ist day of Dec, A.D. 19 18
Division Registrar of Timmins Ont

20 M—6—17.

4-5-a&b: Thomas Ridout (1754-1829) immigrated to Maryland in 1774 where he became a trader. Remaining in the American Colonies after the American Revolution, Ridout, provided with letters of introduction by George Washington, set out to resettle in Kentucky in January 1788. However, en route, his group was captured by a group of Shawnee natives on the Ohio River. The only survivor, Ridout was sold to the British at Fort Detroit. Moving to Upper Canada, he joined the Commissary Department at Newark (Niagara-on-the-Lake) and then served as clerk at the Surveyor General's Office. By 1810, Ridout had become the colony's Surveyor General. He also served as Registrar of York County (1796) and Clerk of the Peace for the Home District (1800).

Wills and estate files are currently processed by the Superior Court of Justice, Estates Division (formerly, the processing was done by the County or District Surrogate Court). The Archives annually acquires estate files, including wills, when the records become forty years old.

DOSSIERS RELATIFS AUX TESTAMENTS ET SUCCESSIONS

4-5-a et b : Thomas Ridout (1754-1829) avait émigré au Maryland en 1774 et y était devenu marchand. Ayant décidé de demeurer dans les colonies américaines après la révolution américaine, Ridout, muni de lettres d'introduction de George Washington, part s'établir au Kentucky en janvier 1788. Chemin faisant, toutefois, les voyageurs sont capturés par un groupe de Shawnees sur l'Ohio. Seul survivant, Ridout est vendu aux Britanniques de Fort Detroit. Il déménage alors dans le Haut-Canada et entre a l'intendance de Newark (Niagara-on-the-Lake), puis travaille comme commis au bureau de l'Arpenteur en chef; en 1810, Ridout devient Arpenteur en chef de la colonie. Il avait auparavant été greffier du comté de York (1796), puis greffier de la paix du district de Home (1800).

Les dossiers relatifs aux testaments et successions sont actuellement traités par la division des successions de la Cour supérieure de justice (antérieurement, c'était la Cour des successions et tutelles du district ou du comté qui s'en chargeait). Les Archives entrent en possession tous les ans de nombreux dossiers de succession, testaments compris, au moment où les documents atteignent leur quarantième année d'existence.

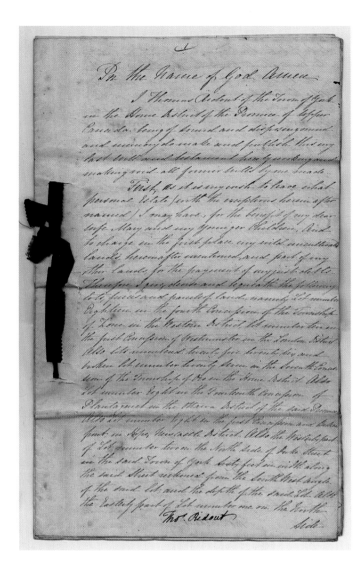

4-5a

Court of Probate
Upper Canada
York to wit

You George Ridout, of York in the Home District and Province of Upper Canada, Esquire and you Thomas Gibbs Ridout, of the same place, Esquire, Executors named in the last Will and Testament of the late Honorable Thomas Ridout, of York aforesaid, His Majesty's Surveyor General, deceased, do severally swear that you are the persons named in the said last Will and Testament, as Executors thereto, that you believe the Paper now shown to you to be the said last Will and Testament, that you will pay all the Debts and Legacies of the deceased as far as the goods shall extend and the law shall bind you, and that you will exhibit a true, full, and perfect Inventory of all and every the goods and chattels, Rights and Credits of the deceased, together with a just and true account into the Registry of the Court of Probate when you shall be lawfully called thereunto.

So help you God

Sworn before me
at York in Upper Canada
this 7 day of March 1829

4-5b

STORK DERBY

4-6: When prominent Toronto lawyer and bachelor Charles Vance Millar died of a heart attack in October 1926, he set off the wildest series of court cases in Ontario legal history. A student of human nature, Millar delighted in exposing greed and hypocrisy. His last will and testament, designed to be 'necessarily uncommon and capricious,' was his final and greatest prank.

The ninth clause of Millar's will awarded his estate, huge even by 1920s standards, to the mother who gave 'birth in Toronto to the greatest number of children as shown by the Registrations under the Vital Statistics Act over the next 10 years.' The media shamelessly commercialized the 'stork derby' and publicly investigated every child who lived or died and the 'ranking' of the mothers involved. Two events then made Millar's estate an even more attractive prize than it already was. First, the free-spending 1920s were followed by the Great Depression of the 1930s, when a third of all working-age Canadians were unemployed. Second, Millar's long-shot investment in the Windsor-Detroit Tunnel became worth $750,000 when the route opened in November 1929. Compared to a minimum wage of $12.50 for a sixty-hour week, the Millar estate now rep-resented more money than most people could imagine. And so his curious bequest suddenly became a source of hope for a few families living in abject poverty.

Meanwhile, the will was unsuccessfully challenged all the way to the Supreme Court of Canada. Millar's distant relatives wondered if the ninth clause was legal and, if not, wanted to claim his estate. A lawyer involved in the case wondered what constituted 'Toronto' and the attorney general wondered whether the stork derby contributed to public immorality and 'feeble-mindedness.' Still others wondered if stillborn or unregistered children counted towards the total (of the five women leading the pack, only thirty-two of their fifty-six children were considered eligible).

The race ended in 1936 when four women (Annie Smith, Kathleen Nagel, Lucy Timleck, and Isabel Maclean) were recognized for having nine properly registered live births apiece. Each received $125,000. Two other mothers who had given birth ten times during the specified period were awarded $12,500 each (Lillian Kenny had two stillbirths while several of Pauline Clarke's children were rejected as illegitimate).

UN DERBY DE LA CIGOGNE

4-6 : Lorsque le brillant avocat torontois et par ailleurs célibataire Charles Vance Millar succombe à une crise cardiaque en octobre 1926, son décès déclenche une kyrielle d'affaires judiciaires rocambolesques, les plus étranges jamais vues en Ontario. Observateur inlassable de la nature humaine, Millar prenait un malin plaisir à dénoncer les manifestations d'hypocrisie et de cupidité de ses semblables. Son dernier testament, qu'il voulait « à toute force fantaisiste et hors du commun », devait être son ultime facétie, de loin la plus percutante.

En neuvième clause de son testament, Millar léguait sa succession, d'une ampleur stupéfiante – même selon les normes des années 1920 – à la citoyenne de Toronto qui [traduction] « aura, au cours de ces dix prochaines années, donné naissance au plus grand nombre d'enfants, selon les registres tenus en vertu de la *Loi sur les statistiques de l'état civil*. » Sans aucune retenue, les médias s'étaient alors empressés de faire mousser ce « derby de la cigogne », menant une enquête publique sur tous et chacun des enfants, survivants ou non, et sur le « classement » des mères en cause. Deux événements avaient alors rendu la succession de Millar plus désirable encore et plus convoitée que jamais. Tout d'abord, les folles dépenses des années 1920 avaient été suivies de la Grande Crise des années 1930, ingrate période pendant laquelle le tiers de tous les Canadiens en âge de travailler avaient été réduits au chômage. En deuxième lieu, la valeur de l'investissement de Millar dans le tunnel Windsor-Detroit, hautement hasardeux, avait subitement atteint les 750 000 $ lors de l'inauguration de l'ouvrage en novembre 1929. Si l'on songe que le salaire minimum était alors de 12,50 $ pour une semaine de soixante heures, la succession Millar représentait une somme faramineuse, inconcevable pour la plupart des gens. Tant et si bien que ce legs saugrenu était brusquement devenu source d'espoir pour quelques familles vivant dans l'indigence.

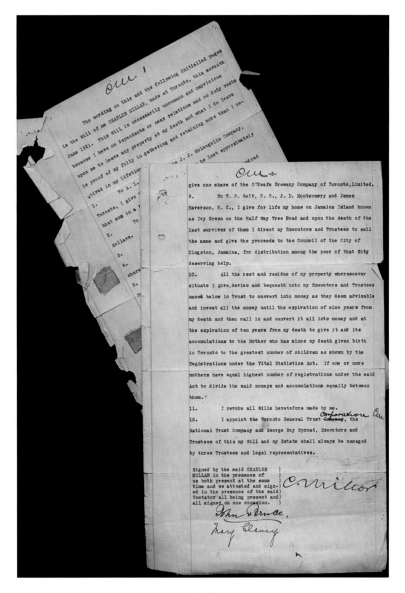

4-6

Entre-temps, le testament était soumis à une série de contestations infructueuses, jusqu'en Cour suprême du Canada. Des parents éloignés de Millar mettaient en doute la légalité de la neuvième clause et, le cas échéant, revendiquaient la succession. Un avocat impliqué dans l'affaire s'interrogeait sur la définition de « Toronto », et le procureur général, pour sa part, se demandait si ce « derby de la cigogne » n'incitait pas la population à l'immoralité, en plus de récompenser la « débilité mentale ». D'autres encore ergotaient, à savoir si les enfants morts-nés et non inscrits au registre ne pourraient pas être inclus dans le total (pour les cinq femmes en tête de liste, seules

trente-deux naissances – sur un total collectif de cinquante-six – étaient considérées comme admissibles).

Le marathon prend fin en 1936, lorsqu'on reconnaît officiellement que quatre des femmes (Annie Smith, Kathleen Nagel, Lucy Timleck et Isabel Maclean) ont chacune mis au monde neuf enfants vivants, dûment inscrits au registre; chacune se voit remettre une somme de 125 000 $. Deux autres mères, ayant accouché dix fois pendant la période stipulée, reçoivent 12 500 $ chacune (Lillian Kenny avait eu deux enfants morts-nés, tandis que plusieurs des nouveau-nés de Pauline Clarke étaient illégitimes et par là non admissibles).

CORONER'S INQUESTS AND INVESTIGATIONS

4-7: Jacob Godbatt met a tragic end in the town of St Marys in 1866. While standing atop a moving train attempting to fix a bell rope, he was struck by a low bridge and killed. Godbatt's death led to a coroner's inquest to investigate the circumstances of the accident. The report recommended that 'owing to the number of accidents of the same nature that has occured [sic] at the same bridge, the jury would reccommend [sic] to the G.T.R.R. Co. to take some steps with regard to this bridge, to prevent a repetition of similar accidents.' Good advice, but too late for Godbatt.

In Ontario, coroners traditionally reported to the Department of the Attorney General (the Ministry of the Solicitor General was not created until 1972).

Locally, the coroner worked under the auspices of the county or district clerk of the peace and any autopsies, investigations, or inquests generated by the coroner were passed to that office. However, before 1963 there was no provincial legislation requiring that the clerk of the peace retain any records from the coroner. In many cases, the clerk of the peace retained only the records of those inquests or investigations that could result in a criminal investigation. Consequently, there are no surviving pre-1963 coroner records for most of Ontario's counties and districts. Coroners' files created after 1962 are held by the Chief Coroner's Office and will be transferred to the Archives when they are fifty years old.

DOSSIERS DE RECHERCHES ET D'ENQUÊTES DU CORONER

4-7 : De son côté, le malheureux Jacob Godbatt connaît une fin tragique en 1866, dans la petite ville de St. Marys. Debout sur un wagon de train en marche, il tente de réparer un cordon de sonnette, lorsque le véhicule s'engouffre sous un viaduc de faible hauteur; il est tué sur le coup. Le décès de Godbatt donne lieu à une enquête du coroner sur les circonstances de l'événement. Le rapport tire une sage conclusion : [traduction] « Attendu le nombre d'accidents de même nature qui sont survenus au même endroit, le jury recommande à la GTRR de prendre des mesures concernant les abords du viaduc, pour éviter que pareil drame ne se reproduise. » Conseil excellent certes, mais de peu d'utilité pour l'infortuné Godbatt.

En Ontario, le coroner relevait traditionnellement du ministère du Procureur général (le ministère du Solliciteur général n'a été institué qu'en 1972). Au palier local, le coroner travaillait sous l'égide du greffier de la paix du comté ou du district, et c'était le greffe qui recevait les résultats des autopsies, recherches ou enquêtes demandées par le coroner. Cependant, avant 1963, aucune loi provinciale n'exigeait du greffier de la paix qu'il conserve les documents remis par le coroner. Dans bien des cas, le greffier de la paix ne conservait que les documents relatifs aux recherches ou enquêtes susceptibles d'aboutir à une enquête criminelle. Par conséquent, en ce qui concerne la période antérieure à 1963, il ne nous est parvenu aucun dossier provenant du coroner pour la plupart des comtés et districts de l'Ontario. Les dossiers du coroner constitués après 1962 sont conservés au Bureau du coroner en chef et seront versés aux Archives lorsqu'ils atteindront leur cinquantième année d'existence.

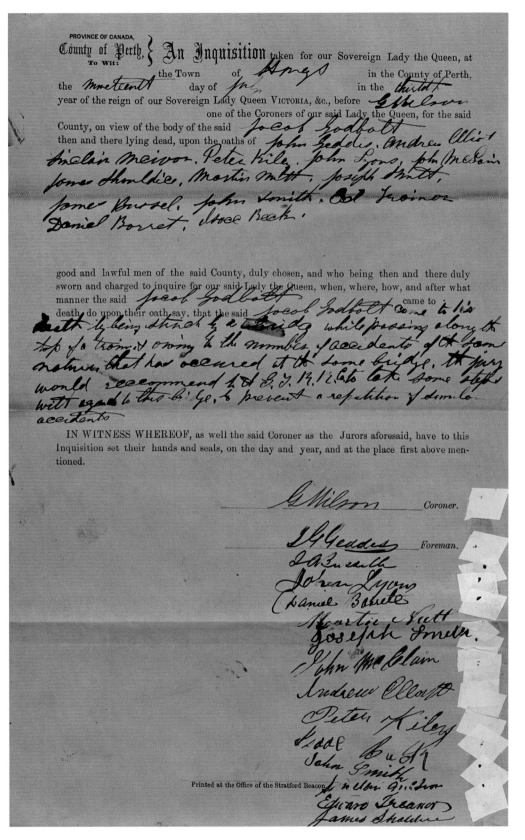

PROVINCE OF CANADA,
County of Perth, } An Inquisition taken for our Sovereign Lady the Queen, at
To Wit:

the Town of _Amys_ in the County of Perth,

the _Nineteenth_ day of _Jn_ in the _thirtieth_

year of the reign of our Sovereign Lady Queen VICTORIA, &c., before _G Wilson_

one of the Coroners of our said Lady the Queen, for the said

County, on view of the body of the said _Jacob Godbolt_

then and there lying dead, upon the oaths of _John Geddie, Andrew Elliot_

Sinclair McIvor, Peter Kiley, John Lyons, John McClain

James Shouldice, Martin Nutt, Joseph Nutt,

James Bursel, John Smith, Ed Treinor

Daniel Borret, Isace Beck.

good and lawful men of the said County, duly chosen, and who being then and there duly
sworn and charged to inquire for our said Lady the Queen, when, where, how, and after what
manner the said _Jacob Godbolt_ came to
death, do upon their oath say, that the said _Jacob Godbolt came to his_
death by being struck by a bridge while passing along the
top of a train & owing to the number of accidents of the same
nature that has occured at the same bridge, the jury
would recommend to the G. T. R. R. Co to take some steps
with regard to this bridge, to prevent a repetition of similar
accidents

IN WITNESS WHEREOF, as well the said Coroner as the Jurors aforesaid, have to this
Inquisition set their hands and seals, on the day and year, and at the place first above mentioned.

G Wilson _____ Coroner.

J G Geddes ____ Foreman.
J A Bursell
John Lyons
Daniel Borrett
Martin Nutt
Joseph Smith.
John McClain
Andrew Elliott
Peter Kiley
Isace Beck
John Smith
Sinclair McIvor
Edward Treanor
James Shouldice

Printed at the Office of the Stratford Beacon

4-7

4-8-a to c: The crown lands records, which document early settlement and land ownership in Ontario, include some of the most important papers held by the Archives. The examples shown here illustrate part of the life story of one of Upper Canada's most illustrious figures, William Hamilton Merritt.

William Hamilton Merritt was born in New York in 1793 but his family moved to the vicinity of St Catharines when he was three years old. Merritt's father served under John Graves Simcoe in the Queen's Rangers during the American Revolution, and in his turn, Merritt fought during the War of 1812. He was captured by the Americans in late July 1814 during the Battle of Lundy's Lane and remained a prisoner until the end of the war. When he returned home, Merritt worked as a merchant, operated a mill, opened a land agency, and even erected a small distillery. His great vision, however, was to build a canal to connect Lake Erie and Lake Ontario. Merritt wanted a more efficient method to move goods from western regions to the trade centre of Montreal, one that would bypass the Niagara Falls portage, and he was also well aware of the threat posed by the rival Erie Canal in the United States. As a result of his lobbying, on 19 January 1824 the Upper Canadian House of Assembly chartered the Welland Canal Company. After many engineering problems and difficulties in raising capital, the Welland Canal was finally completed in 1833.

However, this success was not the end of Merritt's transportation dream. He had quickly moved on from the Welland Canal to envision a complete St Lawrence canal system linking inland waters with the ocean. From 1832 to 1860, Merritt served in the legislature, representing first Haldimand and then Lincoln. He never gave up fighting for his St Lawrence system and for improved trade conditions. In addition, Merritt was an enthusiastic supporter of the Niagara suspension bridge, opened for international travel in 1849, and in the late 1850s he promoted the construction of a railway to connect Port Dalhousie and Port Colborne. Merritt died in 1862 while on board a ship passing through the Cornwall Canal.

The Archives holds the personal papers of William Hamilton Merritt, which include correspondence, memoranda, and other records relating to his personal, business, and political affairs.

[4-8-a] This is a detail of the patent plan of Zorra Township (west and east), which shows three 200-acre lots of land that the crown granted to Merritt in 1820. The lot numbers are 4, 7, and 8 in concession 2. It is likely that Merritt received these lands in reward for his military service in the War of 1812.

LA PROPRIÉTÉ

4-8-a à c : Les dossiers relatifs aux terres de la Couronne, qui portent sur les premiers villages et titres de propriété des biens-fonds de l'Ontario, renferment certains des documents les plus importants qui soient aux Archives. Les spécimens exposés ici évoquent des moments qui ont été marquants pour l'un des personnages les plus illustres du Haut-Canada, William Hamilton Merritt.

Né à New York en 1793, William Hamilton Merritt avait trois ans lorsque sa famille s'est établie dans les environs de St. Catharines. Le père de Merritt avait servi sous le commandement de John Graves Simcoe, dans les Queen's Rangers, pendant la révolution américaine. Merritt est à son tour soldat pendant la guerre de 1812. Fait prisonnier par les Américains à la fin de juillet 1814, au cours de la bataille de Lundy's Lane, il demeure en captivité jusqu'à la fin de la guerre. À son retour, Merritt devient marchand, s'occupe d'un moulin, ouvre une agence d'administration des terres et même une petite distillerie. Son grand rêve, toutefois, est d'aménager un canal qui relierait les lacs Érié et Ontario. Merritt était persuadé qu'il devait y avoir moyen de transporter les marchandises des régions de l'Ouest jusqu'au centre commercial de Montréal en évitant le portage des chutes Niagara, et il était aussi conscient de la menace que représentait, du côté américain, le canal Érié. En conséquence de ses démarches, la Chambre d'assemblée du Haut-Canada sanctionne, le 19 janvier 1824, la constitution de la Welland Canal Company. Une fois surmontés de

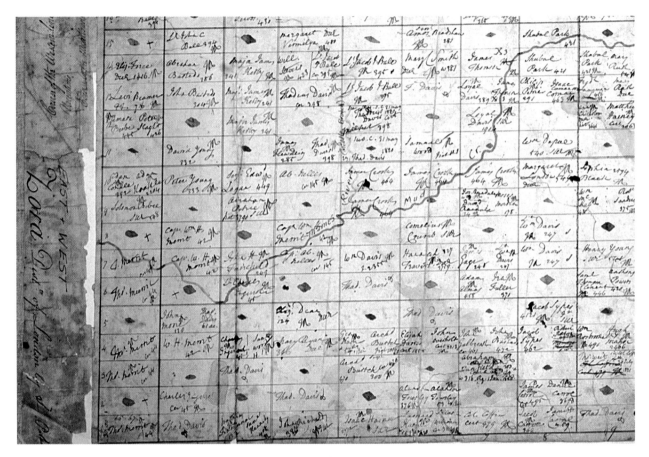

4-8a

nombreux problèmes d'ingénierie et les difficultés que posait la réunion des capitaux nécessaires, le canal Welland est enfin achevé en 1833.

Cependant, cette réussite ne met pas un terme aux ambitions de Merritt en matière de transport. Le canal Welland chose faite, il s'attaque aussitôt à un autre projet d'envergure : il s'agit cette fois d'un vaste réseau de canaux, reliant à l'océan les eaux intérieures du Saint-Laurent. De 1832 à 1860, Merritt siège à l'Assemblée législative comme député, d'abord de Haldimand, puis de Lincoln. Il milite sans relâche pour la réalisation de son réseau du Saint-Laurent et pour l'amélioration des conditions de commerce. En outre, Merritt est un partisan enthousiaste du pont suspendu de Niagara, qui est ouvert à la circulation internationale en 1849, et, à la fin des années 1850, il

contribue à la construction d'un chemin de fer entre Port Dalhousie et Port Colborne. Merritt s'éteint en 1862, à bord d'un navire justement engagé dans le canal de Cornwall.

Les Archives possèdent les papiers personnels de William Hamilton Merritt, lesquels comprennent des lettres, des notes de service et d'autres documents relatifs à ses affaires personnelles, commerciales et politiques.

[4-8-a] On voit ici un détail du plan de concessions du canton de Zorra (ouest et est), délimitant les trois lots de 200 acres cédés à Merritt par la Couronne en 1820. Il s'agit des lots numéros 4, 7 et 8 de la concession 2. Il est probable que Merritt avait reçu ces terres en récompense de ses services de soldat lors de la guerre de 1812.

PROVINCE OF UPPER-CANADA.

GEORGE the *Fourth* by the Grace of GOD, of the United Kingdom of Great-Britain and Ireland, King, Defender of the Faith :—To all to whom these Presents shall come——GREETING:

KNOW YE, That We, of our special Grace, certain Knowledge, and mere Motion, have Given and GRANTED, and by these Presents do Give and GRANT, unto *William Hamilton Merritt of the Township of Grantham in the County of Lincoln in the District of Niagara, as a Captain Commanding a Troop of Provincial Light Dragoons,* heirs and assigns for ever ; ALL that parcel or tract of LAND, situate *in the Township of Zorra in the County of Oxford in the District of London* in our said Province, containing by admeasurement *Eight Hundred Acres,* be the same more or less, being *the East halves of Lots No. Four, Seven & Eight in second Concession and of Eight in the fourth Concession — Also the west halves of Lots No. Four, Seven & Eight in the Second Concession and of Eight in the fourth Concession of the said Township, Reserving to the Crown all navigable waters within the same,*

TOGETHER with all the Woods and Waters, lying and being, under the reservations, limitations and conditions hereinafter expressed ; which said *Eight hundred Acres are* butted and bounded, or may be otherwise known as follows, that is to say *Commencing where a post has been planted at the South east angle of each of the said East half Lots respectively, then north twenty two degrees five minutes west, thirty chains more or less to where a post has been planted at the north east angle of each of the said half Lots, then South sixty eight degrees five minutes, west thirty three chains thirty three links and a half more or less to the Centre of said Concessions — then South twenty two degrees five minutes East thirty chains more or less to the Southern limit of each of the said half Lots, then North sixty eight degrees five minutes, East, thirty three chains thirty three links and a half more or less to the place of beginning in each half Lot Also commencing where a post has been planted at the South west angle of each of the said West half Lots respectively, then north twenty two degrees five west, thirty chains more or less to where a post has been planted at the North west angle of each of the said half Lots, then North sixty eight degrees five minutes, east thirty three chains thirty three links and a half more or less to the Centre of the said Concessions, then South twenty two degrees five minutes, East thirty chains more or less to the Southern limit of each of the said half Lots, then South sixty eight degrees five minutes West thirty three chains thirty three links and a half more or less to the place of beginning in each half Lot—*

H. J. Boulton
S. Genl.

Dundas 24 July 1822

TO HAVE AND TO HOLD, the said parcel or tract of land hereby given and granted to *him* the said *William Hamilton Merritt his* heirs and assigns for ever ; saving nevertheless, to Us, our heirs and successors, all Mines of Gold and Silver, that shall or may be hereafter found on any part of the said parcel or tract of land hereby given and granted as aforesaid ; and saving and reserving to Us, our heirs and successors, all White Pine trees, that shall or may now or hereafter grow, or be growing on any part of the said parcel or tract of land hereby granted as aforesaid. ~~Provided always that if at any time or times hereafter, within the space of three years from the date of these presents, the said~~ ~~by any Deed of Bargain and Sale, release, exchange, or other conveyance, shall grant, bargain, sell, alien, release or convey, all or any part of the said parcel or tract of land hereby granted, then and in such case, this our Grant for such part of the land so given and granted to the said~~ ~~and~~ ~~heirs as aforesaid, shall be null and void, any thing herein before contained to the contrary thereof, in any wise notwithstanding.~~ — PROVIDED ALSO, that no part of the parcel or tract of land hereby given and granted to the said *William Hamilton Merritt* and *his* heirs, be within any reservation heretofore made and marked for Us, our heirs and successors, by our Surveyor General of Woods, or his lawful Deputy, in which case, this our grant for such part of the land hereby given and granted to the said *William Hamilton Merritt* and *his* heirs for ever, as aforesaid, and which shall upon a survey thereof being made, be found within any such reservation, shall be null and void and of none effect, any thing herein contained to the contrary notwithstanding. PROVIDED ALSO that the said *William Hamilton Merritt his* heirs or assigns, shall and do within three years, erect and build, or cause to be erected and built, in and upon some part of the said parcel or tract of land, a good and sufficient dwelling house *as* the said *William Hamilton Merritt* or *his* assigns, not having built, or not being in *his* or their own right, lawfully possessed of a house in our said Province, and be therein, or cause some person to be therein resident, for and during the space of three years, then next ensuing the building of the same. PROVIDED ALSO, that if at any time or times hereafter, the land so hereby given and granted to the said *William Hamilton Merritt* and *his* heirs, shall come into the possession and tenure of any person or persons whomsoever, either by virtue of any Deed of sale, conveyance, enfeoffment or exchange ; or by gift, inheritance, descent, devise or marriage, such person or persons, shall within twelve months next after his, her or their entry into, and possession of the same, take the oaths prescribed by law, before some one of the Magistrates of our said Province, and a certificate of such oath having been so taken, shall cause to be recorded in the Secretary's Office of the said Province. IN DEFAULT of all, or any of which conditions, limitations and restrictions, this said Grant and every thing herein contained shall be, and WE hereby declare the same to be null and void, to all intents and purposes whatsoever ; and the land hereby granted and every part and parcel thereof, shall revert to, and become vested in us, our heirs and successors, in like manner as if the same had never been granted, any thing herein contained to the contrary thereof in any wise notwithstanding.

AND WHEREAS, by an Act of the Parliament of Great-Britain, passed in the thirty-first year of *the Reign of the Late King George the third* entitled, "an Act to repeal certain parts of an Act, passed in the fourteenth year of *His Majesty's Reign* entitled, an Act for making more effectual provision for the Government of the Province of Quebec, in North-America, and to make further provision for the Government of the said Province." It is declared, " that no grant of lands hereafter made, shall be valid or effectual, unless the same shall contain a specification of the lands to be allotted and appropriated, solely to the maintenance of a Protestant Clergy within the said Province, in respect of the lands to be thereby granted,"—Now KNOW YE, that We have caused an allotment or appropriation of *One Hundred and Twelve Acres, and two twenties to be made in Lot No. Four, with the third Concession of the said Township of Zorra.*

GIVEN under the Great Seal of our Province of Upper-Canada. WITNESS our trusty and well beloved *Sir Peregrine Maitland K.C.B. & Governor of our said Province, and Major General Commanding our forces therein* this *Twentieth* day of *June* in the year of our LORD one thousand eight hundred and *twenty two* and *third* of our Reign.

By Command of *His Excellency in Council D. Cameron Sy.*

P. M.
Entered with the Auditor
8 July 1822
Thomas Andrew C.C.C.

O.C. 19 Jan: 1820 accept of Mil: Rank under the Adm: of Sir P. Maitland K.C.B. & Govr. for 800 Acres. Settleme Duty performed

4-8b

A Memorial,

TO be Registered pursuant to the

STATUTE in such case made and provided, of an INDENTURE of BARGAIN and SALE, made at *Oxford* in the County of *Oxford* in the *District of London* and Province of Upper Canada, bearing date the *Nineteenth* day of *July* in the year of our Lord one thousand eight hundred and thirty *Four* **Between** *William Hamilton Merritt of the township of Grantham and system of Niagara District* of the one part, and *George H. Harris of the township of Zorra County District and Province aforesaid* of the other part----Whereby the said *William Hamilton Merritt* for and in consideration of the sum of *One hundred pounds* _____ lawful money of Upper Canada, to *him* in hand paid, by the said *George H. Harris* the receipt whereof is thereby acknowledged *hath* granted, bargained, sold, aliened, transfered, conveyed and confirmed unto the said *George H. Harris his* heirs and assigns, for ever, *all and singular that* certain parcel or tract of land and premises, situate, lying and being in *the township of Zorra* in the county of *Oxford*, in the *District of London* and Province oforesaid, containing, by admeasurement. *One hundred acres of Land being the West half of lot Number Seven in the ____ Concession of the township of Zorra, and is butted and bounded, or May be otherwise known as follows That is to say, Commencing where a Post has been Planted at the South West angle of the Said West half lot, Then North twenty two degrees five Minutes West, Thirty Chains More or less to where a Post has been Planted at the North West angle of the Said half lot, Then North Sixty Eight degrees five Minutes East, Thirty Three Chains, Thirty Three links and a half, More or less to the center of the Said Concession Then South Twenty two degrees five Minutes East, Thirty Chains More or less to the Southern limit of the Said half lot Then South Sixty Eight degrees five Minutes West, Thirty Three Chains Thirty Three links & a half, More or less to the Place of beginning*

Together with all houses, out-houses, woods, ways, waters and water-courses thereon erected, lying and being ; the reversion and reversions, remainder and remainders, rents, issues and profits thereof ; and all the estate, right, title, interest, claim, property and demand whatsoever, either at law or in equity, of *him* the said *William Hamilton Merritt* _____ of, in, to or out of the same, and every part and parcel thereof ; **To have and to hold** the said parcel or tract of land and premises, free and clear, and freed and cleared, of and from all and all manner of incumbrances, to the said *George H. Harris his* _____ heirs and assigns, to the sole and proper use, benefit and behoof of the said *George H. Harris his* _____ heirs and assigns, for ever----under the reservations, limitations and conditions expressed in the original grant from the Crown ; Which said Indenture is witnessed by *Saml Ingersoll Esqr of Oxford and Edward Merigold Merchant Clerk and Daniel Harris & Jerman both of Oxford* and this MEMORIAL thereof is hereby required to be registered, by me, the *Grantee* therein named

Witness ---- hand and seal , this _____ day of _____ in the year of our Lord one thousand, eight hundred and thirty *above written*

SIGNED AND SEALED,
In presence of

Saml Ingersoll
Edward Merigold
Daniel Harris Jur

Wm Hamilton Merritt

88
140
728
11/3

4-8c

4-9: Assessment rolls are particularly useful for researchers. In this sample from the Municipality of Brantford Township for 1876, we can glean these facts: name and occupation of the occupant, name of the owner, lot and concession number of the property, value of the property, the number of dogs, cattle, sheep, hogs, and horses on the land, the number of persons in the family, and their religion.

4-9 : Les rôles d'évaluation sont fort prisés par les chercheurs. De ce spécimen issu de la municipalité du canton de Brantford pour 1876, nous retenons les faits suivants : nom et profession de l'occupant, nom du propriétaire, numéro de lot et de concession de la propriété, valeur de la propriété, nombre de chiens, têtes de bétail, moutons, porcs et chevaux, nombre et religion des membres de la famille

ASSESSMENT ROLL FOR THE MUNICIPALITY OF

	NAMES AND DESCRIPTIONS OF PERSONS ASSESSED.						DESCRIPTION AND VALUE	
1	2	3	4	5	6	7	8	9
Nos.	NAME OF OCCUPANT OR OTHER TAXABLE PARTY.	OCCUPATION.	Freeholder, Householder, or Tenant.	Age of Occupant.	OWNERS AND ADDRESS.	Non-Resident / School Section	No. of Concession, Street, Square, or other designation.	No. of Lot, House, &c.
45	Joseph Downing	Mechanic	F. 65		Mt Vernon	2	4	1
46	Arthur W. Dickie	Farmer	T 27		Thos. Clark Brantf	9	4	21
47	Patrick Donovan	Cooper	T 24		M. Irwin Mt Vernon	2	4	3
48	Charles Dutton	Farmer	T 48		A. Huntington Brantfd	2	4	9
49	Hiram Dickie	"	F. 50		Brantford	9	3	21+22
50	Isaac Dickie	"	F. 53		"	9	3	21+22
51	Geo Douglass	"	F. 36		Mt Vernon	2	4	1
52	Wm Depew	"	F. 45		Paris	1a	1	7+8
53	Stephen Dadson	"	T 40		Phil. Sovereign Paris	1a	1	11
54	Thos. G. Davidson	"	T 30		Geo Anne Woodstock	1	3	3
55	Percy Douglass	"	T 24		J.R. Douglas Mt Vernon	2	3	4+5

Brantford Township FOR 1876

Hart & Rawlinson, Municipal Printers and Publishers, 5 King Street West, Toronto.

OF REAL PROPERTY.				PERSONAL PROPERTY AND INCOME.			AGGREGATE VALUE OF ALL PROPERTY.	STATUTE LABOUR.	DOGS.					RELIGION.	STATISTICS.				
10	11	1	13	14	15	16	17	18	19			20			22	23	24	25	26
No. of Acres, Feet, or other Measurement.	No. of Acres Cleared, Vacant, or Built on.	Value of each Parcel of Real Property.	Total Value of Real Property.	Value of Personal Property other than Income.	Amount of Taxable Income.	Total Value of Personal Property and Taxable Income.	Total Value of Real and Personal Property and Taxable Income.	Persons from 21 to 60 years.	No. of Dogs.	Road Division.	Dogs.	Bitches.	No. of persons in the Family.		No. of Cattle.	No. of Sheep.	No. of Hogs.	No. of	Date of Delivery of Notices under Section 48.
1/4	1/4		225				225	2✓			1		1	P					Feb 19th/76
			200	200	200		2 2				2		1	B	3	7	2	2	" 22nd "
1/4	1/4		200				200	1 2✓			4		1	R.C.					" 25th "
150	120		4000	400	400		4400	48✓	1		10		1	C.E.	11	7	15	5	" 26th "
140	125		4200	700	700		4900	58✓	1		7		1	B	14	40	2	5	" 29th "
70	60		2360	400	400		2760	46✓	1		6		1	B	7	16	2	5	" " "
130	30		2700				2700	1 6✓			1		1						Mrch 2d/76
80	80		3520	138	138		3658	2 6✓			7		1	W.M.	1	6	1	1	" 9th/76
50	29		1800				1800	1 4			2		1	B.	1		1		" 15th "
99	99		3762	127	127		3889	2 7✓	1		4		1	M.	3	10	1	2	" 18th "
200	200		7400	400	400		7800	4 11✓			4		1	E.M.	7	3	2	3	" 21st/76

4-9

4-10-a&b: Company and business records are invaluable sources of information when reconstructing the past. This example from the Company Charter Books shows the first page of the letters patent of incorporation for the Thunder Bay Silver Mining Company in 1868. As can be seen on the accompanying map from 1872, mining of silver, gold, and tin was a growing enterprise in the Thunder Bay area. Two of the principals in the Silver Mining Company were the well-known Montreal merchants Hugh Allan, famous for the Montreal Ocean Steamship Company (known as the Allan Line), and John Redpath, founder of Redpath Sugar.

L'ENTREPRISE

4-10-a et b : Les actes et documents des sociétés et entreprises sont de précieuses sources d'information lorsqu'on veut reconstituer le passé. Le présent spécimen, tiré du registre des chartes de compagnies, est la première page des actes de constitution en personne morale de la Thunder Bay Silver Mining Company, qui date de 1868. Comme on le voit sur la carte de 1872 qui est annexée, l'extraction d'or, d'argent et d'étain prenait de l'ampleur dans la région de Thunder Bay. Deux des actionnaires principaux de la Silver Mining Company étaient les marchands montréalais bien connus Hugh Allan, lié à la Montreal Ocean Steamship Company (l'Allan Line, à l'époque), et John Redpath, fondateur de la Redpath Sugar.

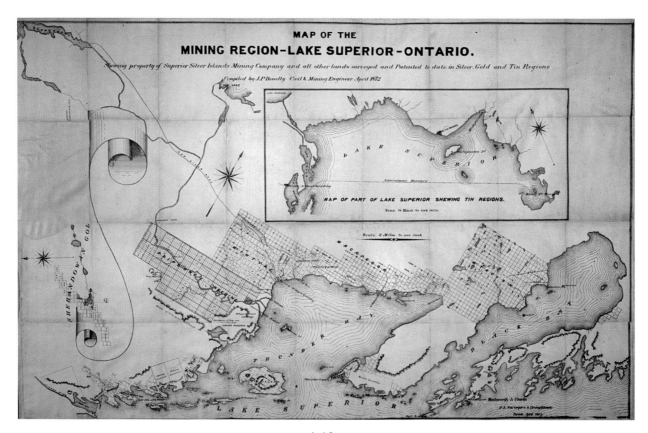

4-10a

(P P)

H Plested

PROVINCE OF ONTARIO.

Victoria, *by the Grace of God, of the United Kingdom of Great Britain and Ireland, QUEEN, Defender of the Faith, &c., &c., &c.*

To all to whom these Presents shall come—GREETING.

Whereas, under and by an Act of our Parliament of the Province of Canada, passed in the session thereof held in the twenty-seventh and twenty-eighth years of Our Reign, and intituled: "An Act to authorize the granting of Charters of Incorporation to Manufacturing, Mining and other Companies," Our Governor General in Council may grant, by letters patent under the Great Seal of Our said Province, a Charter of Incorporation to any number of persons, not less than five, who shall petition therefor, and may constitute such persons and others who may become shareholders in any such company, a body corporate and politic, for any of the purposes therein mentioned.

AND WHEREAS, under the provisions of an Act of the Imperial Parliament, intituled, "An Act for the Union of Canada, Nova Scotia and New Brunswick, and the government thereof, and for purposes connected therewith," Our Lieutenant-Governor of the Province of Ontario in Council may in like manner cause to be issued the said letters patent.

AND WHEREAS, by Petition addressed to Our Lieutenant-Governor of Ontario in Council,

LETTERS PATENT

INCORPORATING

"*Thunder Bay Silver Mining Company.*"

Recorded 3rd June A.D. 1868

No. 11

Thos. Patterson
Deputy Reg'r.

John Redpath, Hugh Allan, Edward W. Hopkins, George Stephen, Thomas Morland, Thomas Reynolds, and Donald Lorn Mac Dougall.

have prayed that a Charter of Incorporation, embodying and setting forth the general provisions of the above in part recited Act,

may be granted to them and to such other persons as are or may become shareholders in a Company formed for the purpose of *Mining for Silver and other Metals and Minerals, and for washing, dressing, smelting and otherwise preparing for market the ores of such metals and for exporting and selling the same.*

AND WHEREAS, in accordance with the provisions of the above in part recited Act, notice was published in the *Canada* Gazette, for at least one month previous to the presentation of the petition hereinbefore mentioned, in which notice it was stated that *John Redpath, Hugh Allan, Edward W. Hopkins, George Stephen, Thomas Morland, Thomas Reynolds and Donald Lorn Mac Dougall, all of the City of Montreal, in the Province of Quebec.*

being *all* ——— of the applicants who have petitioned as aforesaid, intended to apply for such Charter; that the proposed Corporate name of the Company is " *The Thunder Bay Silver Mining Company.*"

that the object or purpose for which Incorporation is sought is *the mining for Silver and other Metals and Minerals and for washing, dressing, smelting and otherwise preparing for market the ores of such metals and for the exportation and sale thereof.*

*J. S. Macdonald.
Attorney General.*

that the *place* where the operations of the Company are to be carried on *is at Thunder Bay, upon Lake Superior, in the Province of Ontario, and at the City of Montreal, in the Province of Quebec.*

that the amount of the nominal capital of the Company is *to be Four hundred thousand dollars.* ———

4-10b

SCHOOL

4-11-a to e: The three photographs of schools presented here illustrate both the evolution of schoolhouses and the importance placed upon education. [4-11-a] A typical one-room schoolhouse of the nineteenth century was a reflection of the relative poverty of rural areas. [4-11-b] In contrast, the magnificent high school of 1890s Belleville shows how the school had become a point of civic pride; education was seen as a sign of progress and prosperity, and so the school, as the outward expression of a community's success, must be of the highest calibre. [4-11-c] By the 1950s, school architecture – typified by this modern building in York Mills – reflected the shift to 'progressive' education.

[4-11-d, e] However, one thing that did not change much was the dreaded examination. On the next pages are excerpts from two history examinations, the first from 1890 and the second from 1958.

L'INSTRUCTION

4-11-a à e : Les photographies de trois écoles présentées ici témoignent de l'évolution du bâtiment scolaire et de l'importance croissante que prend l'instruction. [4-11-a] Au dix-neuvième siècle, l'école à classe unique reflète la pauvreté relative des régions rurales. [4-11-b] Par contraste, dans les années 1890, la magnifique école secondaire de Belleville atteste que le bâtiment scolaire est désormais symbole de fierté civique; l'instruction est considérée comme un signe de progrès et de prospérité, de sorte que l'école, manifestation concrète de la réussite collective, doit être à la hauteur.

[4-11-c] Dans les années 1950, l'architecture scolaire – telle que représentée par cette construction moderne de York Mills – traduit le passage à une instruction « progressiste ».

[4-11-d et e] Mais une chose n'a guère changé : la période si redoutée des examens. Des extraits de deux examens d'histoire, le premier de 1890 et le second de 1958, se trouvent sur les pages suivantes.

4-11a

4-11b

4-11c

University of Toronto.

ANNUAL EXAMINATIONS, 1890.

JUNIOR MATRICULATION.

FACULTY OF MEDICINE.

HISTORY AND GEOGRAPHY.

PASS AND HONORS.

Examiner—T. ARNOLD HAULTAIN, M.A.

NOTE. — *Candidates for Scholarships will take only those questions marked with an asterisk. All other candidates (whether for Pass or Honors) must take the first four questions and any one of the remainder.*

*1. *There are four divisions in which most of the various peoples or races [of Europe] may be classified."* Make a detailed classification of the nationalities of Europe on this basis.

*2. Give a brief but particular account of the various deposits of economic minerals and metals in the several Provinces of Canada. State in general terms the description and magnitude of these deposits.

*3. Describe the main physical features of the Dominion of Canada, and show how these influence (a) the climate of the different Provinces, (b) the distribution of the chief field and forest flora—cereals, grasses, fruits, timber, etc.

*4. *"In outer seeming,"* says Green, *"the Revolution of 1688 had only transferred the sovereignty over England from James to William and Mary. In actual fact, it was transferring the sovereignty from the King to the House of Commons."* Support this assertion and point out at length the changes in the machinery of government which followed this transference.

*5. (a) Describe the material condition of the English nation at the time of Walpole's ascendancy. (b) Remark on his financial policy, substantiating your opinions by references to particular measures advocated by him.

6. Give a concise account of the state of British industry at the time of Pitt's administration.

4-11d

Department of Education, Ontario

Annual Examinations, 1958

GRADE 13

HISTORY

NOTE. *Five questions constitute a complete paper. Candidates must answer two questions from Part A, the question in Part B, and two questions from Part C.*

PART A
(Answer two questions only.)

1. Describe the efforts of the United States to protect her national interests by following a policy of isolation during the period from the adoption of the Constitution, 1789, to the announcement of the Monroe Doctrine, 1823.

2. (a) Account for the vital importance of slavery to the South in the first half of the nineteenth century.

(b) Describe the course of the abolitionist movement in the United States before the Civil War.

3. (a) What were the sources of political discontent in the colonies of Upper and Lower Canada before 1837?

(b) How did Lord Durham's Report propose to remove these difficulties?

4. Discuss *three* important episodes in Canadian-American relations in the period 1867-1911.

PART B

5. Write an account of the effect of the American Civil War on the development of the United States and of British North America to the end of the nineteenth century.

PART C
(Answer two questions only.)

6. By the end of the nineteenth century certain disadvantages had become apparent in the economic system of *laissez-faire.*

(a) What were these disadvantages?

(b) Describe the remedies that were proposed to correct these conditions under *two* of the following:
   (i) state intervention and control;
   (ii) socialism;
   (iii) communism.

7. (a) What were the conditions in Italy, after the First World War, that enabled the Fascist party to gain power?

(b) Describe the policies and activities of the Fascist government of Italy under Benito Mussolini.

8. (a) In what respects was the Second World War unlike any previous war in modern times?

(b) What reasons may be given to support the claim that the year 1942 marked the turning-point in the Second World War?

9. (a) Describe the peace treaties made with (i) Italy, (ii) Japan, after the Second World War.

(b) Describe and account for the incomplete peace settlement with Germany after the Second World War.

4-11e

HEALTH

4-12-a to e: The Ontario government set up the Provincial Board of Health of Ontario in 1882. Its function was to promote and ensure the general health of the province's citizens. This was accomplished in part by the efforts of public-health nurses who travelled around the province making inspections and filing reports on health conditions, particularly regarding the health of mothers and children. These samples of reports and photographs show the work of nurses in some of the most remote regions of Ontario. It is interesting to see how many children had rotten teeth and somewhat frightening to think about the treatment that they would receive.

LA SANTÉ

4-12-a à f : En 1882, le gouvernement de l'Ontario s'était donné un Conseil provincial de la santé. Le rôle de cet organisme était de promouvoir la santé des citoyens et de veiller à son maintien, mandat réalisé en partie par le travail des infirmières hygiénistes. Celles-ci effectuaient des tournées d'inspection et déposaient des rapports sur les conditions d'hygiène, en particulier touchant la santé des mères et des enfants. Ces quelques rapports et photographies montrent les infirmières à l'œuvre, dans certaines des régions les plus reculées de l'Ontario. Il est certes intéressant de dénombrer les enfants qui présentent des caries dentaires, mais on ne peut s'empêcher de frémir en songeant au traitement qui leur est réservé.

4-12a

4-12b

4-12c

Provincial Board of Health
SCHOOL REPORT

Municipality *Fort William* Nurse *Edith Murphy*

Date *December 1925*

SCHOOLS

Findings	Oct 16 Blake #2	Oct 28 Blake S.S.#1	Oct 22 Conmee S.S.2	Nov 2 Gillies S.S.4	Nov 11 O'Conor S.S.H1	Nov 12 O'Conor S.S.No.2	Nov 16 Crooks S.S No4	Dec 1 Gillies No.2	Oct 7 Conmee S.S No1	Nov John St.	Dec	Nov 27 Property	
No. of C. P.	19	24	20	27	12	12	31	38	5				188
" with defective vision	3	1	2	2			1	1	1				11
" " " hearing		2	1	1		1	1	1					7
" " eye disease		1	2	1									4
" " ear "													
" " def. nasal breathing	5	1				1		1					8
" " abnormal tonsils	11	6	2	2	3	4	3	1					32
" " anaemic appearance													
" " def. teeth	8	15	11	15	7	7	18	7	1				89
" " dig. abnormality													
" " enlarged glands													
" " " thyroid	15	12	13	15	9	8	22	20	2				116
" " skin disease													
" " orthopedic defect		1											1
" " malnutrition		2	3										5
" " pulmonary disease													
" " cardiac disease													
" " nervous disorders													
Other—specify *Defective speech*		1											1
Diseases Child Has Had													
Measles													
German Measles													
Scarlet Fever													
Diphtheria													
Whooping Cough													
Chickenpox													
Mumps													
C. S. Meningitis													
Inf. Paralysis													
Rheumatism													
Pneumonia													
Defects Corrected Summary		3	2			5	2	6	6	5		4	33
No. Exam. by Dr.													
" Defs. Found													
" Exam. by Nurse	19	24	20	27	12	12	31	38	5	36			188
" Defs. Found	42	40	36	36	19	21	42	30	5				274
" Ref. Physician	10	6	2	2	1	1	2	4					28
" " Dentist	3	9	6	7	5	4	16	7					57
" " Oculist	2	1	2	1			1	1					8
Class Room talk	1	1		1	1		2	1	1	1	1	1	13
Class-Room Inspections										1	1	1	3
No. Children Inspected	19	24	20	27	12	12	31	38		36	24	36	281
Visits following Inspections	17	29	20	3	2	0	25	10		2	2	0	110

4-12d

Brief Report on Work Done in Rainy River,

by ∨S.M.C.H. Winter and early Summer 1 9 2 6.

By S.M.Carr-Harris,
Public Health Nurse.

RAINY RIVER.

Report on work between end of November 1925 and end of June 1926.

Winter Months.

School: Besides the general routine school work of inspections,
health talks, L.M.L. classes, "NURSES Inspections" out side the class
rooms were made of all children previously seen or newly entered in
the Public School; and the same within the class room in the Seperate
school.

A list of the Defects found was given to each teacher,
and corrections as made, recorded.

The recorded defects and corrections were about as follows at the end
of June:

Eyes: Public: One correction from former recommendation.
               5 newly recommended to Eye Specialist not corrected.
      Seperate: No corrections,
               6 recommended to see Eye Specialist. (None in Rainy)

Ears: 1 correction, a bean removed from the ear of a Continuation
       School boy's ear.
       9 referred to doctor for hearing, obstruction or hardened wax.

Enlarged thyroid: 10 slight cases in the Public School.

Underweight: There were 21 children from 6½ to 22 pounds below average
             "   "   11 "   "   2 " 6½ "   "   "
in the Public School. Data not available for Seperate.

Teeth: 37 corrections, in the Public and one in the Seperate school.
       31 of these were in 1926. This left about 68 in the Public and
       11 in the Seperate school not yet corrected. Some promised to
       have attention during the holidays. The dentist was continuously
       busy and appointments not always easy. Many of these cases
       had teeth too far gone to be corrected.
       Teeth in the Continuation School were in better condition and
       and there were many corrections there which are unrecorded.

Tonsils: 4 corrections. One was done in 1924, not previously recorded.
         Two were done in 1925. One in 1926.

         The Women's Institute were anxious to arrange a tonsil clinic
         but the doctors were not willing to have one.

Social Service: A certain amount of Social Service was done in
         connection with indigents, Influenza cases, and tuberculosis
         cases, two of the latter being sent to Sanitaria from unorgan-
         ized territory; and a number of visits were made to the
         country with the Medical Health Officer, Provincial Police, and
         Children's Aid Officer, in connection with the above.

Conference: A Conference was attended at Sault Ste. Marie in regard
         to School Work with Miss Knox and Miss Jamieson.
Infant and Preschool Conferences were attempted in the Spring with
         very indifferent success. In Winter the weather is too severe
         and in spring the mothers appear too busy or indifferent.

4-12e

4-1: Statue of the Hon. John Sandfield Macdonald, 1909, Walter S. Allward (1876-1955) (Government of Ontario Art Collection, 619879, Tom Moore Photography)

4-2-a: Birth registration for Mary Pickford (far left), born Gladys Louise Smith on University Avenue in Toronto on 8 April 1892 (Office of the Registrar General, Registrations of Births and Stillbirths - Registrations, RG 80-2-0-373 vol.17)

4-2-b: Mary Pickford posing with a group of employees during her visit to the General Engineering Company, June 5, 1943 (General Engineering Company (Canada) fonds, F 2082-1-2-10. I0004930)

4-3: Marriage registration for Gregor McGregor and Susan Robert, 1 May 1796 (Office of the Registrar General, District Marriage Registers, RG 80-27-1-26, 17)

4-4-a: Death Registrations for 1918 for District of Temiskaming (Timmins), 31 Dec. 1918 (Office of the Registrar General, Deaths - Registrations, RG 80-8-0-688)

4-4-b: Men gathered at a funeral [between 1895 and 1910] (Bartle Brothers fonds, C 2-61. I0002522)

4-5-a&b: Estate file for the Hon. Thomas Ridout, probated 7 March 1829, Court of Probate estate files, RG 22-155, Microfilm MS 638 Reel 64, Archives of Ontario

4-6: Will of Charles Vance Millar, 1926 (York County Surrogate Court estate files, RG 22-305, file 55697)

4-7: Coroner's inquest into death of Jacob Godbatt in the town of St Marys, 19 July 1866 (Perth County Coroner Investigations and Inquests, RG 22-4295, Godbatt, Jacob, 1866)

4-8-a: Detail of patent plan of Zorra Township (west and east) [ca. 1840] (Crown Lands, Patent Plans, RG 1-100, C-71, Map A.14, AO 5973)

4-8-b: Letters patent for the lands in Zorra Township granted to William Hamilton Merritt on 20 June 1822 (Land Patent books, London, 1822-4, RG 53-1, vol. B-1, AO 5974)

4-8-c: Deed for the sale of one of Merritt's lots to George H. Harris, 19 July 1834 (Oxford County Instruments and Deeds, RG 61-41, instrument 2761)

4-9: Extract from the assessment roll for the municipality of Brantford Township, Ward 1, 1876 (County of Brant fonds, F 1551-19-0-991, no. 102)

4-10-a: 'Map of the mining region - Lake Superior - shewing property of Superior Silver Islands Mining Company and all other lands surveyed and patented to date in silver, gold and tin regions, J.P. Donnelly, Civil and Mining Engineer, compiler Wadworth and Unwin, Toronto, publisher, 1872' (Miscellaneous Map Collection, C 279-0-0-0-69)

4-10-b: Charter (letters patent of incorporation) for the Thunder Bay Silver Mining Company (Company Charter Books, RG 55-1, vol. 1, 11, AO 5970)

4-11-a: One-room schoolhouse in Oxford County or Township [ca. 1872] (S 14861, Acc. 9434)

4-11-b: Belleville High School, ca. 1890 (Department of Public Works Photographs, RG 15-90-0-0-41. I0002089)

4-11-c: York Mills Collegiate, 1958 (Department of Travel and Publicity photographs, RG 65-35-3, X3091. I0005585)

4-11-d&e: Excerpts from the Annual Exam Books for 1890 and 1958 (Examination Papers for High Schools and Collegiate Institutes, RG 2-116)

4-12-a: Children sitting in a classroom [used to illustrate poor lighting and its effects on children's vision for the Department of Health] [ca. 1905] (Public Health Nursing photographs, RG 10-30-2, 3.03.5. I0005194)

4-12-b: Public-health nurse sitting on a car at South Gillies, Thunder Bay District, 1923 (Public Health Nursing photographs, RG 10-30-2, 2.20.1. I0005230)

4-12-c: This woman was nursing a brother who had typhoid as well as caring for family [notation on back of photo], 1923 (Public Health Nursing historical files, RG 10-30-1, file 1-14, box 1)

4-12-d: Provincial Board of Health School Report, December 1925 (Public Health Nursing historical files, RG 10-30-1, file 1-14, box 1)

4-12-e: Brief Report of Work Done in Rainy River by Public Health Nurse S.M. Carr-Harris, 1926 (Public Health Nursing historical files, RG 10-30-1-1.14)

LÉGENDES

4-1 : Statue de l'hon. John Sandfield Macdonald, 1909, Walter S. Allward (1876-1955) (Collection d'œuvres d'art du gouvernement de l'Ontario, 619879, Tom Moore Photography)

4-2-a : Enregistrement de naissance de Mary Pickford (colonne de gauche), née Gladys Louise Smith, avenue University, à Toronto, le 8 avril 1892 (Bureau du registraire général de l'état civil, Enregistrements des naissances et des naisssances d'enfants morts-nés, RG 80-2-0-373, vol. 17)

4-2-b : Mary Pickford pose avec un groupe d'employés lors de sa visite à la General Engineering Company, le 5 juin 1943 (Fonds General Engineering Company (Canada), F 2082-1-2-10. I0004930)

4-3 : Enregistrement du mariage de Gregor McGregor et Susan Robert, 1er mai 1796 (Bureau du registraire général de l'état civil, Registres des enregistrements de mariages des districts, RG 80-27-1-26, 17)

4-4-a : Enregistrements des décès pour 1918, district de Temiskaming (Timmins), 31 décembre 1918 (Bureau du registraire général de l'état civil, Enregistrements de décès, RG 80-8-0-688)

4-4-b : Rassemblement d'hommes lors d'un enterrement [entre 1895 et 1910] (Fonds Bartle Brothers, C 2-61. I0002522)

4-5-a et b : Dossier de succession pour l'hon. Thomas Ridout, homologué le 7 mars 1829, Dossiers du tribunal des successions, RG 22-155, microfilm MS 638, bobine 64, Archives publiques de l'Ontario

4-6 : Testament de Charles Vance Millar, 1926 (Dossiers de la Cour des successions et des tutelles du comté de York, RG 22-305, dossier 55697)

4-7 : Enquête du coroner sur le décès de Jacob Godbatt, dans la ville de St. Marys, 19 juillet 1866 (Enquêtes et recherches du coroner du comté de Perth, RG 22-4295, Godbatt, Jacob, 1866)

4-8-a : Détail, plan de concessions du canton de Zorra (ouest et est) [vers 1840] (Terres de la Couronne, plans de concessions, RG 1-100, C-71, carte A.14, AO 5973)

4-8-b : Lettres patente relative à la concession de terres octroyée à William Hamilton Merritt dans le canton de Zorra, 20 juin 1822 (Registre des lettres patentes, London, 1822-1824, RG 53-1, vol. B-1, AO 5974)

4-8-c : Acte de vente d'un des lots de Merritt à George H. Harris, 19 juillet 1834 (Actes instrumentaires et actes scellés du comté d'Oxford, RG 61-41, acte 2761)

4-9 : Extrait du rôle d'évaluation de la municipalité du canton de Brantford, quartier 1, 1876 (Fonds Comté de Brant, F 1551-19-0-991, no 102)

4-10-a : *Map of the mining region - Lake Superior - shewing property of Superior Silver Islands Mining Company and all other lands surveyed and patented to date in silver, gold and tin regions*, J.P. Donnelly, Civil and Mining Engineer, compiler Wadworth and Unwin, Toronto, publisher, 1872 (Collection de cartes diverses, C 279-0-0-0-69)

4-10-b : Charte (lettres patentes d'incorporation) de la Thunder Bay Silver Mining Company (Registre des chartes de compagnies, RG 55-1, vol. 1, 11, AO 5970)

4-11-a : École à classe unique, comté ou canton d'Oxford [vers 1872] (S 14861, Acc. 9434)

4-11-b : École secondaire de Belleville, vers 1890 (Photographies du ministère des Travaux publics, RG 15-90-0-0-41. I0002089)

4-11-c : École supérieure de York Mills, 1958 (Photographies du ministère du Tourisme et de la Publicité, RG 65-35-3, X3091. I0005585)

4-11-d et e : Extraits du recueil des examens annuels pour 1890 et 1958 (Questionnaires d'examens des écoles secondaires et supérieures, RG 2-116)

4-12-a : Enfants en classe [pour illustrer les effets d'un mauvais éclairage sur la vue des écoliers, pour le compte du ministère de la Santé] [vers 1905] (Photographies des services infirmiers de santé publique, RG 10-30-2, 3.03.5. I0005194)

4-12-b : Infirmière de la santé publique assise sur le marchepied d'une voiture à South Gillies, district de Thunder Bay, 1923 (Photographies des services infirmiers de santé publique, RG 10-30-2, 2.20.1. I0005230)

4-12-c : Mère de famille qui prenait soin de son frère atteint de fièvre typhoïde tout en s'occupant de ses enfants [annotation au dos de la photo], 1923 (Dossiers historiques des services infirmiers de santé publique, RG 10-30-1, dossier 1-14, boîte 1)

4-12-d : Rapport sur les écoles du Conseil provincial de la santé de l'Ontario, décembre 1925 (Dossiers historiques des services infirmiers de santé publique, RG 10-30-1, dossier 1-14, boîte 1)

4-12-e : Rapport sommaire sur sa visite à Rainy River par l'infirmière de la santé publique S. M. Carr-Harris, 1926 (Dossiers historiques des services infirmiers de santé publique, RG 10-30-1-1.14)

PART II

THE IMPORTANCE OF CONTEXT

L'IMPORTANCE DU CONTEXTE

In its sheer size, the Archives of Ontario's collection of records is daunting to say the least. Besides 3.5 million photographs, 35,000 maps, 23,000 hours of audio, video, and film recordings, and more than 170,000 architectural drawings, the textual records are so voluminous that, if laid end to end, they would encircle the globe several times.

Organizing such a mass of material into an intelligible system would be no simple task if it had to be undertaken from scratch. Fortunately, however, most of the records the Archives acquires are already organized into a system on their arrival, and we try not to interfere with it. Archives are different from libraries and museums for precisely this reason. Whereas those institutions select and group their holdings for the purposes of developing themes and subject areas, archives endeavour to maintain the filing systems and other arrangements that the records' creators devised. In addition, believing that records are understood best when one knows the context of the creators' lives and times, archives try to keep the records of a particular creator together and apart from those of other creators. This rule applies whether the records are those of a government ministry, a company, a family, or an individual.

An understanding of the context of records also enriches our appreciation for them. A photograph of a lovely old mill takes on more resonance when we know that the photographer was Eric Arthur, one of Canada's premier architectural historians, and that he was trying to capture a disappearing landscape. In the same way, we can more easily understand and value the earliest acquisitions of the Government of Ontario Art Collection when we know of the motivations of its founder, Egerton Ryerson. The father of Ontario's school system was convinced that exposure to great works of art would help to transform young student teachers into sophisticated educators.

The five chapters that follow focus on some of the individuals, firms, and government ministries that have created records held at the Archives of Ontario. It is our hope that the work of the artists, writers, photographers, and architects represented on these pages will not only spark curiosity but also help us to understand what their lives and times have in common with our own.

De par sa simple envergure, la collection de documents des Archives publiques de l'Ontario est à tout le moins impressionnante. Abstraction faite des 3,5 millions de photographies, 35 000 cartes, 23 000 heures d'enregistrement audio, vidéo et cinématographique et plus de 170 000 dessins d'architecture qu'elle renferme, les documents textuels à eux seuls sont si volumineux que, mis bout à bout, ils ceintureraient plusieurs fois le globe.

S'il fallait partir de rien, structurer une telle masse de matériel selon un mode intelligible constituerait une tâche considérable. Par bonheur, la plupart des documents acquis par les Archives suivent déjà une certaine organisation, que nous essayons de respecter. C'est précisément pour cette raison que les archives diffèrent des musées et des bibliothèques. Alors que, dans ces établissements, on choisit et regroupe les documents dans le but d'étoffer des thèmes et domaines, on s'efforce aux archives de préserver l'ordre établi par leurs créateurs. De plus, estimant qu'un document est mieux compris lorsqu'il est situé dans le contexte de la vie et l'époque de son créateur, l'archiviste tente de regrouper les documents selon leur provenance, c'est-à-dire en fonction de leur créateur. Cette règle est générale, peu importe que les documents émanent d'un ministère, d'une entreprise, d'une famille ou d'un individu. Cette règle est générale, peu importe que les documents émanent d'un ministère, d'une entreprise, d'une famille ou d'un individu.

La connaissance du contexte des documents donne de la profondeur à leur appréciation. Par exemple, la photographie d'un vieux moulin pittoresque acquiert des résonances si l'on sait que l'auteur en est Eric Arthur, l'un des meilleurs historiens de l'architecture au Canada, qui a voulu ainsi capter un paysage sur le point de disparaître. De façon analogue, il est plus facile de comprendre et d'apprécier les premières acquisitions de la Collection d'œuvres d'art du gouvernement de l'Ontario lorsqu'on connaît les motivations de son fondateur, Egerton Ryerson. Le père du système scolaire de la province était convaincu que la fréquentation des chefs-d'œuvre allait nécessairement pousser les jeunes étudiants à devenir des éducateurs éclairés.

Les cinq chapitres qui suivent portent sur certains des particuliers, entreprises et ministères qui ont été à l'origine des documents conservés par les Archives publiques de l'Ontario. Nous espérons vivement que les œuvres des artistes, écrivains, photographes et architectes représentées au fil de ces pages sauront provoquer l'intérêt et aideront à découvrir ce que leur vie et leur époque ont en commun avec les nôtres.

CITATION

Part II Intro
Young people at the tower, Queen's Park, Toronto, 19 July 1925,
    M.O. Hammond (M.O. Hammond fonds, F 1075, H 1025.
    I0001412)

LÉGENDE

Partie II Intro
Jeunes gens au pied de la tour, Queen's Park, Toronto,
    19 juillet 1925, M. O. Hammond (Fonds M. O. Hammond,
    F 1075, H 1025. I0001412)

5

AMATEUR AND COMMERCIAL PHOTOGRAPHERS

LA PHOTOGRAPHIE AMATEUR ET COMMERCIALE

5-1

Since its inception in 1837, photography has been characterized by continual innovations. Early cameras were bulky and cumbersome and were usually confined to the studio, where the photographer had to prepare his own glass-plate negatives, adjust light levels for exposure, and develop his own prints. The late nineteenth century, however, witnessed a number of developments, notably improvements in cameras and lenses, the introduction of pre-packaged glass-plate negatives and, later, film negatives on a plastic base. Another turning point was the advent, by the turn of the century, of Eastman Kodak's 'Brownie' camera; one of the first 'point and shoot' cameras, it was portable, affordable, and easy to use. The twentieth century saw further changes, including the introduction of colour film, many refinements in cameras, lenses, negatives, and film processing, and, in the 1990s, the introduction and rapid growth of digital photography. In the midst of all this change, the late nineteenth century stands out as the period when photography, once the art form of the few, became widely accessible. The new technology of that era allowed anyone who had the inclination and a little spare money to take photographs, and, in fact, the hobby became so popular that, within a short time, amateur photographers of great talent emerged. The work of certain amateurs, such as John Boyd, M.O. Hammond, or John Macfie, may be distinct from other photographs because of their skill in composition and because of the lengths to which they would go to obtain a perfect shot. Their photographs, and those of a number of other amateurs, can be found at the Archives of Ontario.

The early professional photographers were motivated by the same impulses as the amateurs. Though they were producing photographs for sale, they, too, displayed freshness of vision, genuine interest in their subject matter, and devotion to their craft. Some, like Thomas and John Connon of Elora, ran businesses of their own, while others were employees. The work of the Connons as well as other professional photographers is also available at the Archives.

Ranging from the nineteenth century on, the Archives' collection of photographs numbers in the millions. This chapter presents a few samples which not only portray interesting subjects but also demonstrate technical sophistication and a considerable degree of artistry. The people who took these pictures occupy an important place in the history of photography in Ontario. At the same time, by capturing images of people and places of the past on film, they made an invaluable contribution to the documentary record of the history of the province itself.

Depuis ses débuts en 1837, la photographie se caractérise par une innovation continue. Comme les premiers appareils étaient volumineux et encombrants, ils étaient habituellement confinés à l'atelier ou au studio, où le photographe devait lui-même préparer ses négatifs sur plaque de verre, mesurer le niveau d'éclairage nécessaire à l'exposition et développer ses épreuves. Puis, la fin du dix-neuvième siècle est témoin d'un certain nombre d'améliorations, notamment en matière d'appareils et d'objectifs; il y a apparition des négatifs sur plaque de verre préemballés et, plus tard, des négatifs sur pellicule de plastique. Autre étape marquante, le tournant du siècle voit l'avènement du petit appareil « Brownie » d'Eastman Kodak : portatif, bon marché et facile à utiliser, c'est un des premiers appareils à mise au point automatique. Le vingtième siècle assistera à bien d'autres changements, notamment à l'introduction du film en couleur et au perfectionnement poussé des appareils, objectifs, négatifs et procédés de traitement de la pellicule, qui culmineront pendant les années 1990, lors de l'irruption du numérique et son évolution en accéléré. Parmi tous ces chambardements, le dix-neuvième siècle ressort comme étant la période où la photographie, jusque là forme d'art réservée à une élite, devient largement accessible. La nouvelle technologie de l'époque invite à s'y essayer quiconque en a l'envie et un peu d'argent; en fait, ce hobby devient si populaire que des photographes amateurs de grand talent ne tardent pas à s'imposer. Certains d'entre eux, tels que John Boyd, M. O. Hammond et John Macfie, se distinguent par un sens inné de la composition et aussi par leurs efforts pour arriver à une quasi-perfection. Leurs photographies et celles de nombreux autres amateurs se retrouvent aux Archives publiques de l'Ontario.

On observe chez les premiers photographes professionnels les mêmes qualités et motivations que chez leurs collègues amateurs. À cela près qu'ils visaient la vente, ils manifestent une égale fraîcheur de vision, un vif intérêt pour leur sujet et une véritable ferveur pour leur métier. Certains, dont Thomas et John Connon à Elora, dirigent leur propre entreprise, tandis que d'autres sont employés. Des œuvres des Connon et d'autres professionnels sont également conservées aux Archives.

La collection des Archives compte des millions de photographies, dont une partie remontent au dix-neuvième siècle. Ce chapitre en présente quelques-unes qui, non seulement illustrent des sujets intéressants, mais dégagent une virtuosité technique certaine et un sens artistique considérable. Les auteurs de ces clichés occupent une place d'honneur au panthéon ontarien de la photographie. Par ailleurs, en fixant sur pellicule lieux et visages du passé, ils ont été d'un précieux apport aux annales documentaires de la province.

McCARTHY AERO SERVICE

5-2 to 5-4: McCarthy Aero Services was formed by a number of former Royal Air Force pilots after the First World War and survived only until 1920. The firm took oblique aerial photographs, mostly of urban areas, using Curtis JN-4 aircraft. Most of the photographs were taken at between 60 and 90 metres, providing rare early aerial views of southern Ontario cities and towns.

The Archives holds a remarkable collection of McCarthy Aero Services photographs. The scope of places photographed is broad, including almost all of the cities, towns, and villages along the St Lawrence River and Lake Ontario. There are numerous views of Toronto, Ottawa, and the Niagara Falls/Niagara River region. While contemporary postcard companies used some of their images, the collection as a whole provides an unparalleled visual record documenting urban growth and infrastructure changes in Ontario.

[5-2] The image presented here, showing the pinwheel layout of the town of Goderich, is a fine example of how McCarthy aerial photographs captured urban settings from a singularly informative perspective.

LE STUDIO McCARTHY AERO SERVICE

5-2 à 5-4: Le studio McCarthy Aero Services, fondé après la Première Guerre mondiale par d'anciens pilotes de l'Aviation royale du Canada, n'a existé que jusqu'en 1920. On y pratiquait la photographie aérienne oblique, généralement de régions urbaines, à bord d'un appareil Curtis JN-4. La plupart des photographies étaient prises à une altitude de 60 à 90 mètres; nous avons ainsi hérité d'exceptionnelles vues aériennes des villes du sud de l'Ontario à leurs débuts.

Les Archives possèdent une remarquable collection de photographies du studio McCarthy Aero Services. Des lieux de toutes sortes ont ainsi été photographiés, y compris la quasi totalité des villes et villages qui bordent le lac Ontario et le Saint-Laurent. On y retrouve de nombreuses vues de Toronto et d'Ottawa, de Niagara Falls et de la région de la Niagara. Certains fabricants de cartes postales du temps ont exploité quelques-unes de ces images, mais la collection dans son ensemble constitue un document visuel sans égal en ce qui touche la croissance urbaine et l'évolution de l'infrastructure en Ontario.

[5-2] L'image que nous voyons ici fait ressortir la configuration rayonnante de la ville de Goderich; c'est un superbe exemple de la manière du studio McCarthy, qui croque le cadre urbain depuis une perspective riche d'information.

5-2

[5-3] Toronto's harbour has changed dramatically since this photograph was taken in 1919. Reclamation has extended the land into the lake to put the present-day shoreline nearly at the bottom of the photograph. Today, busy waterfront highways like Lake Shore Boulevard and the Gardiner Expressway are integral to Toronto's infrastructure and carry endless traffic in and out of the city. The aerial photograph is remarkable for its ability to convey the impact of development on the urban landscape.

[5-4] This aerial photograph is equally valuable for its documentation of a town much changed, all in the name of progress. It shows the town of Iroquois, the St Lawrence River, and the shipping canal as it existed in 1919. When the St Lawrence Seaway was being built in 1958, a significant portion of Iroquois was flooded as a result of the construction. Residents of and visitors to Iroquois today will recognize the dramatic transformation of its shoreline, as evidenced in this photograph.

[5-3] Le port de Toronto a radicalement changé depuis la date lointaine de cette photographie, prise en 1919. Le projet de reconquête des terrains sur le lac a fait reculer le trait de côte jusqu'à son emplacement actuel, près du bas de la photographie. De nos jours, des autoroutes riveraines achalandées, telles que le Lake Shore Boulevard et le Gardiner Expressway, font partie intégrante de l'infrastructure torontoise, avec leurs flots incessants de circulation aux portes de la ville. La photographie aérienne n'a pas sa pareille pour visualiser l'impact du développement sur le paysage urbain.

[5-4] Cette photographie aérienne est également intéressante, car elle renseigne sur une collectivité qui a radicalement changé, et ce au nom du progrès. On y voit la petite ville d'Iroquois, le Saint-Laurent et le canal de dérivation tels qu'ils étaient en 1919. Lors des travaux de la voie maritime du Saint-Laurent, en 1958, une grande partie du territoire a été immergé. Les résidents d'Iroquois et les visiteurs qui s'y rendent aujourd'hui pourront, en regardant la photo, mesurer à quel point le rivage a été transformé.

5-3

5-4

CONNON FAMILY

5-5 to 5-7: This collection, containing photographs taken by Thomas Connon and his son, John R. Connon, in Elora, documents the town's early history, including buildings, the surrounding landscape, village life, and prominent residents. There are magnificent views of the mill, the Elora Falls, the Grand River and the Elora Gorge, shop fronts, churches, bridges, and events in addition to numerous portraits of people connected to Elora's early history and to the Connon family.

[5-5] One can almost hear the water rushing over the rocks alongside this mill in Elora. The Connons would have positioned themselves near the rushing water to capture the full effect of the beauty and power of nature.

LA FAMILLE CONNON

5-5 à 5-7 : Cette collection, qui renferme des images de Thomas Connon et de son fils, John R. Connon, documente les débuts de la petite ville d'Elora, ses bâtiments, les paysages des environs, la vie au village et ses notables. On y retrouve des vues magnifiques du cadre – moulin, chutes Elora, rivière Grand et gorge Elora, de même que devantures de commerces, églises, ponts et événements divers – outre de nombreux portraits de personnages qui ont marqué les débuts d'Elora et de connaissances de la famille Connon.

[5-5] On croit entendre le grondement des eaux qui se fracassent sur les rochers, près de ce moulin d'Elora. Les Connon ont dû se placer tout près du torrent pour saisir aussi nettement le dynamisme et la beauté du phénomène.

5-5

5-6

[5-6] The Connons were pioneer photographers and invented much of the photographic equipment they used. In 1881 Thomas Connon invented a roll-holder for cameras, a significant contribution to the transition from glass plate to film negatives, which was later patented by George Eastman as the Kodak camera. Later, in 1887, John R. Connon invented a panoramic camera. This camera also initiated the practice of placing film rolls in the front corners of the camera, which Connon later claimed made it possible to develop small film cameras. The Archives holds textual records of the Connon family, which include correspondence, patents, clippings, a notebook, and financial records. Among these are sketches for the design of John R. Connon's panoramic camera and correspondence with George Eastman.

The aftermath of an ice storm is both beautiful and treacherous - a paradox that this photograph captures in its representation of power lines straining under the pressure and weight of ice after a storm in Elora at the turn of the century.

[5-6] En véritables pionniers, les Connon ont en bonne partie inventé leur équipement. En 1881, Thomas Connon avait conçu un support à rouleaux, ce qui a grandement facilité le passage de la plaque de verre au négatif sur pellicule, procédé ultérieurement breveté par George Eastman, sous le nom de Kodak. Plus tard, en 1887, John R. Connon imaginait l'objectif panoramique. On peut enfin placer les rouleaux de pellicule à l'avant de l'appareil, ce qui, selon les dires ultérieurs de Connon, a permis de mettre au point l'appareil à pellicule de petit format. Les Archives possèdent des documents écrits de la famille Connon, soit un carnet et des lettres, brevets, coupures de journaux et registres financiers. Parmi ces documents, il y a des croquis de John R. Connon pour la mise au point de l'appareil panoramique et des lettres échangées avec George Eastman.

Les effets d'une tempête de verglas frappent d'admiration, mais aussi d'effroi – paradoxe très bien capté par cette photographie du début du siècle à Elora, où des fils électriques gainés de glace ploient sous le fardeau, après la tempête.

5-7

[5-7] This westward view of the Irvine River and the town of Salem evokes a sense of peaceful beauty. The photograph demonstrates the Connons' characteristic appreciation of rural scenes in Ontario.

[5-7] Cette vue à orientation ouest de la rivière Irvine et de la petite ville de Salem dégage une impression de beauté paisible. La photographie témoigne du goût caractéristique des Connon pour les scènes rurales de l'Ontario.

5-8

5-9

CHARLES MACNAMARA

5-8 to 5-10: From 1887 to 1934, photographer Charles Macnamara was employed by the McLachlin Brothers, a lumbering firm located in Arnprior. Macnamara took many photographs of lumbering operations, the Arnprior area, and Royal Navy ships and officers at Quebec. The Archives' collection of his photographs provides a rich visual record of the Ottawa valley and the lumber industry in early-twentieth-century Ontario.

[5-8 to 5-9] In the photographs presented here, Macnamara records the utter desolation left in the wake of a disastrous fire in Ottawa in 1900.

CHARLES MACNAMARA

5-8 à 5-10 : De 1887 à 1934, le photographe Charles Macnamara a été au service de la société d'exploitation forestière McLachlin Brothers, à Arnprior. Macnamara a réalisé de nombreuses photographies des opérations forestières, de la région d'Arnprior, ainsi que de la flotte de la Marine royale et de ses officiers à Québec. La collection de ses photographies conservée par les Archives constitue une riche documentation visuelle sur la vallée de l'Outaouais et l'industrie ontarienne du bois, au début du vingtième siècle.

[5-8 et 5-9] Dans les photographies présentées ici, Macnamara dépeint les suites catastrophiques d'un terrible incendie survenu à Ottawa en 1900.

5-10

[5-10] Macnamara photographed many events demonstrating progress and development in Ontario. Here we see a group of men who are about to lay a pipe across the Madawaska River. One man is ready to dive into the river while his fellow workers hold his air-supply line.

[5-10] Macnamara a photographié de nombreuses scènes attestant la marche du progrès et du développement en Ontario. Nous voyons ici un groupe d'ouvriers sur le point d'installer une conduite d'une rive à l'autre de la Madawaska. L'un d'eux va descendre en profondeur, tandis que ses compagnons tiennent son équipement de plongée.

M.O. HAMMOND

5-11 to 5-14: Melvin Ormond Hammond (1876-1934) was a noted Canadian journalist, editor, writer and amateur photographer. He joined the Toronto Globe in 1895 as a reporter and later became an editor. He worked at the *Globe* until the end of his life.

[5-11] Hammond recognized the value of photography as a journalistic tool and as a vehicle for artistic expression. In the photograph at the upper right, Hammond has captured an interesting juxtaposition of the old and the new. The Oliver Dunn Store, situated on a country road in Westover, can accommodate people travelling by two modes of transportation: there is both a gas pump and a hitching post for horses!

[5-12] In addition, Hammond created and collected a series of portrait photographs of Canadian artists that he made available for sale. Painter Horatio Walker is the subject of several photographs in the Hammond collection, including this one at the lower right showing Walker in his studio.

M. O. HAMMOND

5-11 à 5-14 : Melvin Ormond Hammond (1876-1934) était un journaliste canadien réputé, également rédacteur, éditeur et photographe amateur. Entré comme reporter au *Globe* de Toronto en 1895, il en devient plus tard rédacteur en chef. Il a travaillé au Globe jusqu'à la fin de sa vie.

[5-11] Hammond reconnaissait la valeur de la photographie comme instrument de reportage et comme procédé d'expression artistique. Dans la photographie en haut à droite, Hammond a fixé sur pellicule une pittoresque juxtaposition de l'ancien et du nouveau. Le magasin Oliver Dunn, au bord d'une route de campagne à Westover, dessert deux catégories de voyageurs : la pompe à essence s'adresse aux motorisés, et le poteau d'attache aux chevaux!

[5-12] En outre, Hammond a réalisé et conservé une série de portraits photographiques d'artistes canadiens du dix-neuvième siècle et du début vingtième, qu'il offrait en vente. Le peintre Horatio Walker est le sujet de plusieurs photographies de la collection Hammond, dont celle en bas à droite, où l'artiste pose dans son atelier.

5-11

5-12

[5-13] This photograph of a natural gas well in Fisherville documents an industry that still exists in Ontario.

[5-14] Gone are the days of the travelling fish market. This anecdotal photograph shows a Toronto fish merchant showing off his wares for youngsters.

[5-13] Cette image d'un puits de gaz naturel, à Fisherville, témoigne d'une industrie qui existe toujours en Ontario.

[5-14] Voici un marché aux poissons ambulant, emblème d'une époque révolue. Dans cette photographie anecdotique, un marchand de poissons torontois vante sa marchandise devant des jeunes.

5-13

5-14

5-15

MARSDEN A. KEMP

5-15 to 5-17: Marsden A. Kemp (d. 1943) was an amateur photographer who lived in Kingston and Picton. Little is known about him, other than that he was an avid gardener and outdoorsman. His photographs date mainly from about 1900 to 1914 and depict eastern Ontario communities, recreation, steamships, people, and events. He took many of his pictures while touring the countryside on his bicycle.

[5-15] This image shows officials and workmen dealing with the catastrophe of a fallen bridge span in Cornwall.

MARSDEN A. KEMP

5-15 à 5-17 : Le photographe amateur Marsden A. Kemp (m. 1943) a vécu à Kingston et à Picton. On sait peu de chose à son sujet, sinon que c'était un enthousiaste du jardinage et du plein air. Ses photographies remontent principalement à la période de 1900 à 1914 et ont pour sujets des collectivités de l'Est de l'Ontario, des activités récréatives, des bateaux à vapeur, des personnages et des événements. Beaucoup de ses photos ont été prises lors de promenades à vélo dans la campagne.

[5-15] Cette image montre des fonctionnaires et des ouvriers sur la scène d'une catastrophe : la chute d'une travée de pont à Cornwall.

5-16

5-17

[5-16] In this beautiful image, the reflection of the men and trees on the ice is striking. The men are posing with their sleigh, presumably before going out to cut some ice blocks.

[5-16] Dans cette image très réussie, la glace réfléchit les personnages et les arbres en arrière-plan de façon saisissante. Les hommes posent avec leur traîneau, probablement avant de découper des blocs dans la glace.

[5-17] This photograph illustrates the old method of acquiring ice for cold storage of perishable food items. It recalls a time when life may have been simpler but also was more physically demanding.

[5-17] Cette photographie montre comment, au temps jadis, on se procurait la glace nécessaire à la conservation des aliments périssables. Elle évoque un temps où la vie était peut-être plus simple, mais aussi beaucoup plus exigeante au plan physique.

JOHN BOYD

5-18 to 5-21: John Boyd (1865-1941) was an amateur photographer and railway employee in Toronto and Sarnia. Boyd first grew interested in photography in the 1890s and became a master at capturing the moment, be it staged or spontaneous. His photographs often possess a sense of playfulness.

JOHN BOYD

5-18 à 5-21 : John Boyd (1865-1941), employé des chemins de fer à Toronto et à Sarnia, était aussi féru de photographie. S'étant intéressé à cette technique dès les années 1890, Boyd était passé maître dans l'art de saisir l'instant présent, sur le vif ou mis en scène. Ses tableautins respirent souvent la gaieté et l'enjouement.

5-18

5-19

5-20

5-21

ERIC ARTHUR

5-22 to 5-24: Eric Ross Arthur (1898-1982) was born in Dunedin, New Zealand. He immigrated to Canada in 1923 to take up an appointment as an assistant professor of architecture at the University of Toronto - a position he held until 1966. Arthur was one of Canada's most prominent architects and architectural historians.

[5-22] Most of Arthur's photographs feature buildings and other structures, thus illustrating his love of Ontario's architectural heritage. He photographed all types of buildings, from historic sites such as Fort Henry in Kingston to much simpler structures. This view shows the state of disrepair that Fort Henry fell into after it was last used by troops in 1891. The fort was restored from 1936 to 1938 and is now a living-history museum.

[5-23] No shop was too small or too humble to be unworthy of Arthur's attention.

[5-24] This lovely and tranquil scene is representative of Arthur's attachment to a rural way of life that was fast disappearing.

ERIC ARTHUR

5-22 à 5-24 : Eric Ross Arthur (1898-1982) est né à Dunedin, en Nouvelle-Zélande. Il avait émigré au Canada en 1923, pour entrer à l'Université de Toronto comme professeur adjoint d'architecture – poste qu'il a occupé jusqu'en 1966. Arthur est devenu l'un des plus remarquables praticiens et historiens de l'architecture au Canada.

[5-22] La plupart des oeuvres d'Arthur portent sur des bâtiments et d'autres constructions, dans une prédilection toute naturelle pour le patrimoine architectural de l'Ontario. Il a photographié tous les types d'édifices, ceux de lieux historiques, tels que le Fort Henry de Kingston, mais aussi des structures beaucoup plus modestes. Cette vue montre l'état de délabrement où se trouvait le Fort Henry après que troupes l'arent quitté en 1891. Le fort a été restauré de 1936 à 1938, et abrite aujourd'hui un musée d'histoire vivante.

[5-23] Nulle échoppe n'était trop rustique ou trop humble pour lui servir de sujet.

[5-24] Cette scène aimable et tranquille est représentative de l'attachement qu'éprouvait Arthur pour un mode de vie rurale en voie de disparition accélérée.

5-22

5-23

5-24

JOHN MACFIE

5-25 to 5-28: John Macfie (1925-) was a provincial civil servant who worked in northern Ontario for the Department of Lands and Forests, as well as an author and an amateur photographer. Macfie combined his government work with his personal interest in photography, and, during the ten years he worked in the north, he often carried a camera with him on field trips to record Native people, fellow staff, and interesting events.

[5-25] A good example of his work is this picture of a camp and all its amenities, including the teepee, the drying beaver skin, and a member of the dog team in the immediate foreground.

[5-26] This stark and cold image reminds us how harsh life in the north can be.

JOHN MACFIE

5-25 à 5-28 : John Macfie (1925-) travaillait dans le Nord de l'Ontario, pour le ministère des Terres et Forêts, de même qu'à son propre compte, qu'à son propre compte comme auteur et photographe amateur. Pendant les dix années de son séjour dans le Nord, Macfie a réussi à concilier son goût pour la photographie et son travail de fonctionnaire : lors de ses missions de terrain, il se munissait souvent d'un appareil photo, pour croquer des scènes autochtones, des collègues et les événements qui lui semblaient dignes d'intérêt.

[5-25] Un bon exemple de ses réalisations est cette image d'un campement et de ses installations, où apparaissent un tipi, une peau de castor en cours de séchage et la bonne tête d'un membre de l'attelage de chiens, à l'avant-plan.

[5-26] Cette image de ton sobre et austère symbolise admirablement l'âpreté de la vie dans le Nord.

5-25

5-26

[5-27 & 5-28] Macfie's photographs depict various Cree, Oji-Cree, and Ojibway people and activities at Fort Severn, Attawapiskat, Landsdowne House, Sioux Lookout, Winisk, Gogama, Big Trout Lake, and Sandy Lake. Macfie photographed with a Kodak camera, a Rolleicord, and a Zeiss contax for 35 mm. colour slides. His images show Native people, their dwellings and community buildings, artifacts, and domestic activities such as trapping and tool construction.

[5-27 et 5-28] Les photographies de Macfie campent divers personnages cris, oji-cris et ojibways ainsi que leurs activités, à Fort Severn, Attawapiskat, Landsdowne House, Sioux Lookout, Winisk, Gogama, Big Trout Lake et Sandy Lake. Macfie utilisait des appareils Kodak, Rolleicord et Zeiss contax, ce dernier pour les diapositives 35 mm en couleur. Ses images ont pour thèmes des Indiens, leurs habitations et maisons communautaires, des artéfacts et des activités traditionnelles et artisanales, telles que le piégeage et la fabrication d'outils.

5-27

5-28

RICHARD W. BARROW

5-29 to 5-31: Richard W. Barrow was an active amateur photographer in the Kingston area in the 1870s.

Barrow was accomplished at producing crisp, clear albumen photographs. The high resolution afforded by the albumen photographic process allowed him to capture these magnificent images of Kingston's limestone heritage.

RICHARD W. BARROW

5-29 à 5-31 : Le photographe amateur Richard W. Barrow a beaucoup travaillé dans la région de Kingston dans les années 1870.

Barrow était un virtuose de l'albuminotypie, dont il tirait des clichés nets, d'une précision cristalline. L'excellente définition qui faisait le mérite du procédé se remarque dans ces magnifiques images du patrimoine de pierre calcaire, à Kingston.

5-29

5-30

5-31

5-1: *A backwoods barber shop*, 1894, John Boyd (John Boyd fonds, C 7-1-0-0-20)

5-2: Goderich, ca. 1919, McCarthy Aero Services Limited (McCarthy Aero Services fonds, C 285-1-0-0-228. I0010151)

5-3: Toronto: Harbour, ca. 1919, McCarthy Aero Services Limited (McCarthy Aero Services fonds, C 285-1-0-0-959. I00010217)

5-4: Iroquois, ca. 1919, McCarthy Aero Services Limited (McCarthy Aero Services fonds, C 285-1-0-0-295. I0010217)

5-5: Elora, Falls and Town [186?-190?], Thomas and John Connon (Connon Family fonds, C 286-3-0-4)

5-6: [Elora ?] Power lines down after ice storm [186?-190?], Thomas and John Connon (Connon Family fonds, C 286-3-0-9)

5-7: Salem, view west over Irvine River [186-190-], Thomas and John Connon (Connon Family fonds, C 286-3-0-1)

5-8: Aftermath of the 1900 Ottawa fire, Charles Macnamara (Charles Macnamara fonds, C 120-2-0-0-11. I0004641)

5-9: Burned fire engine from Ottawa fire, 1900, Charles Macnamara (Charles Macnamara fonds, C 120-2-0-0-12. I0004642)

5-10: Men preparing to lay a pipe across the Madawaska River, with a diver in suit ready to work, Arnprior, Ontario, 1911. Charles Macnamara (Charles Macnamara fonds, C 120-3-0-0-45)

5-11: Oliver Dunn store, Westover, July 1930, M.O. Hammond (M.O. Hammond fonds, F 1075-13, H 2215. I0001729)

5-12: Horatio Walker in his studio, Île d'Orléans, July, 1926 (M.O. Hammond fonds, F 1075, H 1329. I0001577)

5-13: Fisherville natural gas well, 10 July 1910, M.O. Hammond (M.O. Hammond fonds, F 1075-13, H 425. I0000935)

5-14: Fish merchant and children, Toronto, July 1929, M.O. Hammond (M.O. Hammond fonds, F 1075-13, H 2012)

5-15: Bridge with fallen span, Cornwall, ca. 1898, Marsden Kemp (Marsden Kemp fonds, C 130-1-0-8-38. I0003959)

5-16: Men on sleigh in Picton harbour, 20 Jan. 1906, Marsden Kemp (Marsden Kemp fonds, C 130-1-0-23-55. I0003984)

5-17: Cutting ice, Picton harbour [ca. 1905], Marsden Kemp (Marsden Kemp fonds, C 130-1-0-23-51. I0003982)

5-18: Boy Scouts 'get caught' bathing near Point Edward, Ontario, 1911, John Boyd (John Boyd fonds, C 7-3, 2483. I0003423)

5-19: Riverdale Zoo animal handler performs before the crowds with the park's tame raccoon [1923], John Boyd (John Boyd fonds, C 7-3, 18383. I0003652)

5-20: *A slight misunderstanding*: two cyclists who have run into each other [189-], John Boyd (John Boyd fonds, C 7-2-0-1-32. I0003797)

5-21: *And are imbedded in the snow*: train locomotive stuck in the snow, 1895, John Boyd (John Boyd fonds, C 7-1-0-0-74. I0003772)

5-22: Fort Henry, Kingston, July 1931, Eric Arthur (Eric Arthur fonds, C 57-1-2-56. I0002554)

5-23: Shoe-repair shop in Cooksville [ca. 1931], Eric Arthur (Eric Arthur fonds, C 57-1-2-168. I0002572)

5-24: Mill in Perth, 17 July 1931, Eric Arthur (Eric Arthur fonds, C 57-1-2-71. I0002560)

5-25: Winter camp of Chief James Msakayash of the Osnaburgh tribe, February 1951, John Macfie (John Macfie fonds, C 330-13-0-0-110. I0000437)

5-26: Hauling firewood home on Big Trout Lake, January 1956, John Macfie (John Macfie fonds, C 330-13-0-0-107. I0000434)

5-27: William Moore of Mattagami Reserve, 1958, John Macfie (John Macfie fonds, C 330-13-0-0-153. I0000480)

5-28: Woman from Moose Factory fleshing a beaver pelt and scraping it during the 'frost-drying' process, 1959, John Macfie (John Macfie fonds, C 330-3-6-0-21. I0000139)

5-29: Courthouse, Kingston [between 1870 and 1900], Richard W. Barrow (Richard W. Barrow fonds, F 4398-0-0-0-2. I0009554)

5-30: Chalmers Church, Earl Street, Kingston [between ca. 1875 and 1889], Richard W. Barrow (Richard W. Barrow fonds, F 4398-0-0-0-8)

5-31: Ontario Street, near Princess (Kingston) [ca. 1878], Richard W. Barrow (Richard W. Barrow fonds, F 4398-0-0-0-20. I0009571)

5-1 : *A backwoods barber shop*, 1894, John Boyd (Fonds John Boyd, C 7-1-0-0-20)

5-2 : Goderich, vers 1919, McCarthy Aero Services Limited (Fonds McCarthy Aero Services, C 285-1-0-0-228. I0010151)

5-3 : Toronto : le port, vers 1919, McCarthy Aero Services Limited (Fonds McCarthy Aero Services, C 285-1-0-0-959. I00010217)

5-4 : Iroquois, vers 1919, McCarthy Aero Services Limited (Fonds McCarthy Aero Services, C 285-1-0-0-295. I0010217)

5-5 : Elora, le torrent et la ville [186?-190?], Thomas et John Connon (Fonds Famille Connon, C 286-3-0-4)

5-6 : [Elora?] Fils électriques endommagés par une tempête de verglas [186?-190?], Thomas et John Connon (Fonds Famille Connon, C 286-3-0-9)

5-7 : Salem, vue vers l'ouest, sur la rivière Irvine [186?-190?], Thomas et John Connon (Fonds Famille Connon, C 286-3-0-1)

5-8 : Au lendemain de l'incendie de 1900 à Ottawa, Charles MacNamara (Fonds Charles MacNamara, C 120-2-0-0-11. I0004641)

5-9 : Voiture-pompe ayant brûlé lors de l'incendie d'Ottawa, 1900, Charles MacNamara (Fonds Charles MacNamara, C 120-2-0-0-12. I0004642)

5-10 : Des ouvriers vont installer une conduite d'une rive à l'autre de la Madawaska, tandis que l'un d'eux, en tenue, s'apprête à plonger, Arnprior, en Ontario, 1911. Charles MacNamara (Fonds Charles MacNamara, C 120-3-0-0-45)

5-11 : Magasin d'Oliver Dunn, Westover, juillet 1930, M. O. Hammond (Fonds M. O. Hammond, F 1075-13, H 2215. I0001729)

5-12 : Horatio Walker dans son atelier de l'île d'Orléans, juillet 1926 (Fonds M. O. Hammond, F 1075, H 1329. I0001577)

5-13 : Puits de gaz naturel à Fisherville, 10 juillet 1910, M. O. Hammond (Fonds M. O. Hammond, F 1075-13, H 425. I0000935)

5-14 : Marchand de poissons et enfants, Toronto, juillet 1929, M. O. Hammond (Fonds M. O. Hammond, F 1075-13, H 2012)

5-15 : Pont dont une travée est tombée, Cornwall, vers 1898, Marsden Kemp (Fonds Marsden Kemp, C 130-1-0-8-38. I0003959)

5-16 : Hommes sur un traîneau dans le port de Picton, 20 janvier 1906, Marsden Kemp (Fonds Marsden Kemp, C 130-1-0-23-55. I0003984)

5-17 : Coupe de la glace, port de Picton [vers 1905], Marsden Kemp (Fonds Marsden Kemp, C 130-1-0-23-51. I0003982)

5-18 : Scouts « surpris » à la baignade, près de Point Edward, en Ontario, 1911, John Boyd (Fonds John Boyd, C 7-3, 2483. I0003652)

5-19 : Un dresseur du zoo de Riverdale fait son numéro devant la foule, avec le raton laveur apprivoisé du parc [1923], John Boyd (Fonds John Boyd, C 7-3, 18383. I0003652)

5-20 : *A slight misunderstanding:* deux cyclistes viennent d'entrer en collision [189?], John Boyd (Fonds John Boyd, C 7-2-0-1-32. I0003979)

5-21 : *And are imbedded in the snow* : locomotive immobilisée par la neige, 1895, John Boyd (Fonds John Boyd, C 7-1-0-0-74)

5-22 : Fort Henry, Kingston, juillet 1931, Eric Arthur (Fonds Eric Arthur, C 57-1-2-56. I0002554)

5-23 : Boutique de cordonnier à Cooksville [vers 1931], Eric Arthur (Fonds Eric Arthur, C 57-1-2-168. I0002572)

5-24 : Minoterie à Perth, 17 juillet 1931, Eric Arthur (Fonds Eric Arthur, C 57-1-2-71. I0002560)

5-25 : Campement d'hiver du chef James Msakayash de la tribu Osnaburgh, février 1951, John Macfie (Fonds John Macfie, C 330-13-0-0-110. I0000437)

5-26 : On rapporte du bois de chauffe à la maison, sur le lac Big Trout, janvier 1956, John Macfie (Fonds John Macfie, C 330-13-0-0-107. I0000434)

5-27 : William Moore, de la réserve de Mattagami, 1958, John Macfie (Fonds John Macfie, C 330-13-0-0-153. I0000480)

5-28 : À Moose Factory, une femme retire la chair d'une peau de castor et la racle au cours de la phase de « dessication par le gel », 1959, John Macfie (Fonds John Macfie, C 330-13-6-0-21. I0000139)

5-29 : Le palais de justice de Kingston [entre 1870 et 1900], Richard W. Barrow (Fonds Richard W. Barrow, F 4398-0-0-0-2. I0009554)

5-30 : L'église Chalmers, rue Earl, à Kingston [entre 1875 et 1889, à peu près], Richard W. Barrow (Fonds Richard W. Barrow, F 4398-0-0-0-8)

5-31 : La rue Ontario, près de la rue Princess (Kingston) [vers 1878], Richard W. Barrow (Fonds Richard W. Barrow, F 4398-0-0-0-20. I0009571)

6

GOVERNMENT OF ONTARIO ART COLLECTION

LA COLLECTION D'ŒUVRES D'ART
DU GOVERNMENT DE L'ONTARIO

6-1

The works of art now displayed in Ontario government buildings comprise a collection that was begun in 1855. The Government of Ontario Art Collection, as it is known, consists of more than 2,300 original works, including paintings, murals, works on paper, and indoor and outdoor sculpture. Found in more than thirty locations across the province, the art collection is the most widely dispersed of all the collections administered by the Archives of Ontario.

The history of the government's art holdings reflects the changing tastes and fashions of the last one hundred and fifty years. Egerton Ryerson, as the architect of Canada West's educational system in the period from the 1840s to the 1870s, created the nucleus of the current collection. Ryerson wished to use art for a didactic purpose: to educate Canadians about European artistic achievements and taste. Building on his early acquisitions, the government initiated a new period of collecting in 1875. This phase, which lasted until 1914, saw the purchase of several hundred paintings from the annual exhibitions of the Ontario Society of Artists. In 1895 Minister of Education George Ross made the acquisition of art the responsibility of his department. This resulted in a number of important acquisitions and commissions; the former included works by future Group of Seven painters Arthur Lismer and J.E.H. MacDonald, and among the latter were original illustrations by C.W. Jefferys for public and secondary school textbooks.

Currently, there are more than two hundred portraits in the collection. Acquired from the 1880s on, these portraits include ones of Ontario premiers, lieutenant-governors, and speakers of the Legislative Assembly. It is the only area of the collection for which new works have continued to be commissioned to the present day, the subjects ranging from John Graves Simcoe and Isaac Brock to Bill Davis, David Peterson, and Bob Rae.

As with most public collections, many fine artworks have been donated by private individuals. These patrons include George Agnew Reid, who donated more than 400 of his own works in 1944. More recently, the Ontario Heritage Foundation has donated fine art (including paintings by Norval Morrisseau), furnishings, and decorative objects to the collection on behalf of individual donors. Of particular note are the works that entered the collection between 1966 and 1995 as a result of the government's Art in Architecture Program. Instituted by Premier John Robarts, this initiative was funded through a percentage of the cost of new government buildings and resulted in the acquisition of both site-specific and movable artworks for more than thirty buildings across Ontario, the artists represented including Harold Town, Jack Bush, and A.J. Casson.

Les œuvres d'art aujourd'hui exposées dans les édifices du gouvernement de l'Ontario font partie d'un ensemble dont les débuts remontent à 1855. C'est la Collection d'œuvres d'art du gouvernement de l'Ontario, qui compte aujourd'hui plus de 2 300 œuvres originales, dont des murales, peintures, œuvres sur papier et sculptures d'intérieur et d'extérieur. Répartie entre plus de 30 établissements de toutes les régions de la province, cette collection est la plus largement dispersée de toutes celles qu'administrent les Archives publiques de l'Ontario.

L'histoire des collections d'œuvres d'art publiques reflète l'évolution du goût et des modes au cours des cent cinquante dernières années. Egerton Ryerson, architecte du système d'instruction publique du Canada-Ouest dans les années 1840 à 1870, a constitué le noyau de la collection actuelle. Ryerson désirait que celle-ci serve à des fins didactiques : faire connaître aux Canadiens le goût et les réalisations artistiques de l'Europe. Afin d'enrichir ce noyau de départ, le gouvernement entame une nouvelle phase de collection en 1875. Cette phase, qui dure jusqu'en 1914, voit l'achat de plusieurs centaines de peintures lors des expositions annuelles de l'Ontario Society of Artists. En 1895, le ministre de l'Éducation George Ross fait relever l'acquisition d'œuvres d'art de son ministère. Il s'ensuit un certain nombre d'acquisitions et de commandes importantes; parmi les premières, citons des œuvres d'Arthur Lismer et de J. E. H. MacDonald, membres du futur Groupe des Sept, et, parmi les secondes, des illustrations originales de C. W. Jefferys, destinées à des manuels d'écoles élémentaires et secondaires.

On dénombre actuellement plus de deux cents portraits dans la collection. Acquis à partir des années 1880, ces tableaux sont à l'effigie notamment des premiers ministres, lieutenant-gouverneurs et présidents de l'Assemblée législative de l'Ontario. Seul secteur de la Collection où l'on a commandé de nouvelles œuvres de façon continue jusqu'ici, la galerie des sujets va de John Graves Simcoe et Isaac Brock à Bill Davis, David Peterson et Bob Rae.

Comme c'est le cas pour la plupart des collections publiques, maintes œuvres marquantes ont été offertes par des particuliers. L'un de ces mécènes, George Agnew Reid, avait fait don de plus de 400 de ses œuvres en 1944. Plus récemment, la Collection recevait de la Fondation du patrimoine ontarien un exceptionnel choix d'œuvres (dont des tableaux de Norval Morrisseau), de pièces de mobilier et d'objets d'art décoratif en provenance de donneurs individuels. Particulièrement dignes d'attention, sont les œuvres qui entrent dans la collection de 1966 à 1995, dans le cadre du Programme de l'art en architecture. Instituée par le premier ministre John Robarts, cette initiative tirait son financement du prélèvement d'un petit pourcentage des budgets de construction des nouveaux édifices publics et a abouti à l'acquisition d'œuvres soit à caractère mobile, soit conçues expressément pour un lieu. Les œuvres étaient destinées à plus de trente édifices de tous les coins de l'Ontario, et leurs auteurs comprennent Harold Town, Jack Bush et A. J. Casson.

6-2

6-2: In order to acquire works of art, Egerton Ryerson set out for Europe in July 1855. Over the next ten months he visited its capital cities where he purchased hundreds of paintings, including copies of old masters and original works, portrait busts, and plaster casts of antique statuary. These 'objects of taste' were sent back to Canada to be put on display in Toronto at the province's first public museum, the Educational Museum of Upper Canada. Opened in 1857, it was located in the Normal School (Teachers' College) in St James Square.

6-2 : C'est dans l'intention d'acquérir des œuvres d'art qu'Egerton Ryerson se rend en Europe en juillet 1855. Pendant les dix mois suivants, il va séjourner dans les grandes capitales, où il achètera des centaines de tableaux, œuvres originales aussi bien que copies de vieux maîtres, ainsi que des bustes et plâtres d'après la statuaire antique. Ces « objets de bon goût » sont expédiés au Canada, pour être plus tard exposés à Toronto, au premier musée des beaux-arts public de la province, l'Educational Museum of Upper Canada. Inauguré en 1857, le musée avait été aménagé dans des locaux de l'École normale, St. James Square.

6-3

6-4

6-3 & 6-4: Today, we can still view some of Ryerson's paintings, although many of his original purchases have been lost. More than twenty of them can be found on display in the Ontario Legislature at Queen's Park.

Ryerson purchased these two paintings, and the one on the previous page, in Rome between 20 and 23 February 1856.

6-3 et 6-4 : Encore aujourd'hui, bien qu'on ait perdu la trace d'un bon nombre des acquisitions de Ryerson, on peut admirer certaines des œuvres réunies par ses soins. Ainsi, plus d'une vingtaine sont toujours exposées au siège de l'Assemblée législative, à

Queen's Park.

C'est à Rome, entre le 20 et 23 février 1856, que Ryerson a fait l'achat des deux tableaux que voici et de celui qui figure à la page précédente.

6-5 & 6-6: Of the several hundred works acquired at exhibitions of the Ontario Society of Artists between 1875 and 1914, a significant number, including the two illustrated here by Gertrude Spurr Cutts and Clara Sophia Hagarty, reflect European subject matter. Many Canadian artists of the period studied abroad in the art schools and academies of Europe and, increasingly, women artists were among them.

6-5 et 6-6 : S'inspirent de thèmes européens une bonne part des centaines d'œuvres acquises lors d'expositions de l'Ontario Society of Artists de 1875 à 1914, dont les deux que nous voyons ici, respectivement de Gertrude Spurr Cutts et de Clara Sophia Hagarty. Une foule d'artistes canadiens de l'époque avaient reçu leur formation dans des académies et écoles de beaux-arts européennes, et la présence des femmes dans leurs rangs allait en s'affirmant.

6-5

6-6

6-7

6-7: This photograph records members of the Ontario Society of Artists (OSA) in 1904. Included in the group are Gertrude Spurr, middle row, fifth from left (who would marry fellow artist William Cutts, second from left, in 1909). George Reid sits, looking to his right, in the middle row, seventh from left, while C.W. Jefferys stands behind Owen Staples in the back row, seventh from left. The Archives holds the OSA's records, which include details of membership and meetings from its founding in 1872.

6-7 : Cette photographie représente des membres de l'Ontario Society of Artists (OSA), en 1904. Dans le groupe, on remarque Gertrude Spurr, rangée du milieu, cinquième depuis la gauche (elle devait, en 1909, épouser un autre artiste, William Cutts, deuxième depuis la gauche). George Reid est assis, le regard tourné vers sa droite, rangée du milieu, septième depuis la gauche, tandis que C. W. Jefferys est debout derrière Owen Staples, dernière rangée, septième depuis la gauche. Les Archives sont dépositaires des dossiers de l'OSA, qui comprennent les listes de membres et les procès-verbaux d'assemblées depuis sa fondation en 1872.

6-8

6-8: As the Government of Ontario Art Collection grew, it acquired a number of paintings by future members of the Group of Seven, including Arthur Lismer and J.E.H. MacDonald.

British-born Lismer arrived in Canada in 1911 and over the next few years became acquainted with the other artists who would form the Group of Seven in 1920. *The Clearing* most likely depicts a scene recorded by the artist on one of his Sunday sketching trips to York Mills, just north of Toronto. It was the favourite haunt at the time of Lismer and fellow artist Tom Thomson.

6-8 : Au fur et à mesure de sa formation, la Collection du gouvernement de l'Ontario incorpore des œuvres de ceux qui allaient bientôt constituer le Groupe des Sept, notamment d'Arthur Lismer et de J. E. H. MacDonald.

Le Britannique Lismer était arrivé au Canada en 1911 et, au cours des années suivantes, s'était lié d'amitié avec d'autres artistes; ensemble, ils institueront le Groupe des Sept en 1920. *The Clearing* dépeint probablement une scène rapportée par l'artiste d'une de ses tournées de croquis du dimanche à York Mills, à peu de distance au nord de Toronto. C'était là un des lieux favoris de Lismer et de son collègue Tom Thomson.

6-9 & 6-10: J.E.H. MacDonald's *By the River (Early Spring)* was purchased at the OSA's Toronto exhibition of 1911. It depicts loggers at work as they drive the timber down the upper reaches of the Humber River. This was a common sight in the nineteenth century but became less so in the twentieth as the building of dams interrupted the free flow of the river's waters.

MacDonald's moody, low-keyed painting can be contrasted with another OSA purchase, C.W. Jefferys's *Wheat Stacks on the Prairies*. A bright, luminous work, Jefferys's canvas depicts the clear air and strong light of the Manitoba prairies he visited in 1906. Although the artist executed an extensive body of similar works, he is probably better known for his historical illustrations. Often completed in pen and ink, these drawings were used to illustrate public- and secondary-school textbooks and have remained popular with scholars and publishers to this day.

6-9 et 6-10 : Le tableau *By the River (Early Spring)* de J. E. H. MacDonald avait été acquis lors de l'exposition de l'OSA de 1911, à Toronto. Il représente des draveurs qui acheminent des trains de bois flottés jusqu'en amont de la rivière Humber. Cette scène, courante au dix-neuvième siècle, allait devenir plus rare au vingtième, où des barrages vont contrarier le courant par endroits.

Le ton sobre et pensif du tableau de MacDonald fait contraste avec celui d'un autre acheté aussi lors de l'exposition de l'OSA, *Wheat Stacks on the Prairies*, de C. W. Jefferys. La vigueur et l'éclat de cette dernière oeuvre rend bien l'ambiance tonique et la lumière éblouissante des prairies du Manitoba, où Jefferys avait séjourné en 1906. L'artiste nous a laissé quantité d'œuvres analogues, mais il est probablement mieux connu pour ses images à caractère historique. Souvent retouchés à l'encre, ces dessins devaient illustrer des manuels d'écoles primaires et secondaires, et ils sont toujours appréciés des chercheurs et des éditeurs d'aujourd'hui.

6-9

6-10

6-11

6-11: Jefferys' *Battle of Lundy's Lane* was published in G.M. Wrong's *Ontario Public School History of Canada* (Toronto: Ryerson Press 1921).

6-11 : La *Battle of Lundy's Lane* de Jefferys a paru dans l'ouvrage *Ontario Public School History of Canada*, de G. M. Wrong (Toronto, Ryerson Press, 1921).

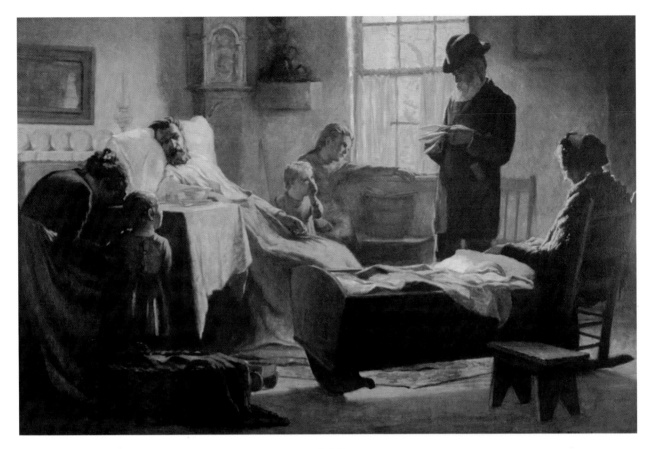

6-12

6-12: In 1944 artist and teacher George Reid made a generous gift of 459 of his own works to the Ontario government. Thus, he is the best-represented artist in the collection. His large-scale genre scenes and small oils reflect the artist's farming roots and the beauty of Ontario's varied landscape.

In *Foreclosure of the Mortgage*, a work the artist repainted in 1935 following the destruction by fire of an earlier version, a distraught family is shown gathered around the bed of the invalid father as they listen to the bailiff read from a notice of repossession. Based in part on his own experience, the painting, with its cool tones coupled with the family's obvious despair, creates a sombre and moving portrait of rural life.

6-12 : En 1944, le peintre et enseignant George Reid a généreusement offert au gouvernement de l'Ontario 459 de ses œuvres, ce qui en fait l'artiste le mieux représenté dans la Collection. Ces petites huiles et scènes de genre grand format reflètent les origines terriennes de l'artiste et célèbrent la beauté du paysage multiforme de l'Ontario.

Dans *Foreclosure of the Mortgage*, œuvre dont le peintre a exécuté une nouvelle version en 1935 après la destruction par le feu de la première, une famille accablée est réunie au chevet du père invalide, pour apprendre du huissier la saisie de son bien. En partie d'inspiration personnelle, le tableau, dont les teintes graves sont en harmonie avec l'affliction manifeste de la famille, brosse un portrait sombre et émouvant de la vie rurale.

6-13

6-13: Less emotional are many of Reid's smaller works depicting scenes he encountered on his travels across the province and during summers spent in the Catskill Mountains of upstate New York. In 1891 Reid and his wife, fellow artist Mary Hiester Reid (who has five works in the collection), made their first visit to the Catskills. They were to enjoy many summers there painting and teaching. *Hills and Clouds* is representative of Reid's work during this period.

6-13 : Moins chargées d'affectivité, beaucoup de formats réduits de Reid dépeignent des scènes glanées au fil de ses voyages dans la province et pendant les étés passés dans les monts Catskill, dans le nord de l'État de New York. En 1891, Reid et sa femme, l'artiste Mary Hiester Reid (dont la Collection possède cinq oeuvres), font leur premier séjour dans les Catskill. C'est là qu'ils passeront de nombreux étés, occupés à l'enseignement et à leurs propres travaux. *Hills and Clouds* est représentatif des œuvres de Reid pendant cette période.

6-14

6-14: Mary Hiester died in 1921, and the following year Reid married artist Mary Wrinch, whose work may also be found in the collection. They, too, enjoyed travelling and painting together and Reid often recorded the local scenery in small oil sketches.

In 1925 the couple visited Algoma and the valley of the Agawa River for the first time. After trips to Quebec the next year, the Reids once again returned to Algoma in 1927. Subsequently, they continued to travel throughout Ontario's northland where Reid sought to capture the area's rugged beauty in works such as *The Valley of the Agawa*. By the mid-1930s, however, these activities were curtailed by Reid's desire to concentrate on his mural commissions.

6-14 : Mary Hiester s'éteint en 1921; l'année suivante, Reid épouse la peintre Mary Wrinch, dont des oeuvres se retrouvent également dans la Collection. Le couple se plaît à voyager et à peindre de concert, et Reid prend souvent le panorama local pour de petits croquis à l'huile.

En 1925, ils se rendent une première fois en Algoma et dans la vallée de l'Agawa. Après des excursions au Québec l'année suivante, les Reid retournent en Algoma en 1927. Par la suite, ils vont continuer leurs pérégrinations dans tout le Nord de l'Ontario, région dont Reid cherche à traduire l'âpre beauté, dans des œuvres telles que *The Valley of the Agawa*. Vers le milieu des années 1930, toutefois, ces activités sont mises en veilleuse, car le peintre veut se consacrer à l'exécution des murales qu'on lui a commandées.

6-15: In addition to donations from artists themselves, the collection has been fortunate to receive gifts made through the Ontario Heritage Foundation (OHF). The OHF, a not-for-profit agency of the Ontario government, was created in 1967 to preserve and promote the province's cultural heritage. While the Foundation has concentrated recently on Ontario's architectural and natural landmarks, it has facilitated the transfer of important and relevant works of art and antiques to the collection by a number of new and familiar artists.

These artists include George Reid, Lucius O'Brien, Frederick Verner, Norval Morrisseau, Kosso Eloul, Colin Forbes, and Elizabeth Bradford Holbrook.

In 1886 Lucius O'Brien exhibited his watercolour *Oinatchouan Falls* at the Royal Academy in Ottawa. The following year T.G. Blackstock purchased it for $100. It remained in her family until 1985, when it was donated by Blackstock's granddaughter to the government's collection through the OHF.

6-15 : La Collection bénéficie, outre des dons personnels de certains artistes, de ceux effectués par le biais de la Fondation du patrimoine ontarien (FPO). Cet organisme sans but lucratif du gouvernement de l'Ontario a vu le jour en 1967, dans le but de préserver et promouvoir le patrimoine culturel de la province. Bien que la Fondation ait récemment privilégié les sites naturels et les œuvres architecturales de l'Ontario, elle a dans le passé facilité le passage à la Collection d'antiquités et d'œuvres d'art importantes et pertinentes de nombreux artistes d'hier et d'aujourd'hui.

De ce nombre, on peut entre autres citer George Reid, Lucius O'Brien, Frederick Verner, Norval Morrisseau, Kosso Eloul, Colin Forbes et Elizabeth Bradford Holbrook.

En 1886, Lucius O'Brien exposait son aquarelle *Oinatchouan Falls* à l'Académie royale, à Ottawa; l'année suivante, T. G. Blackstock en faisait l'acquisition, au prix de 100 $. L'œuvre devait demeurer dans la famille de celle-ci jusqu'en 1985, date à laquelle sa petite-fille l'a offerte à la Collection du gouvernement par l'entremise de la FPO.

6-15

6-16: Official portraits of premiers, speakers, and lieutenant-governors form an important element of the collection, providing a record not only of the subject's physical appearance but also of his or her contribution to the political life of the province. While the government's acquisition of portraits may not always have been motivated by aesthetic or historical concerns (rather by the more practical desire to fill the walls of official buildings), the tradition of commissioning such works has now become firmly established. Today, more than two hundred portraits are included in the collection's inventory, many completed by the foremost portrait artists of their day.

On becoming lieutenant-governor in 1880, the Honourable John Beverley Robinson realized that few of his predecessors had been commemorated in this way. Beginning in the year of his installation, Robinson set out to commission their portraits retroactively, often going to great lengths to acquire the necessary images of his subjects. Starting with a painting of the first lieutenant-governor, John Graves Simcoe, he went on to commission a further nineteen portraits. Fashionable society artist George Theodore Berthon painted many of these.

Because Berthon's task was to paint portraits of people who had been dead for many years, he was often forced to work from second-hand images. For example, when Berthon began work on his portrait of Sir Isaac Brock, more than seventy years had elapsed since the illustrious military leader had been killed at the Battle of Queenston Heights. Berthon thus had to turn to Brock's family in Guernsey for help in determining what he looked like. The family responded by making available a miniature of the major-general, which was sent to England to be copied in oil. It was then photographed and tinted before being forwarded to Canada for Berthon's use.

6-16 : Les portraits officiels d'anciens lieutenants-gouverneurs, premiers ministres et présidents de l'Assemblée législative forment un volet important de la Collection, rappel non seulement de la physionomie des sujets, mais avant tout de leur contribution à la vie politique de la province. L'acquisition de portraits par les pouvoirs publics n'a pas toujours été motivée par des soucis d'ordre historique ou esthétique (mais bien plutôt par la prosaïque nécessité de garnir l'intérieur des édifices publics), mais la tradition voulant que l'on commande ce type d'œuvre est aujourd'hui fermement ancrée. À l'heure actuelle, la Collection compte plus de deux cents portraits, dont nous devons un bon nombre aux artistes les plus accomplis du genre à leur époque.

À son entrée en fonction comme lieutenant-gouverneur en 1880, l'honorable John Beverley Robinson se rend compte que bien peu de ses prédécesseurs ont vu leur mémoire ainsi honorée. À compter de l'année de son installation, Robinson passera donc commande de leurs portraits rétroactivement, se donnant parfois beaucoup de mal pour dénicher l'effigie de ses sujets. Débutant par le portrait du premier lieutenant-gouverneur, John Graves Simcoe, il en commandera dix-neuf autres par la suite. Peintre en vogue dans la bonne société, George Theodore Berthon hérite d'un bon nombre de ces commandes.

Comme Berthon avait pour tâche de dépeindre des personnes disparues parfois depuis longtemps, il était souvent forcé de travailler par images interposées. Par exemple, lorsque Berthon entame son portrait de Sir Isaac Brock, plus de soixante-dix ans se sont écoulés depuis la mort au champ d'honneur de l'illustre chef militaire, lors de la bataille de Queenston Heights. L'artiste se tourne alors vers la famille de Brock, à Guernesey, pour obtenir des précisions sur son apparence. La famille met à sa disposition une miniature du major-général, laquelle est envoyée en Angleterre pour sa reproduction à l'huile; une fois photographiée et teintée, cette copie est expédiée au Canada, à l'intention de Berthon.

6-16

6-17 & 6-18: [6-17] There is often more than meets the eye in archival holdings - a point well illustrated in Mildred Peel's portrait of War of 1812 heroine Laura Secord. This portrait was displayed for years outside Ontario's legislative chamber, but a persistent rumour that it had in fact once portrayed George Ross, premier of Ontario from 1899 to 1905, would not go away. Finally, in 1936, Premier Mitchell Hepburn ordered the portrait to undergo x-ray examination. The result, seen below, reveals the ghostly image of Premier George Ross.

[6-18] The artist who created the original portrait of Premier Ross is unknown; however, Mildred Peel, the artist who painted Laura Secord's image over Ross, was also his wife. It is possible that Peel painted the original portrait herself. That might explain why it was believed to have hung in the Ross household for several years before Peel painted over it.

AU-DELÀ DES APPARENCES – À PROPOS DE LAURA SECORD

6-17 et 6-18 : [6-17] Les documents d'archives réservent parfois des surprises – ce que démontre bien le portrait, exécuté par Mildred Peel, de Laura Secord, l'héroïne de la guerre de 1812. Ce portrait a été exposé pendant de longues années à l'extérieur de l'Assemblée législative de l'Ontario; or, selon la rumeur, l'œuvre aurait antérieurement été un portrait de George Ross, premier ministre de l'Ontario de 1899 à 1905. Le bruit persistant, le premier ministre Mitchell Hepburn ordonne enfin, en 1936, l'examen du portrait aux rayons X. Comme on peut le constater ci-dessous, l'image sous-jacente est bien celle du premier ministre George Ross.

[6-18] On ne connaît pas l'auteur du portrait initial, à l'effigie du premier ministre Ross; cependant, Mildred Peel, qui a superposé le portrait de Laura Secord à celui de Ross, était l'épouse de ce dernier. Il est donc possible que Peel ait elle-même signé le portrait d'origine. Cela justifierait qu'on ait cru l'œuvre en possession du ménage Ross pendant plusieurs années avant que Peel ne s'en serve pour un autre portrait.

6-17

6-18

6-19 to 6-21: Today, the tradition of portraiture continues and is made somewhat easier by the use of photography, as well as the usual availability of the sitter. Portraits have more recently tended towards a relaxed style and often include references to the subject's family and private life.

Istvan Nyikos's 1989 portrait of Bill Davis shows the former premier not stiffly facing the viewer in a darkened anonymous interior but in an office flooded with natural light. Although he is dressed in suit and tie, a somewhat casual demeanour is conveyed by the angle of the sitter's body and the crossed-legged pose. This less formal approach to portraiture is further emphasized in two subsequent premier's portraits, those of David Peterson and Bob Rae.

6-19 à 6-21 : La tradition du portrait se poursuit de nos jours, ce que facilite jusqu'à un certain point la photographie, de même que l'accessibilité habituelle des sujets. Ces dernières années, les portraits ont adopté un style plus détendu et incorporent souvent des renvois à la vie personnelle et à la famille du sujet.

Le portrait de l'ancien premier ministre Bill Davis, réalisé en 1989 par Istvan Nyikos, s'écarte du poncif qui fige le sujet face au spectateur, dans une pose artificielle et dans un décor sombre et anonyme, pour miser sur l'affabilité des traits et un doux éclairage naturel. Le personnage porte le complet traditionnel, mais l'angle de la posture et les jambes croisées dénotent aisance et bonhomie. Cette approche beaucoup moins compassée s'affirme encore davantage dans deux autres portraits d'ex-premiers ministres, ceux de David Peterson et de Bob Rae.

6-19

6-20

6-21

6-22: In 1963 the Ontario government made a significant commitment to purchase works of art for a complex of new government buildings slated for construction in downtown Toronto. This commitment heralded the beginning of the Art in Architecture Program, the goals of which were to improve the working environment of new Ontario government buildings, promote and showcase Ontario art and artists, and illustrate the culture and heritage of the province.

Completed during the term of Premier John Robarts, the artworks installed in the Macdonald Block complex at Bay and Wellesley streets represent thirty commissions made to twenty-nine Canadian artists. Sculpture, large-scale murals, and wall hangings in a variety of media include the work of artists such as Harold Town, Micheline Beauchemin, Kazuo Nakamura, Gerald Gladstone, Jack Bush, and A.J. Casson.

Casson's *Untitled*, an oil-on-linen mural, is located on the first floor (west side) of the Macdonald Block. Casson included his daughter and grandchildren in the composition; they can be seen hurrying past the church located near the top of the mural.

6-22 : En 1963, le gouvernement de l'Ontario prenait un engagement considérable, soit l'achat d'œuvres d'art pour tout un ensemble de nouveaux édifices gouvernementaux qu'on projetait de construire au centre de Toronto. C'était le coup d'envoi du Programme de l'art en architecture, dont les objectifs étaient d'améliorer la qualité de vie au travail dans les nouveaux édifices publics de l'Ontario, de promouvoir et de faire connaître l'art et les artistes ontariens, de même que d'illustrer la culture et le patrimoine de la province.

Achevées pendant le mandat du premier ministre John Robarts, les œuvres qui parent le complexe Macdonald, à l'angle des rues Bay et Wellesley, font suite à trente commandes, octroyées à vingt-neuf artistes canadiens. Ces sculptures, pièces et murales à grande échelle, réalisées dans toute une gamme de techniques, sont des œuvres entre autres de Harold Town, Micheline Beauchemin, Kazuo Nakamura, Gerald Gladstone, Jack Bush et A. J. Casson.

La murale *Untitled* de Casson est une huile sur toile de lin, disposée au rez-de-chaussée (côté ouest) de l'édifice Macdonald. L'artiste a intégré sa fille et ses petits-enfants à la composition, sous la forme des minuscules personnages qui se hâtent devant l'église, placée près du haut de la murale.

6-22

6-23

6-23: Gerald Gladstone's fountain *The Three Graces* was the last work to be installed in the Macdonald complex. It forms a visual centrepiece to the treed seating area that occupies the prominent northeast corner of the lot. The bronze figures represent the three sister goddesses of Greek mythology said to be the givers of charm and beauty. Instead of following the usual practice of turning to foundries in the United States, the artist had *The Three Graces* cast in a small industrial foundry in Georgetown.

6-23 : La fontaine *The Three Graces* de Gerald Gladstone a été la dernière œuvre à prendre place au complexe Macdonald. La pièce forme un centre d'attraction visuelle remarquable dans l'aire de repos bordée d'arbres qui occupe l'angle nord-est du la propriété. Les figures de bronze représentent des divinités de la mythologie grecque, trois sœurs réputées être les dispensatrices du charme et de la beauté. Au lieu de s'adresser, comme c'était l'habitude, à des fonderies américaines, l'artiste a fait couler *The Three Graces* dans une petite fonderie industrielle de Georgetown.

6-24

6-24: In 1986 further contemporary works entered the collection through the Northern Ontario Relocation Program (NORP). This program resulted in the construction of seven new government buildings across northern Ontario, in Sudbury, North Bay, Sault Ste Marie, and Thunder Bay. As part of NORP, art-selection committees were appointed in these four cities. Comprised of individuals with art expertise, the committees were responsible for eleven major commissions and the purchase of hundreds of works of art created mostly by artists from the region.

In 1991 artist Dennis Geden was commissioned to produce work for the North Bay Court House and Land Registry Office. The result was this large figurative oil painting, *Portage of a Pointer*, which now hangs in the main lobby of the building.

6-24 : En 1986, d'autres œuvres contemporaines font leur entrée dans la Collection, par le biais du Programme de déménagement dans le Nord de l'Ontario (PDNO). Ce programme a abouti à la construction de sept nouveaux immeubles publics dans le Nord de l'Ontario : à Sudbury, North Bay, Sault Ste Marie et Thunder Bay. Dans le cadre du PDNO, ces quatre villes se sont donné chacune un comité de sélection. Composés de personnes versées dans les arts, les comités ont été chargés de onze commandes majeures et de l'achat de centaines d'œuvres, principalement d'artistes de la région.

En 1991, on commandait à l'artiste Dennis Geden une œuvre destinée au palais de justice et bureau d'enregistrement immobilier de North Bay. C'est ainsi qu'une grande peinture à l'huile figurative, *Portage of a Pointer*, orne maintenant le hall principal de l'édifice.

6-25: In 1912 the government decided to decentralize the collection by sending out many of the works to normal schools across the province. This policy, along with a lack of proper record keeping and the dispersal of the artworks from the Provincial Museum of Ontario (as the Educational Museum had been renamed) in 1933, resulted in the loss of many fine works. It was only in the late 1970s that a serious attempt was made to document what remained of a scattered collection.

In 1978, after the Ministry of Government Services initiated a project to catalogue the remaining artworks in its care, a broad effort was undertaken to repatriate and document hundreds of works of art, with a partic- ular focus on tracing those artworks that had been dispersed in 1912 and on relocating those that had been stored in various locations in the Legislative Building. The repatriation program made provision for the systematic cataloguing, researching, and photographing of the recovered works. In addition, the art was conserved and restored, as funds would allow.

This effort culminated in 1984 with the publication by Fitzhenry and Whiteside of Fern Bayer's *The Ontario Collection*, a project of the Ontario Heritage Foundation commemorating the province's bicentennial. The book reviews in great detail the fascinating story of the collection's history.

6-25 : En 1912, le gouvernement décidait de décentraliser la Collection, en distribuant un certain nombre d'œuvres à des écoles normales de tous les coins de la province. Cette politique, aggravée par l'absence de registres correctement tenus et par la dispersion du fonds du Provincial Museum of Ontario (ainsi qu'on avait rebaptisé l'Educational Museum) en 1933, devait se solder par la disparition de maintes œuvres de valeur. Ce n'est qu'à la fin des années 1970 qu'on s'est sérieusement efforcé de documenter ce qui restait d'une collection dispersée aux quatre vents.

En 1978, après le lancement par le ministère des Services gouvernementaux d'un projet de catalogage des œuvres qui demeuraient de son ressort, on a mis en œuvre un programme concerté de rapatriement et de documentation de centaines d'œuvres d'art, en s'attachant surtout à retracer celles qui avaient été éparpillées en 1912 et à relocaliser celles qui avaient été entreposées en divers endroits dans l'édifice de l'Assemblée législative. Le programme de rapatriement prévoyait un effort systématique de catalogage, de recherche et de photographie des œuvres retrouvées. De plus, les œuvres devaient, dans toute la mesure des ressources, être restaurées.

En 1984, l'aboutissement du programme est couronné par la publication, chez Fitzhenry et Whiteside, de l'ouvrage *La Collection d'œuvres d'art de l'Ontario* de Fern Bayer, projet de la Fondation du patrimoine ontarien pour la commémoration du bicentenaire de la province. L'ouvrage relate dans le plus grand détail la fascinante histoire de la Collection.

6-25

6-1: Portrait of the Rev. Aldolphus Egerton Ryerson [ca. 1850-1], Theophile Hamel (1817-70) (Government of Ontario Art Collection, 622107, Thomas Moore Photography, Toronto)

6-2: *Carnival in Rome* [ca. 1856], Ippolito Caffi (1809-66) (Government of Ontario Art Collection, 694037, Thomas Moore Photography, Toronto)

6-3: *St George Killing the Dragon* [ca. 1856], Guiseppe Mazzolini (after Paris Bordone, 1500-71) (Government of Ontario Art Collection, 692678, Thomas Moore Photography, Toronto)

6-4: *L'Aurora* [ca. 1856], Augusto Ratti (after Guido Reni, 1575-1642) (Government of Ontario Art Collection, 622032, Thomas Moore Photography, Toronto. I0007641)

6-5: *The Vale of Tintern*, 1893, Gertrude Spurr Cutts, OSA, ARCA. (1858-1941) (Government of Ontario Art Collection, 622089, Thomas Moore Photography, Toronto. I0007644)

6-6: *Flower Market*, Paris, 1900, Clara Sophia Hagarty, OSA, ARCA (1871-1958) (Government of Ontario Art Collection, 622097, Thomas Moore Photography, Toronto. I0007645)

6-7: The Ontario Society of Artists, 1904 (Ontario Society of Artists fonds, F1140-7-0-2.1)

6-8: *The Clearing*, 1913, Arthur Lismer, OSA, RCA, CGP (1885-1969) (Government of Ontario Art Collection, 622110, Thomas Moore Photography, Toronto. I0007647)

6-9: *By the River (Early Spring)*, 1911, J.E.H. MacDonald, OSA, RCA. (1873-1932) (Government of Ontario Art Collection, 622106, Thomas Moore Photography, Toronto. I0007646)

6-10: *Wheat Stacks on the Prairies*, 1907, C.W. Jefferys (1869-1951) (Government of Ontario Art Collection, 619864, Thomas Moore Photography, Toronto)

6-11: *The Battle of Lundy's Lane* [ca. 1921], C.W. Jefferys, OSA, RCA, CSPWC (1869-1951) (Government of Ontario Art Collection, 621234, Thomas Moore Photography, Toronto. I0007669)

6-12: *Foreclosure of the Mortgage*, 1935, George A. Reid, OSA, RCA, CSPWC (1860-1947) (Government of Ontario Art Collection, 619809, Thomas Moore Photography, Toronto. I0007648)

6-13: *Hills and Clouds, Catskills*, 1914 George A. Reid, OSA, RCA, CSPWC (1860-1947) (Government of Ontario Art Collection, 621192, Thomas Moore Photography, Toronto. I0007650)

6-14: *The Valley of the Agawa*, 1932 George A. Reid, OSA, RCA, CSPWC (1860-1947) (Government of Ontario Art Collection, 619837, Thomas Moore Photography, Toronto. I0007649)

6-15: *Oinatchouan Falls*, 1885 Lucius O'Brien, OSA, RCA (1832-99). Donated by the Ontario Heritage Foundation, gift of Cicely Mary Blackstock, 1985 (Government of Ontario Art Collection, 638769, Thomas Moore Photography, Toronto. I0007664)

6-16: Portrait of Major-General Sir Isaac Brock [ca. 1883], George Theodore Berthon (1806-92) (Government of Ontario Art Collection, 694158, Thomas Moore Photography, Toronto)

6-17: X-ray detail of Portrait of Laura Secord [ca. 1984] (Thomas Moore Photography, Toronto)

6-18: Portrait of Laura Secord, 1904, Mildred Peel (1856-1920) (Government of Ontario Art Collection, 619796, Thomas Moore Photography, Toronto)

6-19: The Hon. William Grenville Davis, PC, CC, QC, Istvan Nyikos (b. 1942) (Government of Ontario Art Collection, 654446, Thomas Moore Photography, Toronto)

6-20: The Hon. David R. Peterson, PC, QC, C St J, DU, LLD, 1998, Linda Kooluris Dobbs (b. 1949) (Government of Ontario Art Collection, 100095, Thomas Moore Photography, Toronto. I0007652)

6-21: The Hon. Robert Keith Rae, PC, QC, 1998, Phil Richards (b. 1951), (Government of Ontario Art Collection, 100094, Thomas Moore Photography, Toronto. I0007653)

6-22: *Untitled*, 1966-8, A.J. Casson, OSA, CSPWC, CGP (1898-1992) (Government of Ontario Art Collection, 619772, Thomas Moore Photography, Toronto. I0007655)

6-23: *The Three Graces*, 1971, Gerald Gladstone, OSA, RCA (b. 1929) (Government of Ontario Art Collection, 619768, Thomas Moore Photography, Toronto. I0007657)

6-24: *Portage of a Pointer*, 1992, Dennis Geden (b. 1944), Commission for Courthouse and Land Registry Office, North Bay, 1991 (Government of Ontario Art Collection, 661734, Photographer: Ed Eng Photography, North Bay. I0007660)

6-25: Untitled [ca. 1991], Roy Thomas (b. 1949), Purchase for Ontario Government Building, 189 Red River Road, Thunder Bay, 1991 (Government of Ontario Art Collection, 661729, Photographer: Patrick Doyle, Thunder Bay. I0007676)

LÉGENDES

6-1 : Portrait du rév. Aldolphus Egerton Ryerson [vers 1850-1851], Théophile Hamel (1817-1870) (Collection d'œuvres d'art du gouvernement de l'Ontario, 622107, Thomas Moore Photography, Toronto)

6-2 : *Carnival in Rome* [vers 1856], Ippolito Caffi (1809-1866) (Collection d'œuvres d'art du gouvernement de l'Ontario, 694037, Thomas Moore Photography, Toronto)

6-3 : *St George Killing the Dragon* [vers 1856], Guiseppe Mazzolini (d'après Paris Bordone, 1500-1571) (Collection d'œuvres d'art du gouvernement de l'Ontario, 692678, Thomas Moore Photography, Toronto)

6-4 : *L'Aurora* [vers 1856], Augusto Ratti (d'après Guido Reni, 1575-1642) (Collection d'œuvres d'art du gouvernement de l'Ontario, 622032, Thomas Moore Photography, Toronto. I0007641)

6-5 : *The Vale of Tintern*, 1893, Gertrude Spurr Cutts, OSA, ARAC. (1858-1941) (Collection d'œuvres d'art du gouvernement de l'Ontario, 622089, Thomas Moore Photography, Toronto. I0007644)

6-6 : *Flower Market*, Paris, 1900, Clara Sophia Hagarty, OSA, ARAC (1871-1958) (Collection d'œuvres d'art du gouvernement de l'Ontario, 622097, Thomas Moore Photography, Toronto. I0007645)

6-7 : L'Ontario Society of Artists, 1904 (Fonds Ontario Society of Artists, F 1140-7-0-2.1)

6-8 : *The Clearing*, 1913, Arthur Lismer, OSA, ARC, CGP (1885-1969) (Collection d'œuvres d'art du gouvernement de l'Ontario, 622110, Thomas Moore Photography, Toronto. I0007647)

6-9 : *By the River (Early Spring)*, 1911, J. E. H. MacDonald, OSA, ARC (1873-1932) (Collection d'œuvres d'art du gouvernement de l'Ontario, 622106, Thomas Moore Photography, Toronto. I0007646)

6-10 : *Wheat Stacks on the Prairies*, 1907, C. W. Jefferys (1869-1951) (Collection d'œuvres d'art du gouvernement de l'Ontario, 619864, Thomas Moore Photography, Toronto)

6-11 : *The Battle of Lundy''s Lane* [vers 1921], C. W. Jefferys, OSA, ARC, SCPA (1869-1951) (Collection d'œuvres d'art du gouvernement de l'Ontario, 621234, Thomas Moore Photography, Toronto. I0007669)

6-12 : *Foreclosure of the Mortgage*, 1935, George A. Reid, OSA, ARC, SCPA (1860-1947) (Collection d'œuvres d'art du gouvernement de l'Ontario, 619809, Thomas Moore Photography, Toronto. I0007648)

6-13 : *Hills and Clouds,* Catskills, 1914 George A. Reid, OSA, ARC, SCPA (1860-1947) (Collection d'œuvres d'art du gouvernement de l'Ontario, 621192, Thomas Moore Photography, Toronto. I0007650)

6-14 : *The Valley of the Agawa*, 1932 George A. Reid, OSA, ARC, SCPA (1860-1947) (Collection d'œuvres d'art du gouvernement de l'Ontario, 619837, Thomas Moore Photography, Toronto. I0007649)

6-15 : *Oinatchouan Falls*, 1885 Lucius O'Brien, OSA, ARC (1832-1899). Offert par la Fondation du patrimoine ontarien, don de Cicely Mary Blackstock, 1985 (Collection d'œuvres d'art du gouvernement de l'Ontario, 638769, Thomas Moore Photography, Toronto. I0007664)

6-16 : Portrait du major-général Sir Isaac Brock [vers 1883], George Theodore Berthon (1806-1892) (Collection d'œuvres d'art du gouvernement de l'Ontario, 694158, Thomas Moore Photography, Toronto)

6-17 : Détail aux rayons X du *Portrait of Laura Secord* [vers 1984] (Thomas Moore Photography, Toronto)

6-18 : *Portrait of Laura Secord*, 1904, Mildred Peel (1856-1920) (Collection d'œuvres d'art du gouvernement de l'Ontario, 619796, Thomas Moore Photography, Toronto)

6-19 : L'hon. William Grenville Davis, PC, CC, CR, Istvan Nyikos (né en 1942) (Collection d'œuvres d'art du gouvernement de l'Ontario, 654446, Thomas Moore Photography, Toronto)

6-20 : L'hon. David R. Peterson, PC, CR, C St J, DU, LLD, 1998, Linda Kooluris Dobbs (née en 1949) (Collection d'œuvres d'art du gouvernement de l'Ontario, 100095, Thomas Moore Photography, Toronto. I0007652)

6-21 : L'hon. Robert Keith Rae, PC, CR, 1998, Phil Richards (né en 1951), (Collection d'œuvres d'art du gouvernement de l'Ontario, 100094, Thomas Moore Photography, Toronto. I0007653)

6-22 : *Untitled*, 1966-1968, A. J. Casson, OSA, SCPA, CGP (1898-1992) (Collection d'œuvres d'art du gouvernement de l'Ontario, 619772, Thomas Moore Photography, Toronto. I0007655)

6-23 : *The Three Graces*, 1971, Gerald Gladstone, OSA, ARC (né en 1929) (Collection d'œuvres d'art du gouvernement de l'Ontario, 619768, Thomas Moore Photography, Toronto. I0007657)

6-24 : *Portage of a Pointer*, 1992, Dennis Geden (né en 1944), commande destinée au palais de justice et bureau d'enregistrement immobilier de North Bay, 1991 (Collection d'œuvres d'art du gouvernement de l'Ontario, 661734; photographe : Ed Eng Photography, North Bay. I0007660)

6-25 : *Untitled* [vers 1991], Roy Thomas (né en 1949), achat destiné à l'Édifice du gouvernement de l'Ontario, 189 Red River Road, Thunder Bay, 1991 (Collection d'œuvres d'art du gouvernement de l'Ontario, 661729; photographe : Patrick Doyle, Thunder Bay. I0007676)

7

THE ARCHITECTURAL RECORD

LES DOCUMENTS ARCHITECTURAUX

7-1

The Archives of Ontario's collection of architectural records consists of approximately 170,000 items ranging from the 1820s to the present day. It includes records both of private architectural firms and of various departments of the Ontario government.

The architectural drawings in the collection may represent different stages of a project, from proposal to competition to contract. Genres of drawings include perspectives, sketches, site plans, specifications, construction photographs, and printed designs. The drawings may also document mechanical systems in buildings, landscape, interior design, decorative arts, and engineering works such as dams, bridges, and canals.

The most significant private collection in the Archives' holdings is the J.C.B. and E.C. Horwood drawings, covering the period from 1829 to 1969, with a high proportion of the many thousands of items dating from the twentieth century. This collection represents the firm Horwood & White (originally Burke, Horwood & White) and encompasses as well the work of more than sixty other noted architects, such as Edmund Burke, Frederic W. Cumberland, D.B. Dick, Henry Langley, and William G. Storm. Among the records in the Horwood Collection are drawings of schools, churches, government or institutional buildings, department stores, commercial and industrial facilities, bridges, skating rinks, funerary installations, and private homes. These drawings chart the construction of early Toronto buildings such as Osgoode Hall, University College, the first Robert Simpson Store, and St James Cathedral.

In 2001 the Archives acquired a large collection of records from Moriyama & Teshima Architects.

Known internationally for buildings such as the Canadian Embassy in Tokyo, this firm has also designed a wide variety of public buildings in Ontario, and the Archives' collection of its records concern such significant government structures as the Ontario Science Centre, Science North in Sudbury, and the Peterborough headquarters of the Ministry of Natural Resources.

The government records are no less varied. In the 1960s the Department of Public Works began transferring the records of demolished, obsolete, or alienated government facilities to the Archives. These drawings, by such noted architects as Francis R. Heakes, John G. Howard, Kivas Tully, and George W. Gouinlock, are of psychiatric hospitals, correctional facilities, courthouses and office structures, teachers' colleges and special schools, legislative and viceregal buildings, and engineering works. The Ministry of Labour records relate to workplaces and factories, while those of the Ministry of Transportation include designs for bridges, road construction, and maintenance equipment. Blueprints for most motion-picture theatres, opera houses, and auditoriums are found in the Film Review and Theatre Inspection Records.

The Archives' collection of architectural records reveals the evolution of design and construction in Ontario, from elaborate Second Empire style residences and richly decorated classical-revival edifices built of stone or brick to the iron, steel, glass, and reinforced-concrete structures of the twentieth century. In doing so, the collection highlights not only dramatic changes to architectural taste and fashion but also the transformation of Ontario's built environment.

Les Archives publiques de l'Ontario détiennent une imposante collection de documents architecturaux, qui rassemble quelque 170 000 plans, dessins et autres, datant des années 1820 à aujourd'hui. Ces documents proviennent de cabinets privés et de divers ministères du gouvernement de l'Ontario.

Les plans et dessins d'architecture de la collection font souvent voir un projet à différents stades, de la proposition au concours, puis au contrat. Tous les genres s'y retrouvent : perspectives, croquis, plans de masse et de situation, spécifications, photographies de constructions en chantier et plans imprimés. On y relève des dessins relatifs aux installations techniques internes, à l'aménagement paysagiste et à l'aménagement intérieur, à la conception d'ameublement et de décor, de même qu'à des ouvrages d'art tels que ponts, barrages et canaux.

La collection privée la plus importante des Archives, celle de J. C. B. et E. C. Horwood, illustre la période de 1829 à 1969, une forte proportion des milliers d'articles provenant du vingtième siècle. Dans cette collection figurent des spécimens de la firme Horwood & White (à l'origine Burke, Horwood & White) ainsi que d'une soixantaine d'autres architectes de renom, dont Edmund Burke, Frederic W. Cumberland, D. B. Dick, Henry Langley et William G. Storm. La collection Horwood réunit les destinations les plus diverses : écoles, églises, immeubles publics et institutionnels, grands magasins, installations industrielles et commerciales, ponts, patinoires, établissements funéraires et résidences privées. Ces plans et dessins permettent de retracer la construction de quelques-uns des premiers immeubles de Toronto : Osgoode Hall, University College, le premier grand magasin Robert Simpson et la cathédrale St. James.

En 2001, les Archives acquéraient une vaste collection de documents de la firme Moriyama & Teshima Architects. Ce cabinet, dont la réputation internationale est liée à la réalisation d'immeubles tels que l'ambassade canadienne à Tokyo, a aussi conçu les plans d'un vaste éventail d'immeubles publics en Ontario, et cette collection des Archives documente des constructions gouvernementales de marque, ainsi le Centre des sciences de l'Ontario, Science Nord à Sudbury et le siège du ministère des Richesses naturelles à Peterborough.

Les documents gouvernementaux sont tout aussi diversifiés. Pendant les années 1960, le ministère des Travaux publics commençait à verser aux Archives les documents relatifs aux installations gouvernementales démolies, périmées ou aliénées. Ces dessins, signés par des architectes de renom, par exemple Francis R. Heakes, John G. Howard, Kivas Tully et George W. Gouinlock, ont trait à tous les types de structures : hôpitaux psychiatriques, établissements correctionnels, palais de justice et immeubles à bureaux, écoles normales et écoles spécialisées, bâtiments législatifs et vice-royaux ainsi qu'ouvrages d'art. Les documents du ministère du Travail se rapportent à des usines et autres lieux de travail, tandis que ceux du ministère des Transports englobent des plans de ponts, de routes et de matériel d'entretien. Les plans directeurs de la plupart des cinémas, opéras et auditoriums de la province se retrouvent parmi les documents relatifs à l'examen des films et à l'inspection des cinémas.

La collection de documents architecturaux des Archives relate l'évolution de l'architecture et de la construction dans la province, depuis les résidences Second Empire très ornées et les édifices de pierre ou de brique à riche décor néoclassique jusqu'aux structures contemporaines mariant fer, acier, verre et béton armé. Grâce à cet éclectisme, la collection met en lumière non seulement les métamorphoses du goût et de la mode en architecture, mais également la transformation de l'environnement bâti en Ontario.

Front Elevation

7-2

7-2: In early Ontario, the courthouse, often referred to as a 'palace of law,' was an essential component of the architectural scene since its construction was necessary once a provincial district or county was established. The illustration presented here shows the Newcastle District courthouse and gaol (jail), located in Cobourg.

James G. Chewett's drawings of this structure date to 1828, making them the earliest architectural drawings of a courthouse held by the Archives. The courtroom and clerks' and judges' chambers occupied the upper levels of the courthouse, while the lower level contained the cells for prisoners.

7-2 : Dans l'Ontario des débuts, le tribunal, qu'on appelait communément « palais de justice », était un composant essentiel du paysage architectural, puisque sa construction devenait nécessaire dès l'instauration d'un comté ou d'un district provincial. Cette image représente le palais de justice (où loge la prison) du district de Newcastle, situé à Cobourg. Les plans de

James G. Chewett pour ce bâtiment remontent à 1828; ce sont donc les dessins architecturaux de palais de justice les plus anciens des Archives. Le tribunal, le greffe et le cabinet des juges occupaient les étages supérieurs, tandis que les cellules des détenus se trouvaient au rez-de-chaussée.

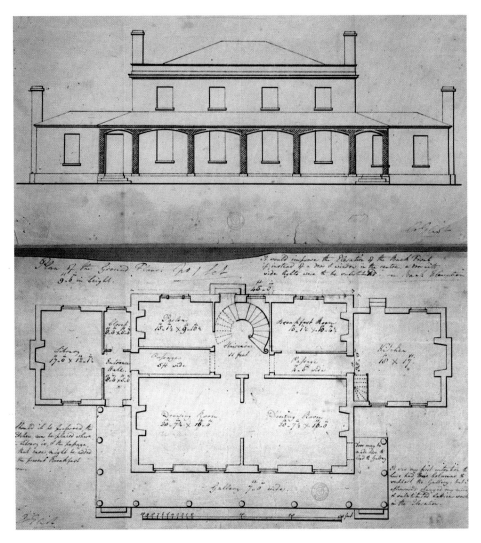

7-3

7-3: These house plans, prepared on paper water-marked 1821, are attributed to Charles Eliot, a British half-pay lieutenant of the 43rd Regiment who settled at Petite Côte, presently called LaSalle, in 1825. The plans are believed to be the earliest residential designs held by the Archives. The elevation of the house depicts a façade with a colonnaded porch, which has a simple but elegant Georgian line. The ground-floor plan, with its circular staircase and symmetrical rooms flanking a central rotunda, is reminiscent of the courthouses of the period.

7-3 : Ces plans de résidence, préparés sur un papier portant en filigrane la date de 1821, sont attribués à Charles Eliot, lieutenant britannique en demi-traite-ment du 43e Régiment, qui s'était établi à Petite Côte (aujourd'hui LaSalle) en 1825. On croit que ces plans de résidence sont les plus anciens conservés par les Archives. L'élévation de la façade montre une véranda à colonnade, dans un style simple mais élégant du dix-huitième siècle. Le plan du rez-de-chaussée, avec son escalier en spirale et des salles symétriques de chaque côté d'une rotonde centrale, est dans le goût des palais de justice du temps.

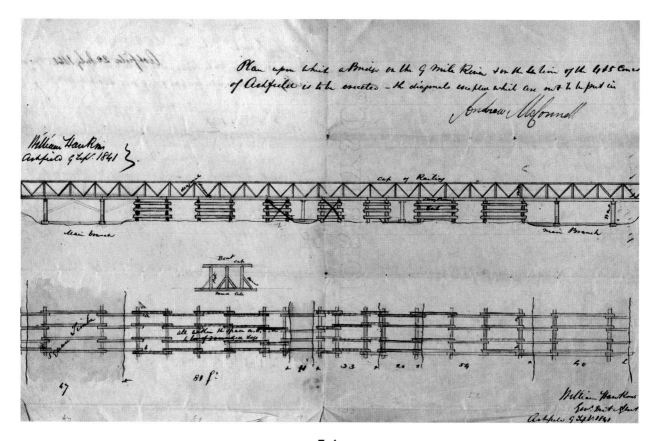

7-4

7-4: This crude drawing from 1841 is attached to a contract for the construction of a wooden bridge in Ashfield Township by William Hawkins.

7-4 : Ce dessin rudimentaire de 1841 est annexé à un contrat visant la construction par William Hawkins d'un pont de bois, dans le canton d'Ashfield.

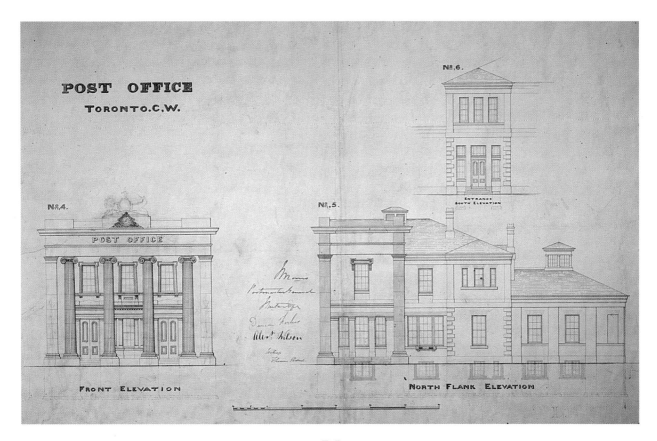

7-5

7-5: This is the Seventh Post Office, located at 10 Toronto Street in Toronto and designed by Cumberland & Ridout to resemble a classical temple. The drawing is part of a suite of contract drawings signed and dated July 1851. The façade, with its columnar arrangement, reflects the Greek revival style that was popular for official buildings in Upper Canada at that time. In 1874 Henry Langley made minor renovations. Much later, in 1959, Argus Corporation bought the building and converted it to private offices.

7-5 : Voici le Seventh Post Office de Toronto, 10, rue Toronto, qui a été conçu par Cumberland & Ridout sur le modèle d'un temple classique. Ce plan fait partie d'une série de dessins contractuels, signés et datés de juillet 1851. La façade, ponctuée de colonnes, est dans la veine néoclassique qui prévalait à l'époque pour les immeubles publics du Haut-Canada. En 1874, Henry Langley apporte des rénovations mineures à la construction. Beaucoup plus tard, en 1959, l'Argus Corporation achète le bâtiment pour y aménager des bureaux privés.

7-6: Osgoode Hall houses the Law Society of Upper Canada and, as the centre of law for the province, was given a majestic design. Subsequent additions, including a major renovation in 1857 to the central section, were designed by Cumberland & Storm. Behind the second-floor façade is the great library, a magnificent example of basilica-type interior architecture with massive columns supporting a vaulted ceiling. This drawing depicts a mirror over the fireplace but that space is now occupied by a portrait of Sir John Beverley Robinson, appointed acting attorney general of Upper Canada in 1812 and chief justice in 1829. At the other end of the room, there is a memorial of the First World War.

7-6 : Osgoode Hall héberge la Société du barreau du Haut-Canada et, en sa qualité de foyer du droit dans la province, s'est valu une conception majestueuse. Des ajouts ultérieurs, notamment lors des importantes rénovations effectuées en 1857 dans le bâtiment central, ont été dessinés par Cumberland & Storm. À l'étage, l'intérieur de la spacieuse et imposante bibliothèque est de type basilique, des colonnes massives soutenant un plafond en voûte. Dans ce dessin, une glace surmonte la cheminée, espace aujourd'hui occupé par un portrait de Sir John Beverley Robinson, nommé procureur général suppléant du Haut-Canada en 1812 et juge en chef en 1829. À l'autre extrémité de la salle s'élève un monument commémoratif de la Première Guerre.

7-6

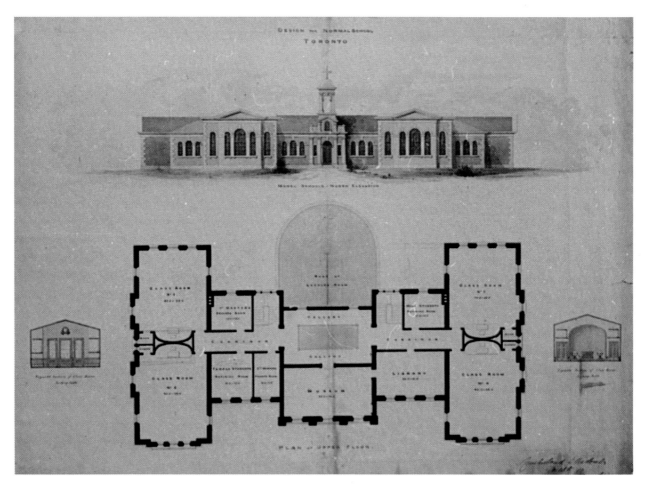

7-7

7-7: The educational building shown here is the Toronto Normal School, founded by Egerton Ryerson as the first teacher-training facility in the province. Built by Cumberland & Ridout in the 1850s, it is an excellent example of the eclectic nature of architectural design in this period. In addition to classrooms, the building housed offices, a library, and a museum. While the façade illustrates a mixture of symmetrical Palladian elements and Romanesque details, the interior was largely Gothic in style. In order to make way for the main campus of Ryerson University, the school was demolished in 1963 except for the main portico, which remains on the campus as an architectural remnant.

7-7 : Le bâtiment scolaire qu'on voit ici est l'École normale de Toronto, fondée par Egerton Ryerson, qui a été le premier institut pédagogique de la province. Érigé par Cumberland & Ridout dans les années 1850, c'est une excellente illustration de l'éclectisme qui régnait alors en architecture. Outre les classes, l'immeuble abritait des bureaux, une bibliothèque et un musée. La façade allie des éléments de style palladien à des détails d'architecture romane, tandis que l'intérieur est d'inspiration surtout gothique. En 1963, l'aménagement du campus principal de l'Université Ryerson a exigé la démolition de l'École, exception faite du grand portique, seue vestige de l'ancien édifice.

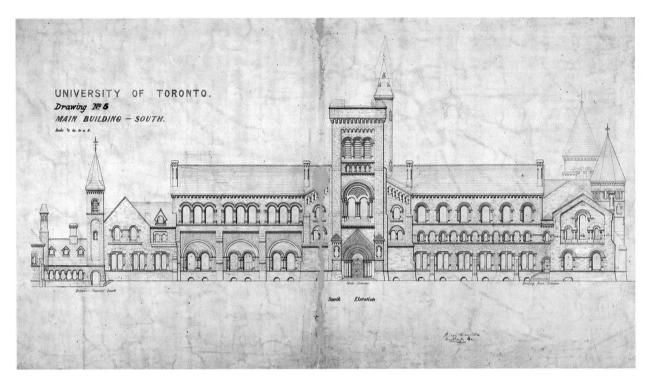

7-8

7-8: Similarly, University College, pictured above, began life on the drawing board in the English Gothic style, but the governor-general of the day preferred that it be Byzantine. It ended up as a fantastically beautiful building, part Romanesque, part medieval, and part classical. It is often described as picturesque, with its charming exterior stone towers and arches and mouldings, all enhanced with gorgeous carvings.

7-8 : De façon analogue, l'University College (ci-dessus), a d'abord été dessiné dans le style gothique anglais, mais le gouverneur général du moment avait un faible pour le byzantin. On a néanmoins abouti à un immeuble d'une beauté fantastique, en partie roman, en partie médiéval et en partie classique. On le décrit souvent comme « pittoresque », avec ses charmantes tours, arcs et moulures extérieurs en pierre, que rehaussent des sculptures fastueuses.

7-9: St James Cathedral, which currently occupies the northwest corner of King and Church streets in Toronto, is actually the fourth church of that name to have been constructed there. Its immediate precursor burned to the ground in 1849. The architectural firm Cumberland & Ridout (later Cumberland & Storm) emerged as the winning candidate for the building contract after competing against colleagues such as Kivas Tully and William Thomas. This watercolour of St James Cathedral is a striking perspective drawing that Cumberland & Storm prepared about 1858.

Though its English Gothic façade may appear quite traditional, there were a number of unusual arrangements in the design of the cathedral. The organ was placed in the south entrance rather than in the chancel and the orientation of the cathedral was north-south rather than the traditional east-west. For these and other reasons, St James Cathedral was an architectural statement that challenged traditional practice. The building project was completed in 1875 with the installation in the towers of a magnificent chiming clock, a gift from the people of Toronto.

7-9 : La cathédrale St. James, actuellement sise à l'angle nord-ouest des rues King et Church à Toronto, est en fait la quatrième église du nom sur ce même emplacement, la précédente ayant été rasée par les flammes en 1849. Le cabinet d'architectes Cumberland & Ridout (plus tard Cumberland & Storm) s'était vu adjuger le contrat de construction, l'emportant sur des collègues tels que Kivas Tully et William Thomas. Cette aquarelle de la cathédrale emploie un dessin de perspective saisissant, préparé vers 1858 par Cumberland & Storm. La façade de style gothique anglais peut sembler tout à

fait conventionnelle, mais le plan de la cathédrale comportait un certain nombre de traits inédits. Ainsi, l'orgue était placé dans l'entrée sud plutôt que dans le chœur, et l'orientation du bâtiment était nord-sud et non pas est-ouest, comme l'aurait voulu la tradition. Pour ces raisons parmi d'autres, la cathédrale St. James constituait une réalisation architecturale qui défiait la coutume. Le projet a été achevé en 1875, avec l'installation dans le clocher d'une magnifique horloge à carillon, don de la population torontoise.

7-9

7-10: The architectural perspective is an artistic rendering of the final design of the building in all its grandeur. Exterior and interior perspectives play an important role in helping clients to understand the process of design, and the former also serves as a form of promotion for the architect's work and the client's business. To this end, perspectives often were coupled with idealized settings, with the surrounding streetscape minimized or the subject building cast in a picturesque style or landscape.

A fine example is this 1890 chromolithograph of the Confederation Life Building at Yonge and Richmond streets in Toronto. This print by the Toronto lithography firm of Rolph, Smith and Company closely follows the builder's presentation drawing, which had been published in various sources. The 'Confed Life' building was executed in a Romanesque revival style with elements of French Gothic. It was considered a landmark edifice at the time and continues to be so today despite the scaling back of portions of the towers and turrets because of roof repairs and fire damage.

7-10 : En architecture, la perspective est un rendu artistique du concept final, dans toute sa splendeur. Les perspectives intérieure et extérieure jouent un rôle important, car elles aident le client à comprendre le processus de conception, et la seconde peut aussi être une forme de promotion, pour l'architecte comme pour l'entreprise cliente. Dans cette visée, on assortissait souvent les perspectives de décors idéalisés, en atténuant le caractère urbain du paysage ou en plaçant la construction dans un paysage de style pittoresque.

Un bel exemple en est cette chromolithographie de 1890, qui a pour sujet l'édifice de la Confederation Life de Toronto, sis à l'angle des rues Yonge et Richmond. Cette gravure du cabinet de lithographie torontois Rolph, Smith and Company suit étroitement le dessin de présentation du constructeur, qui avait paru dans diverses publications. Le bâtiment a été exécuté dans un style néoroman, relevé de gothique français. Considéré comme remarquable à l'époque, il continue de l'être aujourd'hui, bien que certaines parties des tours et tourelles soient moins imposantes qu'à l'origine, en raison d'incendies et des réparations apportées à la toiture.

7-10

7-11

7-11: In 1878 Joseph Ades Fowler prepared this preliminary watercolour perspective of the Building and Loan Association Offices. The painting was submitted as a competition drawing for the commission and did not reflect the actual structure as built. The architects who executed the commission were Langley, Langley & Burke and the offices were constructed at the northeast corner of Toronto and Court streets in Toronto. Unfortunately, that building, a beautiful example of high Victorian architecture, was demolished in 1961.

7-11 : En 1878, Joseph Ades Fowler avait préparé à l'aquarelle cette perspective préliminaire des bureaux de la Building and Loan Association. Le plan avait été présenté au concours tenu pour la commande et ne reflète pas le bâtiment tel qu'il a été construit. Les architectes qui ont exécuté la commande étaient Langley, Langley & Burke, et les bureaux ont été édifiés à l'angle nord-est des rues Toronto et Court, à Toronto. Fait à déplorer, cet excellent spécimen de la grande époque victorienne a été démoli en 1961.

7-12

7-12: The Canada Permanent Building (1928-30) blends modern classical flourishes with New York setbacks. Situated at the southwest corner of Bay and Adelaide streets, it was known for its striking exterior elevations with sculpted roof line and floral and leaf forms, and for the award-winning lobby and banking hall. These interior details are worked in polished brass and bronze with lavish marble walls and decorative allusions to the tomb of Tutankhamun.

7-12 : Le Canada Permanent Building (1928-1930) allie une ornementation moderne de goût classique à des retraits de style new-yorkais. Sis à l'angle sud-ouest des rues Bay et Adelaide, l'édifice était réputé pour ses élévations extérieures frappantes, dotées d'une ligne de toiture sculpturale, à décor de fleurs et frondaison, ainsi que pour son hall et son comptoir bancaire primés. Les détails de l'intérieur sont sur cuivre et bronze polis, et de somptueux murs de marbre font valoir une ornementation évocatrice du tombeau de Toutankhamon.

7-13

7-13: A century before health clubs, mass-spectator sports, and personal trainers, the local YMCA was the focal point of community athletics and sport. This watercolour perspective of the west end 'Y' at College and Dovercourt streets in Toronto may have been rendered as a presentation drawing for the clients or to showcase the Horwood firm's work at the Canadian National Exhibition. The building still functions as a vibrant community YMCA, after extensive renovation in 1981-2 when the entranceway was moved to the northwest corner.

7-13 : Un siècle avant l'apparition des sports de masse ou de spectacle, des centres de conditionnement physique et des entraîneurs personnels, le YMCA était le foyer de l'athlétisme et du sport dans la collectivité. Cette perspective à l'aquarelle du « Y » de l'ouest de Toronto, à l'angle des rues College et Dovercourt, a pu servir de dessin de présentation destiné aux clients ou d'exemple des réalisations du cabinet Horwood à l'Exposition nationale canadienne. L'immeuble loge toujours un dynamique YMCA communautaire, après des rénovations considérables en 1981-1982, date à laquelle le hall d'entrée a été réaménagé dans la partie nord-ouest.

7-14a

7-14b

7-14-a & b: Here we have other examples of exterior
and interior perspectives.

7-14-a à b : Voici d'autres spécimens de perspectives
intérieures et extérieures.

7-15a

7-15b

7-15-a & b: Langley & Burke built a number of picturesque cottages, such as the one at the top for Paul Campbell, in the Lorne Park Estates (situated in present-day Mississauga). The firm used the elaborate logo above to advertise the cottages and their firm.

7-15-a à b : La firme Langley & Burke a construit, pour le compte de Paul Campbell, un certain nombre de bungalows pittoresques, tels que celui au haut de la page, dans les Lorne Park Estates (emplacement de l'actuel Mississauga). Le logo un peu fleuri ci-dessus annonçait les bungalows et services de la firme.

7-16

7-16: The Peleg Howland residence was constructed around 1905 in Rosedale in Toronto and is attributed to Burke & Horwood. This plan shows the colour perspective flanked by smaller inserts indicating the floor plans.

7-16 : La résidence Peleg Howland, édifiée vers 1905 dans le quartier Rosedale de Toronto, est attribuée à Burke & Horwood. Ce plan donne une perspective en couleur, accompagnée de plans d'étage en annotations.

7-17

7-17: This property at 122 Dawlish Avenue, originally the Charles A.G. Matthews House (1924), was located in the fashionable new subdivision of Lawrence Park in Toronto, an area that highlighted the work of many creative architects, such as Chadwick & Beckett. The house as it is presented in this image represents a modest Depression-era renovation by Murray Brown.

Brown immigrated to Canada in 1914 and began working for Charles S. Cobb shortly thereafter. By the 1930s, he had started his own practice and was known for his sensitive and artistic designs of houses, theatres, and public buildings, which incorporated arts and craft and art deco features.

7-17 : Cette propriété du 122, avenue Dawlish, à l'origine résidence de Charles A. G. Matthews (1924), était située dans le nouveau lotissement torontois en vogue de Lawrence Park, quartier regroupant des œuvres de plusieurs architectes novateurs, dont Chadwick & Beckett. Telle qu'on la voit ici, la maison présente une modeste rénovation datant de la Crise, signée

Murray Brown. Ce dernier avait émigré au Canada en 1914, pour entrer au service de Charles S. Cobb peu après. Au début des années 1930, il avait son propre cabinet, et on le recherchait pour l'originalité et le cachet artistique de ses dessins de résidences, théâtres et immeubles publics, qui intégraient des éléments art déco et « arts and crafts ».

7-18

7-18: Galt-area architect Ray M. Hall did most of his work in southwestern Ontario. This 1939 pen and watercolour drawing depicts a movie theatre in the art deco style. The proposal drawing was done for David J. Fleming, a Galt insurance representative of Sun Life Assurance, who possibly saw the project as an investment venture to take advantage of the rage for Hollywood films.

7-18 : L'architecte Ray M. Hall, de la région de Galt, a travaillé surtout dans le sud-ouest de l'Ontario. Ce dessin à la plume avec lavis de 1939 dépeint un cinéma dans le style art déco. Le dessin de la proposition était destiné à David J. Fleming, représentant de la Sun Life Assurance, qui discernait peut-être dans ce projet le moyen de tirer un parti avantageux de l'engouement du temps pour le cinéma hollywoodien.

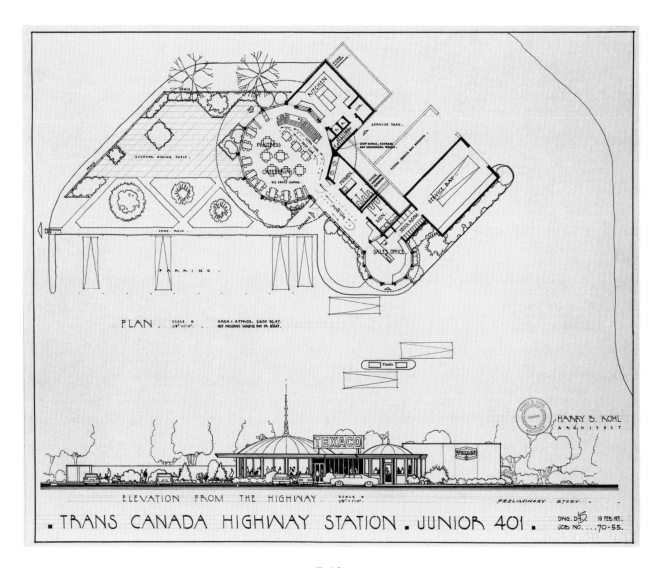

PLAN. SCALE ¼ ⅛"=1'-0". AREA: APPROX. 2400 SQ.FT.
NOT INCLUDING SERVICE BAY OR BSMT.

ELEVATION FROM THE HIGHWAY. SCALE ⅛"=1'-0". PRELIMINARY STUDY.

. TRANS CANADA HIGHWAY STATION . JUNIOR 401 . DWG. D.W. 19 FEB 1971.
JOB NO. ...70-55.

HARRY B. KOHL
ARCHITECT

7-19

7-19: Harry Kohl emerged as a leading architect in Toronto during the building boom of the 1950s and 1960s. He designed this prototype for Texaco Canada highway gas and service centres in 1971. There was an overall concept for both the structures and the landscape in his design.

7-19 : Harry Kohl s'est imposé comme l'un des meilleurs architectes de Toronto pendant la florissante période de construction des années 1950 et 1960. Il a mis au point ce prototype en 1971, pour le compte des centres routiers essence-services de Texaco Canada. Il s'agissait d'un concept d'ensemble, pour les structures et l'aménagement paysager.

7-20

7-20: Museum design has come a long way from the neo-classical or fortress-like Romanesque styles of the nineteenth century. Science North in Sudbury, designed by Moriyama & Teshima, resembles a snowflake on the unforgiving landscape of the Canadian Shield. Moriyama has shown that modern buildings, despite their often monumental scale, do not have to be authoritarian or intimidating. Open central spaces such as atria can foster human interaction in public buildings and may feel more democratic than the temple or palace of old.

7-20 : L'image du musée a bien changé depuis le style néoclassique et la forteresse néoromane du dix-neuvième siècle. Science North, à Sudbury, dessiné par le cabinet Moriyama & Teshima, figure un flocon de neige géant sur le fond d'un implacable Bouclier canadien. Moriyama a su démontrer que l'immeuble moderne, en dépit d'une échelle souvent monumentale, n'est pas forcément intimidant ni oppressant. Des aires centrales ouvertes – atriums par exemple – favorisent l'interaction humaine dans les édifices publics et dégagent un sentiment peut-être plus démocratique que le temple ou le palais d'antan.

7-1: Presentation ceremony for Horwood Collection, with E.C. Horwood and Premier William Davis, March 1979 (Archives of Ontario photographs, RG 17-43, Horwood Donation file, #3-31)

7-2: Gaol and courthouse, front elevation, 1828, James Grant Chewett (Measured Drawings Collection, D1212)

7-3: Plan of ground floor and front elevation of a house for Charles Eliot [location unknown: Sandwich?] [ca. 1825] (Miscellaneous Collection, F 775, MU 2095, n.d., 40)

7-4: Plan and elevation for a wooden bridge over Nine Mile River, Ashfield Township, Canada West, 9 Sept. 1841 (Miscellaneous Collection, F 775, MU 2108, 1841, 8)

7-5: Post Office, 10 Toronto Street, front, north flank, and south elevations, Cumberland & Ridout, 1851 (J.C.B. and E.C. Horwood Collection, C 11-62-0-1 [76] 4)

7-6: Osgoode Hall, library, interior perspective, Cumberland & Storm [ca. 1857-9] (J.C.B. and E.C. Horwood Collection, C 11-102-0-6 [747] 2)

7-7: Design for Normal School, Toronto, Cumberland & Ridout, 1850-2 (J.C.B. and E.C. Horwood Collection, C 11-67-0-1 [79] 4)

7-8: University College in Toronto, Cumberland & Storm [ca. 1855-1859] (J.C.B. and E.C. Horwood Collection, C 11-101-0-7 [114] 15)

7-9: St James Cathedral in Toronto, Cumberland & Storm [ca. 1858] (J.C.B. and E.C. Horwood Collection, C 11-49-0-5 [750] 2)

7-10: Head Office, Confederation Life Association Building, Toronto, Rolph, Smith and Company [ca. 1890] (Documentary Art Collection, C 281-0-0-0-1)

7-11: Building and Loan Association Offices, Joseph A. Fowler, 1878 (J.C.B. and E.C. Horwood Collection, C 11-588-0-1 [311b] 1)

7-12: Canada Permanent Building, F. Hilton Wilkes (architect), Mathers & Haldenby (associate architects), Sproatt & Rolph (consulting architects) [between 1928 and 1931] (Sproatt and Rolph fonds, C 292-1-0-316)

7-13: West End YMCA in Toronto, Burke, Horwood & White [ca. 1911-12] (J.C.B. and E.C. Horwood Collection, C 11-949, K-498)

7-14a: Sketch of house for D.E. Thomson at Queen's Park, Langley & Burke, 1887 (J.C.B. and E.C. Horwood Collection, C 11-36-0-3 [579] 3)

7-14b: View of staircase for D.E. Thomson residence at Queen's Park, Langley & Burke [1888] (J.C.B. and E.C. Horwood Collection, C 11-36-0-3 [579] 1)

7-15a: Paul Campbell Cottage in Lorne Park, Langley & Burke, 1887 (J.C.B. and E.C. Horwood Collection, C 11-535-0-2 [584] 1)

7-15b: Summer Cottages in Lorne Park, Langley & Burke [ca. 1890] (J.C.B. and E.C. Horwood Collection, C 11-593-0-0-1 [568] 1)

7-16: Peleg Howland residence in Rosedale, Burke & Horwood [ca. 1905] (J.C.B. and E.C. Horwood Collection, C 11-1120 [1662])

7-17: Alterations to the residence of C.A.G. Matthews, Lawrence Park, Toronto, Murray Brown, 1936 (William E. Fleury fonds, C 19, A-3)

7-18: Front elevation of proposed movie theatre for D.J. Fleming, Ray M. Hall, 1939 (Ray M. Hall fonds, C 28, A-1, project 39023)

7-19: Texaco Junior Service Centre on 410 Highway at Lancaster, Ont., Harry B. Kohl, 1971 (Harry B. Kohl fonds, C 15, project 7055)

7-20: Photograph of an illuminated model of Science North in Sudbury, Ont., Moriyama & Teshima [198-] (Moriyama & Teshima Architects fonds, F 2187-1-69, project 8016)

7-1 : Cérémonie de présentation de la collection Horwood, où sont présents E. C. Horwood et le premier ministre William Davis, mars 1979 (Photographies des Archives publiques de l'Ontario, RG 17-43, dossier « Horwood Donation », no 3-31)

7-2 : Palais de justice et prison, élévation avant, 1828, James Grant Chewett (Collection des relevés architecturaux, D1212)

7-3 : Plan du rez-de-chaussée et élévation avant d'une résidence, pour le compte de Charles Eliot [emplacement inconnu : Sandwich?] [vers 1825] (Collection mixte, F 775, MU 2095, s. d., 40)

7-4 : Plan et élévation d'un pont de bois sur la rivière Nine Mile du canton d'Ashfield, Canada-Ouest, 9 sept. 1841 (Collection mixte, F 775, MU 2108, 1841, 8)

7-5 : Bureau de poste, 10, rue Toronto, élévations frontale et latérales (nord et sud), Cumberland & Ridout, 1851 (Collection J. C. B. et E. C. Horwood, C 11-62-0-1 [76] 4)

7-6 : Bibliothèque d'Osgoode Hall, perspective de l'intérieur, Cumberland & Storm [vers 1857-9] (Collection J. C. B. et E. C. Horwood, C 11-102-0-6 [747] 2)

7-7 : Plan pour l'École normale, Toronto, Cumberland & Ridout, 1850-1852 (Collection J. C. B. et E. C. Horwood, C 11-67-0-1 [79] 4)

7-8 : University College, à Toronto, Cumberland & Storm [vers 1855-1859] (Collection J. C. B. et E. C. Horwood, C 11-101-0-7 [114] 15)

7-9 : Cathédrale St. James, à Toronto, Cumberland & Storm [vers 1858] (Collection J. C. B. et E. C. Horwood, C 11-49-0-5 [750] 2)

7-10 : Siège social, édifice de la Confederation Life Association, à Toronto, Rolph, Smith & Company [vers 1890] (Collection d'art documentaire, C 281-0-0-0-1)

7-11 : Bureaux de la Building and Loan Association, Joseph A. Fowler, 1878 (Collection J. C. B. et E. C. Horwood, C 11-588-0-1 [311b] 1)

7-12 : Édifice de la Canada Permanent, F. Hilton Wilkes (architecte), Mathers & Haldenby (architectes associés) et Sproatt & Rolph (architectes-conseils) [entre 1928 et 1931] (Fonds Sproatt & Rolph, C 292-1-0-316)

7-13 : Le YMCA de l'ouest de la ville, à Toronto, Burke, Horwood & White [vers 1911-12] (Collection J. C. B. et E. C. Horwood, C 11-949, K-498)

7-14a : Croquis de la résidence de D. E. Thomson, à Queen's Park, Langley & Burke, 1887 (Collection J. C. B. et E. C. Horwood, C 11-36-0-3 [579] 3)

7-14b : Vue d'un escalier, résidence de D. E. Thomson, à Queen's Park, Langley & Burke [1888] (Collection J. C. B. et E. C. Horwood, C 11-36-0-3 [579] 1)

7-15a : Chalet de Paul Campbell, à Lorne Park, Langley & Burke, 1887 (Collection J. C. B. et E. C. Horwood, C 11-535-0-2 [584] 1)

7-15b : Chalets d'été, Lorne Park, Langley & Burke [vers 1890] (Collection J. C. B. et E. C. Horwood, C 11-593-0-0-1 [568] 1)

7-16 : Résidence de Peleg Howland, à Rosedale, Burke & Horwood [vers 1905] (Collection J. C. B. et E. C. Horwood, C 11-1120 [1662])

7-17 : Rénovations de la résidence de C. A. G. Matthews, Lawrence Park, Toronto, Murray Brown, 1936 (Fonds William E. Fleury, C 19, A-3)

7-18 : Élévation avant d'un cinéma, projet de D. J. Fleming, Ray M. Hall, 1939 (Fonds Ray M. Hall, C 28, A-1, projet 39023)

7-19 : Centre de service Texaco Junior, sur la route 410, à Lancaster (Ontario) Harry B. Kohl, 1971 (Fonds Harry B. Kohl, C 15, projet 7055)

7-20 : Photographie d'une maquette lumineuse de Science Nord, à Sudbury (Ontario), Moriyama & Teshima [198?] (Fonds Moriyama & Teshima Architects, F 2187-1-69, projet 8016)

8

GOVERNMENT PUBLICITY AND PROMOTIONAL MATERIAL

LES DOCUMENTS DE PROMOTION ET DE PUBLICITÉ DU GOUVERNMENT

8-1

The government of Ontario has always publicized its new initiatives and continuing programs. Today, it does so primarily through television and government websites, but in earlier times it communicated its message to the public through printed materials such as posters and brochures and also through photographs and motion-picture films.

The Archives of Ontario holds a large collection of records of this kind, totalling well over 500,000 items in all. Portraying such varied activities as teaching, forestry, mining, farming, highway construction, and tourism, government-produced textual and visual material performed an equally diverse range of functions: educating the public about government programs, documenting activities and announcing new developments in different economic sectors, monitoring progress in infrastructure growth, ensuring public safety, and promoting tourism and immigration. Just as obvious as the material's informational function, however, is its high degree of technical and even artistic skill, which is particularly evident in the photography and film records. Of course, government photographers and filmmakers likely had an advantage that others did not, in that they may well have been granted access to remote locations and to specific industries which were off-limits to their amateur and even professional counterparts.

The illustrations in this chapter show material, both printed and visual, that was produced by the government for specific reasons. For example, in 1905 the Bureau of Mines had an interest in documenting the mineral resources of northern Ontario, and in 1940 the Travel and Publicity Bureau wanted to promote American tourism. Yet, beyond the purposes that this material served in the short term, the Archives' collection of government-produced textual and visual records has lasting historical significance. Besides documenting the social, cultural, and economic development of Ontario, the collection preserves images of technologies and work settings that now are vastly changed, if they exist at all.

Le gouvernement de l'Ontario a toujours fait l'annonce de ses nouvelles initiatives et programmes permanents. Aujourd'hui, cette annonce passe principalement par la télévision et les sites Web, alors que, dans le passé, les messages parvenaient à la population par le biais d'imprimés, tels que brochures et affiches, et aussi de photographies et films animés.

Les Archives publiques de l'Ontario possèdent une abondante collection de documents de ce type, au total plus de 500 000 articles. Par la description et la représentation d'activités aussi diverses que l'enseignement, la foresterie, l'extraction minière et l'exploitation agricole, la construction routière et le tourisme, le matériel visuel et textuel produit par le gouvernement visait une gamme également diversifiée de fonctions : informer la population sur les programmes gouvernementaux, documenter les activités se déroulant dans différents secteurs économiques et en annoncer les nouvelles orientations, effectuer le suivi des progrès en implantation de l'infrastructure, assurer la sécurité publique et promouvoir le tourisme et l'immigration. La fonction informative de ce matériel est assez évidente, tout comme d'ailleurs la haute qualité technique et artistique dont témoignent les documents photographiques et cinématographiques. Il est vrai que les photographes et cinéastes du gouvernement avaient une longueur d'avance sur leurs homologues amateurs et même professionnels, ayant probablement accès à des lieux éloignés et à certains secteurs réservés.

Le présent chapitre s'illustre de documents, tant visuels qu'imprimés, qu'avait publiés le gouvernement à des fins précises. Ainsi, en 1905, le bureau des Mines voulait faire connaître les ressources minérales du Nord de l'Ontario, et, en 1940, le bureau du Tourisme et de la Publicité souhaitait promouvoir le tourisme chez les Américains.

Cependant, au-delà des objectifs à court terme du matériel, la collection de documents visuels et textuels produits par le gouvernement que possèdent les Archives a une portée historique durable. En plus de documenter le développement économique, social et culturel de l'Ontario, la collection conserve des images de technologies et de milieux de travail qui ont aujourd'hui énormément changé s'ils ne sont pas déjà disparus.

8-2

8-3

EDUCATION

8-2 & 8-3: The Ottawa Normal School was established in 1875 to provide training for teachers, and later became the Faculty of Education at the University of Ottawa. These photographs feature the kind of training the teachers received. Note the atypical genders in the home economics and shop classes.

L'ÉDUCATION

8-2 et 8-3 : L'École normale d'Ottawa, fondée en 1875 comme institut pédagogique, est plus tard devenue la Faculté d'éducation de l'Université d'Ottawa. Ces photographies illustrent le type de formation que recevaient les futurs enseignants. Notons une répartition des sexes inusitée dans les classes de métiers et d'arts ménagers.

8-4

8-5

FORESTRY

8-4 & 8-5: [8-4] The Ministry of Natural Resources and its predecessors used photographs to document activities such as forest-fire fighting, reforestation and timber management, and forest-ranger education and training. Here the men are assembling a log boom, a chain of connected floating logs that surrounds loose logs. The log boom would then be towed to the mill by a tug.

[8-5] In this photograph, hard-working loggers can be seen using poles to move a raft of logs along a river.

LA FORESTRIE

8-4 et 8-5 : [8-4] Le ministère des Richesses naturelles et les organismes qui l'ont précédé se servaient de photographies pour la documentation de ses activités de lutte contre les incendies de forêts, de reboisement et de gestion des matières ligneuses, de même que pour la formation des gardes forestiers. On voit ici des travailleurs assembler une allingue, pour encadrer les billes perdues. L'allingue est ensuite acheminée vers la scierie par remorqueur.

[8-5] Dans cette photographie, de vaillants bûcherons guident la descente d'un train de billes sur l'eau à l'aide de gaffes.

8-6

8-7

8-8

8-6 to 8-8: These two booklets were produced by the Ontario Department of Lands and Forests and written by E.J. Zavitz, above, the province's first provincial forester and a man passionate about forestation. Zavitz felt that tree farming in the deserted areas of Ontario could make better use of the land while ensuring a wood supply, protecting the headwaters of streams, and providing habitats for local animals. To further this goal, Zavitz saw to it that tens of millions of tree seedlings were planted in areas of the province devastated by erosion.

8-6 à 8-8 : Ces deux brochures du ministère des Terres et Forêts de l'Ontario avaient été rédigées par E.J. Zavitz, ci-dessus premier « forestier de la province », qui était un fervent du reboisement. Selon Zavitz, l'établissement de fermes forestières dans les zones incultes était la clé d'une meilleure utilisation des terres : on garantirait par là un bon approvisionnement en bois, tout en protégeant la source des petits cours d'eau et en assurant un habitat à la faune de la région. Dans ce but, Zavitz avait ordonné la plantation de millions de jeunes arbres dans des parties de la province dévastées par l'érosion.

8-9

TRANSPORTATION

8-9: The Ministry of Transportation used photographs to monitor routine activities such as road construction and maintenance, as well as to document changes in rapid-transit technology and to record urban growth and infrastructure development. This early photo-graph of north Yonge Street shows three men taking a break from their roadwork to pose for the camera. There is a wealth of information in this image regarding types of equipment, modes of dress, and the homes and automobiles of the day.

LES TRANSPORTS

8-9 : Le ministère des Transports faisait appel à la pho-tographie pour assurer le suivi d'activités usuelles telles que la construction et l'entretien des routes, de même que pour documenter l'évolution des technologies du transport rapide, la croissance urbaine et les progrès de l'infrastructure. Cette photographie ancienne du nord de la rue Yonge fait voir trois ouvriers qui inter-rompent leurs travaux de voirie le temps de poser pour le photographe. Cette image est une mine d'informa-tion sur les types d'équipements, de vêtements, de résidences et de véhicules qui avaient cours à l'époque.

8-10 to 8-12: [8-10] Films by the Ministry of Transportation and its predecessors document the construction of Ontario's highway system from the Queen Elizabeth Way in the 1930s to the present, often making note of the specific engineering methods used. This early film pointed out that prison labour was used in building Highway 11 between Hearst and Geraldton.

[8-11 & 8-12] The Ministry of Transportation often employed cartoon figures and animation to promote road safety in creative ways. Elmer the Safety Elephant filmstrips were shown to thousands of Ontario school children. *Superplow* was one of several animated television commercials reminding drivers to pay attention to snowplows on highways.

8-10 à 8-12 : [8-10] Les films du ministère des Transports et des organismes qui l'ont précédé documentent l'aménagement du réseau routier de l'Ontario, depuis le Queen Elizabeth Way des années 1930 jusqu'à nos jours, souvent avec des explications sur les méthodes d'ingénierie employées. Ce film des débuts note qu'on a fait appel à des détenus pour construire le tronçon Hearst-Geraldton de la route 11.

[8-11 et 8-12] Le ministère des Transports a souvent utilisé l'animation et des personnages de bande dessinée pour promouvoir la sécurité routière de façon imaginative. Des milliers d'écoliers ontariens ont applaudi les films fixes mettant en vedette Elmer l'éléphant prudent. Plusieurs commerciaux animés étaient destinés à la télévision; voici *Superplow*, qui rappelle aux conducteurs de prendre garde aux chasse-neige.

8-10

8-11

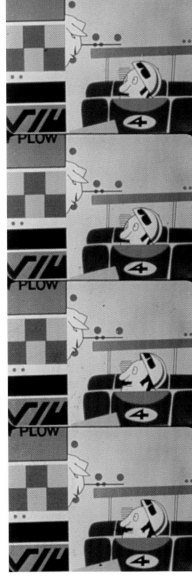

8-12

MINING

8-13 to 8-15: The Department of Mines and Northern Affairs, and its predecessors, produced many of its photographs during field investigations to document mining activities and equipment. This photograph below provides a glimpse into the harsh working environment of the miners. One is struck by the way the miners almost blend into their surroundings, except for those faces captured by the glare of the camera's flash.

LES MINES

8-13 et 8-15 : Un grand nombre des photographies du ministère des Mines et Affaires du Nord et des organismes qui l'ont précédé ont été prises au cours d'enquêtes sur le terrain visant à documenter les activités minières et l'équipement utilisé. La photographie ci-dessous donne une idée des dures conditions de travail des mineurs. Détail frappant : les visages qui se détachent sous l'éclair du flash, alors que les mineurs semblent ne faire qu'un avec le sombre décor.

8-13

8-14

8-15

HEALTH

8-16 & 8-17: [8-16] Even though many decades have elapsed since this photograph was taken, it demonstrates that at least some elements of a medical examination have not changed. As the nurse listens to the child's chest, family members anxiously look on.

[8-17] One cannot help but sympathize with these children as they nervously clutch their arms at an immunization clinic.

LA SANTÉ

8-16 et 8-17 : [8-16] Plusieurs décennies se sont écoulées depuis la prise de cette photographie, mais certains côtés de l'examen médical n'ont pas changé. Ici, l'infirmière ausculte un enfant, sous le regard anxieux des parents.

[8-17] On ne peut que s'attendrir à la vue de ces enfants, qui se palpent nerveusement le bras lors d'une séance de vaccination.

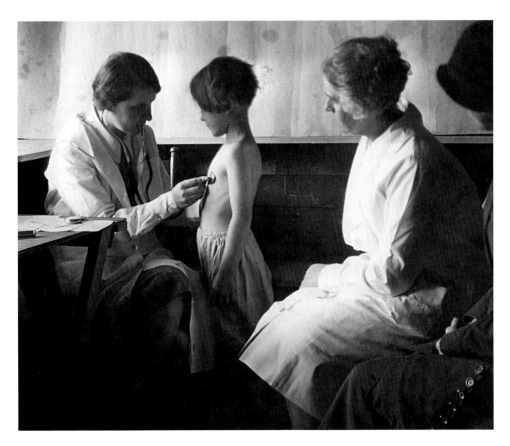

8-16

8-17

TOURISM

8-18 & 8-19: [8-18] Ontario has a long history of celebrating its natural tourist attractions and rich heritage. Here we see a couple visiting one of the province's many tourist bureaus.

[8-19] This photograph depicts a young man enjoying one of Ontario's natural pleasures: ice fishing.

LE TOURISME

8-18 et 8-19 : [8-18] C'est de longue date que l'Ontario fait valoir ses attraits touristiques et son riche patrimoine naturel. Voici un couple venu se renseigner dans l'un des nombreux bureaux de tourisme de la province.

[8-19] Dans cette photographie, un jeune homme s'adonne aux joies du plein air : la pêche blanche.

8-18

8-19

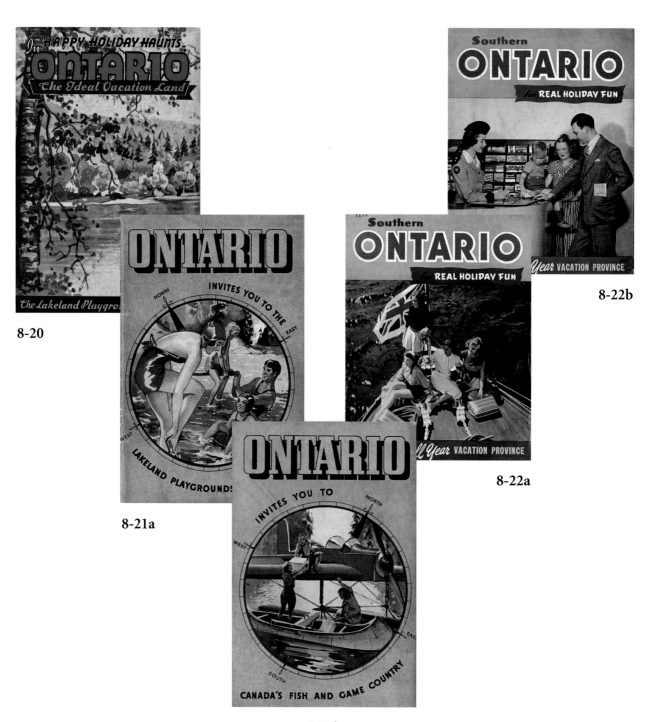

8-20

8-21a

8-21b

8-22a

8-22b

8-20 to 8-22: The Department of Travel and Publicity used these brochures to attract visitors to the province. Notice their lively colours and portrayal of idyllic scenes.

8-20 à 8-22 : Le ministère du Tourisme et de la Publicité diffusait ces brochures pour stimuler le tourisme dans la province. On remarque les scènes idylliques, aux brillantes couleurs.

8-23

8-23: This Ontario Travel and Publicity Bureau film, entitled *Holiday Horizons*, filmed in 1940, is the Archives' earliest government-produced tourism film. As was often the case with such tourism films, its opening narration made clear that the intended audience were Americans: 'Just over the border lies Ontario, America's playground'. The filmmakers were careful to include a car in the scene to draw attention to the high standards of Ontario's highways.

An examination of a series of Ontario tourism films over time would reveal changing attractions and marketing strategies. Whereas images of Niagara Falls have remained an enduring staple in the tourist trade, the Dionne quintuplets, who are also featured in *Holiday Horizons*, were unique to this era of Ontario's history.

8-23 : Ce film du Bureau du tourisme et de la publicité de l'Ontario, tourné en 1940 sous le titre *Holiday Horizons*, est le film touristique gouvernemental le plus ancien que possède les Archives. Comme c'est souvent la règle dans ce genre de document, on précise dès le départ le public visé, en l'occurrence les Américains : [traduction] « Il suffit de traverser la frontière pour se trouver en Ontario, ce grand terrain de jeu de l'Amérique. » Les producteurs ont eu soin de placer une automobile dans le tableau, pour attirer l'attention sur la qualité des routes de l'Ontario.

L'examen sur une certaine période des films touristiques de l'Ontario atteste l'évolution des attractions et des stratégies de commercialisation. Les chutes Niagara sont demeurées une valeur sûre pour le commerce touristique, alors que les quintuplées Dionne, en vedette dans *Holiday Horizons*, s'identifient à cette tranche de l'histoire ontarienne.

AGRICULTURE

8-24 to 8-26: [8-24] The Ontario government campaigned to attract new immigrants by distributing pamphlets such as the one shown here. Their aim to encourage farmers in particular is clear from the title shown on the cover.

[8-25 & 8-26] Government agricultural representatives throughout the province documented farm and rural scenes. The farm workers and families featured in these photographs stand proudly amidst the bounty of their crops.

L'AGRICULTURE

8-24 à 8-26 : [8-24] Le gouvernement de l'Ontario s'efforçait d'attirer de nouveaux immigrants, en distribuant des brochures analogues à celle-ci. L'intention de recruter des agriculteurs est claire, ainsi que l'exprime le titre en couverture.

[8-25 et 8-26] Dans toutes les parties de la province, les représentants du ministère de l'Agriculture documentaient la vie dans les campagnes et dans les fermes. Les travailleurs agricoles et leurs familles qu'on voit ici posent avec fierté, sur un fond de généreuses moissons.

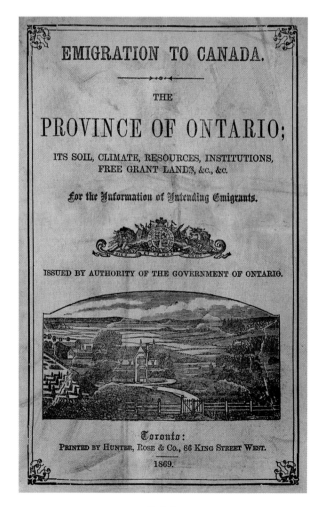

8-24

8-25

8-26

8-27 & 8-28: [8-27] The Ontario Farm Service Force was established in 1941 and until 1955, continued to organize and provide farm labour, particularly during the harvest season. This image illustrates that many of those who participated in the program were women.

[8-28] Those who grew up in eastern Canada have childhood memories of visiting the sugar bush. The children in this photograph look on with fascination as they watch the transformation of maple sap to syrup.

8-27 et 8-28 : [8-27] Le service d'ouvriers agricoles, qui a existé de 1941 à 1955, avait pour but de recruter de la main-d'œuvre, en particulier pour la saison des récoltes. Cette image témoigne qu'un bon nombre des participants au programme étaient des femmes.

[8-28] Pour qui a grandi dans l'Est du Canada, les parties de sucre de son enfance sont inoubliables. Les enfants de cette photographie sont fascinés par la transformation de l'eau d'érable en sirop.

8-27

8-28

8-29 & 8-30: [8-29] Women's institutes were a vitally important source of information and support for farm families.

[8-30] This stark and beautiful image of farm women also features some impressive corn. Many farmers over the years have striven to win awards for their crops – which compete for recognition as the biggest, the tallest, or the best in their category.

8-29 et 8-30 : [8-29] Les Women's Institutes (instituts féminins) constituaient une source d'éducation et de soutien cruciale pour les familles d'agriculteurs.

[8-30] Dans cette belle et sobre image, les deux fermières sont flanquées d'impressionnants spécimens de maïs. Depuis toujours, les fermiers rivalisent pour les prix et médailles des plus belles réussites – c'est à qui remporterait la palme du plus gros, du plus grand ou du meilleur spécimen de sa catégorie.

Ontario Department of Agriculture

WOMEN'S INSTITUTES

BULLETIN 186

CHILDREN

Their Care, Training and Happiness as Future Citizens

BY

J. J. KELSO, Superintendent of Neglected Children, Province of Ontario

Printed by L. K. CAMERON, Printer to the King's Most Excellent Majesty, TORONTO, ONT., December, 1910.

8-29

8-30

8-31 & 8-32: The Department of Agriculture was the first arm of the Ontario government to recognize the potential of motion pictures as a means of reaching its clientele. Until the 1960s, the department's film productions were made at the Ontario Agricultural College in Guelph. The film about potatoes on the near right is representative of the many instructional films that were made with a rural, agricultural audience in mind.

Reflecting a changing Ontario, the ministry's films began to target the urban Ontario audience by the late 1960s, as in the film on the far right, which profiles the vegetable growing and packing industry of the Holland Marsh. These later films informed Ontarians about how food reached the grocery stores and then their dinner plates.

8-31 et 8-32 : Le ministère de l'Agriculture a été le premier organisme du gouvernement de l'Ontario à exploiter le film cinématographique pour rejoindre sa clientèle. Jusqu'aux années 1960, les productions filmées du ministère ont été réalisées au Collège d'agriculture de l'Ontario, à Guelph. Le documentaire tourné sur les pommes de terre (image de gauche), est représentatif de nombreux films éducatifs visant une audience rurale et agricole.

Reflets de l'évolution de l'Ontario, les films du ministère commençaient, à la fin des années 1960, à cibler la population urbaine, comme le montre celui sur la culture des légumes et l'industrie de l'emballage à Holland Marsh (image de droite). Ces films plus récents renseignaient les Ontariens sur les étapes que devaient franchir les aliments avant d'arriver sur les tablettes de l'épicerie et, en dernier lieu, sur la table familiale.

8-31

8-32

8-33 to 8-35: Movie theatres from across Ontario submitted photographs to the Motion Picture Censorship and Theatre Inspection Branch, part of the Ontario Treasury Department, as visual proof of compliance with safety standards. These examples from Windsor and Ottawa are but three such photographs in the Archives' large collection.

LA DIRECTION DES CINÉMAS

8-33 à 8-35 : Dans toute la province, les cinémas devaient présenter des photographies à la Direction de la censure des films et de l'inspection des cinémas, qui faisait partie du ministère du Trésor de l'Ontario, comme preuve visuelle de leur conformité aux normes de sécurité. Ces trois photographies, de Windsor et d'Ottawa, sont exemplaires de la vaste collection des Archives.

8-33

8-34

8-35

ECONOMIC DEVELOPMENT

8-36 & 8-37: [8-36] During the 1960s, Ontario actively marketed itself to the world. While the Department of Economics and Development was busy sending its minister on 'trade crusades' to Europe, Asia, and elsewhere, Ontario television ads encouraged Canadians at home to 'buy Canadian' to support Ontario manufacturing jobs. This ad says: 'Buy a hippo if you must, but for almost everything else buy Canadian.'

[8-37] The world came to Canada and Montreal in 1967. The film *A Place to Stand*, which showcased Ontario's natural resources, economic potential, and recreational activities, played endlessly in the Ontario Pavilion at Expo '67. Those who saw the film may remember it primarily for its catchy title song with the refrain: 'Ontari-ari-ari-o.' However, the film was also noteworthy for its innovative use of multiple images, as seen in this shot. The film won the Canadian Film of the Year Award and an Academy Award.

DÉVELOPPEMENT ECONOMIQUE

8-36 et 8-37 : [8-36] Pendant les années 1960, l'Ontario a voulu se faire connaître en menant, dans le monde entier, de vigoureuses campagnes de commercialisation. Le ministère de l'Économie et du Développement dépêchait son ministre en « mission commerciale » dans divers pays d'Europe, d'Asie et d'ailleurs, tandis que des annonces à la télévision ontarienne incitaient les Canadiens à « l'achat chez-nous » comme appui à l'emploi dans le secteur manufacturier. Selon cette annonce : [traduction] « Sauf si vous cherchez une girafe, vous pouvez faire pratiquement tous vos achats au Canada ».

[8-37] En 1967, l'univers fait son entrée à Montréal et au Canada. Le film *A Place to Stand*, qui faisait valoir les ressources naturelles, le potentiel économique et les activités de loisirs de la province, était projeté en continu au pavillon de l'Ontario d'Expo 67. Ceux qui ont vu le film n'ont pas oublié son entraînante chanson-titre et le refrain : « Ontari-ari-ari-o ». Mais, comme le montre ce plan, le film se démarquait par une utilisation nouvelle de l'image composite; couronné par un oscar, il a été consacré « film canadien de l'année ».

8-36

8-37

8-1: Oxen hauling tree-length logs [between 1920 and 1925], E.J. Zavitz (Ministry of Natural Resources Photo Library Collection, RG 1-448-1, 370. I0006770)

8-2: Male students in a home-economics class at the Ottawa Normal School [ca. 1950] (Ministry of Education, Photographs and historical files / Ottawa Normal School, RG 2-251)

8-3: Female students in a shop class at the Ottawa Normal School [ca. 1950] (Ministry of Education, Photographs and historical files / Ottawa Normal School, RG 2-251)

8-4: Men driving logs on the water during the yellow-birch boom [ca. 1915], E.J. Zavitz (Ministry of Natural Resources Photo Library collection, RG 1-448-1, 358. I0006763)

8-5: Loggers poling a raft [ca. 1900], E.J. Zavitiz (Ministry of Natural Resources, Photo Library collection, RG 1-448-1, 372. I 0006773)

8-6: E.J. Zavitz [ca. 1953] (Ministry of Natural Resources, Photo Library collection, RG 1-448-1, 131)

8-7: *Fifty Years of Reforestation in Ontario, 1958, E.J. Zavitz, Ontario* Department of Lands and Forests (Archives of Ontario Library, Gov. Doc. L&F, misc. box 16)

8-8: *Hardwood Trees of Ontario with Bark Characteristics,* 1959, E.J. Zavitz, Ontario Department of Lands and Forests (Archives of Ontario Library, Gov. Doc. L&F, misc. box 16)

8-9: Men and tractor doing road construction on Yonge Street North [ca. 1920] (Highways historical collection, RG 14-162-5-168, vol. 5, 69)

8-10: Title frames from the motion-picture film *Closing the Gap in the Highway across Canada, 1941-1942* (Ministry of Transportation, Audio visual productions, RG 14-152-1-9)

8-11: Frames from film *Elmer our hero* [1968?] (Ministry of Transportation, Audio visual productions, RG 14-152-1-22)

8-12: Frames from animated television commercial *Superplow* [197-] (Public Service Announcements / Ministry of Transportation and Communications, RG 14-154-1-5)

8-13: Group of miners in a mine [ca. 1905] (Department of Mines and Northern Affairs publication photographs, RG 13-30-1-4. I0004648)

8-14: Second level of the Creighton mine [ca. 1905] (Department of Mines and Northern Affairs publication photographs, RG 13-30-1-5. I0004649)

8-15: *1954: A Year of Achievement for Ontario Mines*, 1954, preliminary report of the Ontario Department of Mines (Archives of Ontario Library, Gov. Doc. Mining, 1954 Reports)

8-16: Child receiving a medical examination, New Liskeard, Ontario, 1929 (Department of Health, public health nursing records, RG 10-30-2, 2.18.7. I0005227)

8-17: Children lined up to receive their needles at an immunization clinic in Algoma District, 1932 (Department of Health, public health nursing records, RG 10-30-2, 2.15.3. I0005225)

8-18: Scene of tourists visiting an information booth, 27 January 1949 (Department of Travel and Publicity, Tourism-promotion photographs, RG 65-35-1, 5-B-759. AO3942)

8-19: Man ice-fishing, 5 February 1959 (Department of Travel and Publicity, Tourism-promotion photographs, RG 65-35-1, 10999-5-B-759)

8-20: *Happy Holiday Haunts: Ontario: The Ideal Vacation Land*, 1934 (Archives of Ontario Library, Gov. Doc. T&P, box 2, no. 10)

8-21 a & b: *Ontario Invites You to the Lakeland Playgrounds of Canada* [ca. 1950] (Archives of Ontario Library, Gov. Doc. T&P, box 2, no. 13)

8-22 a & b: *Southern Ontario: Real Holiday Fun*, 1949 (Library collection, Gov. Doc. T&P, box 2, no. 25)

8-23: Opening images from motion-picture film *Holiday Horizons,* 1940 (Mitchell F. Hepburn fonds, F 10-1-0-8)

8-24: *Emigration to Canada. The Province of Ontario: Its Soil, Climate, Resources, Institutions, Free Land Grants, etc. For the Information of Intending Emigrants,* 1869, Government of Ontario (Archives of Ontario Library, Gov. Doc. A, misc. box 2, no. 1, copy 2)

8-25: Family of three standing in a wheat field in Essex [between 1909 and 1930] (Department of Agriculture, Agricultural Representative Photograph Albums, RG 16-274, Album 1, 8)

8-26: Men and one woman standing in a field of tobacco in Essex [between 1909 and 1930] (Department of Agriculture, Photograph Albums, RG 16-274, Album 1, 8. AO 5936)

8-27: Female farm workers sitting on the bed of a truck, ca. 1950 (Department of Agriculture. Ontario Farm Service Force records, RG 16-20-0-10. I0006645)

8-28: Children touring a sugar bush, Mountsberg, Ontario, 1979 (Department of Agriculture, Photographs of the Communications Branch of the Ministry of Agriculture and Food, RG 16-276-1, 79-B67. I0004487)

8-29: *Children: Their Care, Training and Happiness as Future Citizens*, 1910, Women's Institutes, Bulletin no. 186, Ontario Department of Agriculture (Archives of Ontario Library, Pamphlet 1910, no. 75)

8-30: Two women standing beside very tall stalks of corn [ca. 1920] (Department of Agriculture, Agricultural Representative Photograph Albums, RG 16-274, Album 3, 59. AO 5940)

8-31: Frames from motion-picture film *Potatoes from Planting to Harvesting* [1955?] (Ministry of Agriculture and Food motion-picture films, RG 16-35-0-39-1)

8-32: Frames from motion-picture film *Black Magic*, 1974 (Ministry of Agriculture and Food motion-picture films, RG 16-35-0-250-1)

8-33: The Imperial Theatre, Ottawa, 1938 (Motion Picture Censorship and Theatre Inspection Branch, Theatre photographs, RG 56-11-0-179-5. AO 2376)

8-34: The Capitol Theatre, Windsor, 1948 (Motion Picture Censorship and Theatre Inspection Branch, Theatre photographs, RG 56-11-0-353-2)

8-35: The Centre Theatre, Windsor, 1949 (Motion Picture Censorship and Theatre Inspection Branch, Theatre photographs, RG 56-11-0-354-3)

8-36: Frames from Ontario Trade Crusade television ad, *Hippo*, 1965 (Ontario economic-development television commercials, RG 9-134-0-1)

8-37: Frames from motion-picture film *A Place to Stand*, 1967 (Department of Trade and Development special-projects films, RG 9-136-1-4-1)

LÉGENDES

8-1 : Bœufs de trait attelés à un charroi de grumes [entre 1920 et 1925], E. J. Zavitz (Collection de la photothèque du ministère des Richesses naturelles, RG 1-448-1, 370. I0006770)

8-2 : Étudiants dans une classe d'arts ménagers, à l'École normale d'Ottawa [v. 1950] (Ministère de l'Éducation, Photographies et documents historiques/École normale d'Ottawa, RG 2-251)

8-3 : Étudiantes dans une classe de métiers, à l'École normale d'Ottawa [v. 1950] (Ministère de l'Éducation, Photographies et documents historiques/École normale d'Ottawa, RG 2-251)

8-4 : Des draveurs assemblent une chaîne de billes, du temps où le bouleau jaune était en vogue [v. 1915], E. J. Zavitz (Collection de la photothèque du ministère des Richesses naturelles, RG 1-448-1, 358. I0006763)

8-5 : Des draveurs font avancer un radeau de billes à la gaffe [v. 1900], E. J. Zavitz (Collection de la photothèque du ministère des Richesses naturelles, RG 1-448-1, 372, I0006773)

8-6 : E. J. Zavitz [v. 1953] (Collection de la photothèque du ministère des Richesses naturelles, RG 1-448-1, 131)

8-7 : *Fifty Years of Reforestation in Ontario*, 1958, E. J. Zavitz, ministère des Terres et Forêts de l'Ontario (Bibliothèque des Archives publiques de l'Ontario, Gov. Doc. L&F, boîte mixte 16)

8-8 : *Hardwood Trees of Ontario with Bark Characteristics*, 1959, E. J. Zavitz, ministère des Terres et Forêts de l'Ontario (Bibliothèque des Archives publiques de l'Ontario, Gov. Doc. L&F, boîte mixte 16)

8-9 : Ouvriers et tracteur pendant des travaux de voirie, rue Yonge Nord [v. 1920] (Collection historique sur les routes, RG 14-162-5-168, vol. 5, 69)

8-10 : Images de titres du film *Closing the Gap in the Highway across Canada, 1941-1942* (Productions audio-visuelles du ministère des Transports, RG 14-152-1-9)

8-11 : Images du film *Elmer our hero* [1968?] (Productions audio-visuelles du ministère des Transports, RG 14-152-1-22)

8-12 : Images tirées de l'annonce télévisée *Superplow* [197?] (Messages d'intérêt public du ministère des Transports et des Communications, RG 14-154-1-5)

8-13 : Au deuxième niveau de la mine Creighton [v. 1905] (Photographies de publications du ministère des Mines et Affaires du Nord, RG 13-30-1-5. I0004649)

8-14 : Groupe de mineurs dans une mine [v. 1905] (Photographies de publications du ministère des Mines et Affaires du Nord, RG 13-30-1-4. I0004648)

8-15 : 1954: *A Year of Achievement for Ontario Mines*, 1954, rapport préliminaire du ministère des Mines de l'Ontario (Bibliothèque des Archives publiques de l'Ontario, Gov. Doc. Mining, rapports de 1954)

8-16 : Un enfant au contrôle médical, New Liskeard (Ontario), 1929 (Ministère de la Santé, dossiers des services infirmiers de santé publique, RG 10-30-2, 2.18.7, I0005227)

8-17 : Des enfants font la queue lors d'une séance de vaccination, dans le district d'Algoma, 1932 (Ministère de la Santé, dossiers des services infirmiers de santé publique, RG 10-30-2, 2.15.3, I0005225)

8-18 : Touristes dans un bureau de renseignements, 27 janvier 1949 (Photographies de promotion touristique du ministère du Tourisme et de la Publicité, RG 65-35-1, 5-B-759. AO3942)

8-19 : À la pêche blanche, 5 février 1959 (Photographies de promotion touristique du ministère du Tourisme et de la Publicité, RG 65-35-1, 10999-5-B-759)

8-20 : *Happy Holiday Haunts: Ontario: The Ideal Vacation Land*, 1934) (Bibliothèque des Archives publiques de l'Ontario, Gov. Doc. T&P, boîte 2, no 10)

8-21 a et b : *Ontario Invites You to the Lakeland Playgrounds of Canada* [v. 1950] (Bibliothèque des Archives publiques de l'Ontario, Gov. Doc. T&P, boîte 2, no 13)

8-22 a et b : *Southern Ontario: Real Holiday Fun*, 1949 (Collection de la bibliothèque, Gov. Doc. T&P, boîte 2, no 25)

8-23 : Premières images du film *Holiday Horizons*, 1940 (Fonds Mitchell F. Hepburn, F 10-1-0-8)

8-24 : *Emigration to Canada. The Province of Ontario: Its Soil, Climate, Resources, Institutions, Free Land Grants, etc. For the Information of Intending Emigrants*, 1869, Gouvernement de l'Ontario (Bibliothèque des Archives publiques de l'Ontario, Gov. Doc. A, boîte mixte 2, no 1, exemplaire 2)

8-25 : Petite famille dans un champ de blé, comté d'Essex [entre 1909 et 1930] (Albums de photos de représentants agricoles du ministère de l'Agriculture, RG 16-274, Album 1, 8)

8-26 : Des hommes et une femme posent dans un champ de tabac, comté d'Essex [entre 1909 et 1930] (Albums de photos de représentants agricoles du ministère de l'Agriculture, RG 16-274, Album , 8. AO 5936)

8-27 : Travailleuses agricoles assises sur la plateforme d'un camion, v. 1950 (Ministère de l'Agriculture, dossiers des Forces du service agricole de l'Ontario, RG 16-20-0-10, I0006645)

8-28 : Des enfants en partie de sucre, Mountsberg (Ontario) 1979 (Photographies de la Direction des communications du ministère de l'Agriculture et de l'Alimentation, RG 16-276-1, 79--67, I0004487)

8-29 : *Children: Their Care, Training and Happiness as Future Citizens*, 1910, Women's Institutes, Bulletin no 186, Ministère de l'Agriculture de l'Ontario (Bibliothèque des Archives publiques de l'Ontario, brochure 1910, no 75)

8-30 : Deux femmes debout, à côté de gigantesques tiges de maïs [v. 1920] (Albums de photos de représentants agricoles du ministère de l'Agriculture, RG 16-274, album 3, 59. AO 5940)

8-31 : Images du film *Potatoes from Planting to Harvesting* [1955?] (Films cinématographiques du ministère de l'Agriculture et de l'Alimentation, RG 16-35-0-39-1)

8-32 : Images du film *Black Magic*, 1974 (Films cinématographiques du ministère de l'Agriculture et de l'Alimentation, RG 16-35-0-250-1)

8-33 : Le cinéma Imperial, Ottawa, 1938 (Direction de la censure des films et de l'inspection des cinémas, photographies des cinémas, RG 56-11-0-179-5. AO 2376)

8-34 : Le cinéma Capitol, Windsor, 1948 (Direction de la censure des films et de l'inspection des cinémas, photographies des cinémas, RG 56-11-0-353-2)

8-35 : Le cinéma Centre, Windsor, 1949 (Direction de la censure des films et de l'inspection des cinémas, photographies des cinémas, RG 56-11-0-354-3)

8-36 : Images d'une annonce télévisée (*Hippo*) de la campagne de promotion commerciale de l'Ontario, 1965 (Commerciaux télévisés visant le développement économique de l'Ontario, RG 9-134-0-1)

8-37 : Images du film *A Place to Stand*, 1967 (Films des projets spéciaux, ministère du Développement économique et du Commerce, RG 9-136-1-4-1)

9

PHOTOJOURNALISM

LE PHOTOJOURNALISME

9-1

Pictures are noticeably absent from the pages of nineteenth-century newspapers, apart from the occasional engraving amidst a sea of minute type. Readers of the time who wanted to see pictures along with a news story had to buy an 'illustrated' journal, which appeared less frequently than the average newspaper and thus had less in the way of current news, not just by our standards but even by those of the period.

All this changed around 1880. With the introduction of small, lightweight cameras and the half-tone press (which allowed photographs to be reproduced on the same page as text), the news business was completely transformed. Photography became popular for use in newspapers and magazines – and also signalled the beginning of the end for engravers and illustrators. Technological innovations in photography, as well as the wire transmission of news stories across the globe, meant that the people of Ontario were informed of world events faster than ever before. By the 1930s, the number of outlets for publishing news or human-interest stories had exploded and the photojournalist had a large market at hand for photographs of natural and man-made disasters, political campaigns and protests, achievements by local artists and athletes, and visiting celebrities.

The photojournalists of the mid-twentieth century used photographs to tell a story. Their skills were considerable, as was apparent in many instances when a photograph not only decorated a news story but enhanced its content; indeed, some photographs were so evocative that they could stand on their own as a photo essay, rendering words redundant. In this period, the heyday of photojournalism, newspaper and magazine photographs helped the public understand difficult issues such as poverty and racial intolerance and also shed light on social movements such as feminism.

The Archives of Ontario has acquired the work of several talented photojournalists – Herb Nott, Gordon W. Powley, Gilbert A. Milne, Julien LeBourdais, and others – who worked for a variety of papers and popular magazines, including the Toronto *Daily Star*, the *Star Weekly Magazine*, *Liberty Magazine*, the Toronto *News*, the *Globe and Mail*, and *Maclean's* magazine. Their photographs in the following pages – just a small sample of a collection consisting of more than 300,000 images – portray a variety of well-known people, underscore the transformation of journalism in the twentieth century, and depict a mid-century Ontario in the midst of far-reaching change: the war effort of the 1940s, the urban and industrial growth of the 1950s, and the peace marches of the 1960s.

Dans les journaux du dix-neuvième siècle, l'absence d'illustrations saute aux yeux – exception faite de rares gravures, noyées dans un océan de caractères microscopiques. Les lecteurs qui voulaient voir leurs actualités accompagnées d'images devaient se procurer un journal « illustré », à parution moins fréquente et aux nouvelles logiquement moins fraîches, d'après les standards non seulement d'aujourd'hui mais aussi du temps.

Tout cela devait changer vers 1880. L'apparition d'appareils photo maniables, plus légers, et de la similigravure (pour la reproduction de photographies sur la même page que le texte) vient révolutionner la sphère de l'actualité. Les photographies deviennent courantes dans les journaux et revues, ce qui réduit d'autant le rôle des graveurs et illustrateurs. Grâce aux innovations technologiques en photographie doublées de la transmission télégraphique des reportages partout dans le monde, la population ontarienne est mise au courant de ce qui se passe, dans tous les coins du globe et plus rapidement que jamais. Vers 1930, les débouchés pour les nouvelles et les chroniques spécialisées se multiplient, et le photojournaliste dispose d'un vaste marché pour ses images de catastrophes naturelles et drames humains, campagnes et manifestations politiques, exploits sportifs, réalisations artistiques et célébrités de passage.

Les photojournalistes du milieu du vingtième siècle mettent la photographie au service du reportage. Ils y font preuve d'une compétence remarquable, de sorte que, bien souvent, la photographie cristallise la teneur d'un d'article en plus de l'illustrer. En fait, certaines images ont une telle puissance d'évocation qu'elles peuvent à elles seules exprimer un contenu, rendant le texte inutile : c'est la naissance du reportage photographique. Pendant cet âge d'or du photojournalisme, les photos des journaux et revues aident les citoyens à prendre conscience des difficiles problèmes de pauvreté et d'intolérance raciale et mettent en lumière certains mouvements sociaux, dont le féminisme.

Les Archives publiques de l'Ontario possèdent des œuvres de plusieurs photojournalistes éminents, Herb Nott, Gordon W. Powley, Gilbert A. Milne et Julien LeBourdais pour ne citer que ceux-là, qui publiaient dans toute une gamme de journaux et de revues populaires, entre autres le *Daily Star*, le *Star Weekly Magazine*, le *Liberty Magazine*, le *News* de Toronto, le *Globe and Mail* et le *Maclean's*. Au fil des pages suivantes, un choix de leurs photographies – mince échantillon d'une collection qui renferme plus de 300 000 images – forme une galerie de personnalités, illustre la transformation du journalisme au vingtième siècle et dépeint l'Ontario du milieu de ce siècle dans les remous de phénomènes à longue portée : effort de guerre des années 1940, explosion industrielle et urbaine des années 1950, manifestations pacifistes des années 1960.

9-2 to 9-4: In his lengthy career as a professional photographer, Herb Nott shot more than 130,000 pictures. Beginning in the late 1930s as a studio photographer with Roy Kemp and Christina Huidekoper, he produced mostly college graduation portraits before entering into a long association with the Toronto *Star*, which hired him to cover the British royal visit of 1939. He later undertook many contract assignments with the *Star* while continuing to expand his studio.

After the war, Nott focused mainly on corporate and portrait photography, producing photos of executives, products, and buildings for annual reports and advertisements. He also undertook numerous contract assignments with *Liberty Magazine*, the Toronto *Star Weekly*, the Montreal *Standard*, and *Weekend Magazine*.

[9-2 to 9-4] The town of Iroquois, situated on the shores of the St Lawrence River near Brockville, was entirely relocated during the construction of the St Lawrence Seaway. By 1957, many buildings in Iroquois had been relocated, with some moved to Upper Canada Village. Much of the town was flooded and today foundations and parts of other structures from the old town of Iroquois are under water.

Nott photographed the town in 1941 for a story in the Toronto *Star Weekly*. This series of photos is reminiscent of the photo essays appearing in the magazines *Life* and *Look*, which were popular in Canada.

LES ANNÉES 1940

9-2 à 9-4 : Au cours de sa longue carrière, Herb Nott a pris plus de 130 000 clichés. Débutant à la fin des années 1930 à titre de photographe de studio chez Roy Kemp et Christina Huidekoper, il réalise principalement des portraits de finissants de collèges avant de conclure une association à long terme avec le *Star* de Toronto; ce journal avait d'abord retenu ses services en 1939, pour couvrir la visite du couple royal britannique. Il devait par la suite effectuer de nombreux travaux pour le compte du *Star*, tout en travaillant à l'expansion de son entreprise.

Après la guerre, Nott exécute surtout des portraits et photographies d'entreprises : images de dirigeants, de produits et d'immeubles destinées aux rapports annuels et à la publicité. Il accepte également maintes commandes pour le *Liberty Magazine*, le *Star Weekly* de Toronto, le *Standard* de Montréal, et le *Weekend Magazine*.

[9-2 à 9-4] Pendant la construction de la voie maritime, la petite ville d'Iroquois, sur la rive du Saint-Laurent à proximité de Brockville, est entièrement déménagée. En 1957, nombre d'édifices se dressent sur un nouvel emplacement, alors que d'autres sont passés à l'Upper Canada Village. La ville a été immergée en grande partie et, aujourd'hui, les fondations et certaines parties d'autres constructions du vieux centre ont disparu sous l'eau.

Nott a photographié la ville en 1941, pour illustrer un article du *Star Weekly* de Toronto. Cette série de photos rappelle les reportages photographiques que faisaient paraître les magazines *Life* et *Look*, populaires au Canada.

9-2

9-3

9-4

9-5 to 9-8: Gordon W. Powley's collection of approximately 1,900 negatives depicts Toronto people and events from the early 1940s to the mid-1960s. Powley began his career in 1938 as a staff writer and later a photographer with the *Globe and Mail*. He opened his own studio in 1942 and did freelance work for several publications, including the Toronto *Daily Star*, *Star Weekly Magazine*, *Liberty Magazine*, the Toronto *News*, and the *Globe and Mail*.

Powley's photographic legacy includes many formal portraits of well-known Ontarians and visiting celebri-ties. He also focused on industrial development, arts and sporting events, recreational and leisure activities, election campaigns, labour disputes, urban growth, resource exploitation in northern Ontario, and the domestic war effort during the Second World War.

In fact, photojournalists played an integral role in documenting and supporting the domestic war effort. There are numerous images promoting the sale of victory bonds, documenting the female workforce, and depicting life on the home front.

9-5 à 9-8 : La collection Gordon W. Powley réunit quelque 1 900 clichés, qui représentent des personnages et événements du début des années 1940 au milieu des années 1960, à Toronto. En 1938, Powley entre d'abord au service du *Globe and Mail*, à titre de rédacteur attitré, puis de photographe. Il ouvre son propre studio en 1942 et travaille à titre autonome pour plusieurs publications, dont le *Daily Star* de Toronto, le *Star Weekly Magazine*, le *Liberty Magazine*, le *News* de Toronto et le *Globe and Mail*.

Le legs photographique Powley renferme de nombreux portraits officiels d'Ontariens connus et de célébrités de passage. Le photographe s'est attaché à dépeindre également le développement industriel, les événements artistiques et sportifs, les activités récréatives, les campagnes électorales, les conflits ouvriers, la croissance urbaine, l'exploitation des ressources dans le nord de la province ainsi que l'effort de guerre intérieur pendant la Deuxième Guerre mondiale.

En fait, les auteurs de reportages photographiques ont joué un rôle important de documentation et de soutien de l'effort de guerre intérieur. Quantité de ces images annoncent les obligations de la Victoire, documentent le travail féminin et décrivent le quotidien sur le front civil, au pays.

9-5

9-6

9-7

9-8

9-9

9-9: In 1947, the United Nations General Assembly passed a resolution marking 24 October as United Nations Day in order to garner support for and publi- cize the aims and achievements of the UN. Huge crowds turned out to watch parades and celebrations held to mark the occasion.

9-9 : En 1947, une résolution de l'Assemblée générale des Nations Unies consacre le 24 octobre comme fête des Nations Unies, dans le but de faire connaître les objectifs et réalisations de l'organisation et de lui rallier des appuis. Des foules monstres se pressent dans les rues pour voir les défilés et participer aux manifesta- tions tenues à cette occasion.

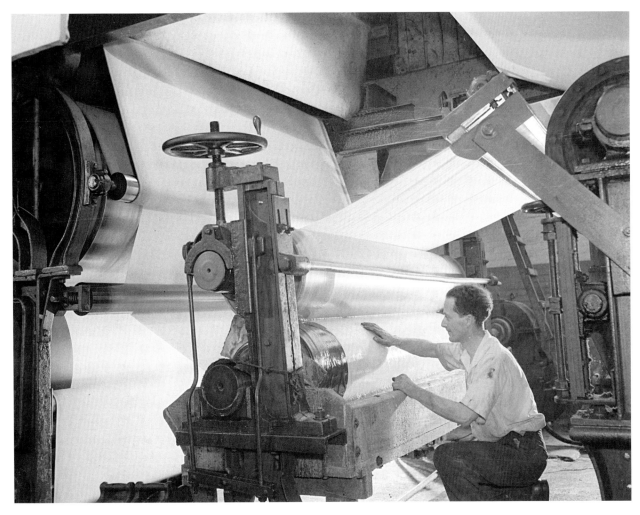

9-10

9-10: The availability of cheap hydro-electric power from nearby Niagara Falls encouraged many heavy industries such as the pulp and paper mill depicted here, to move to the Thorold/St Catharines area, leading to increased prosperity for the region.

9-10 : La disponibilité d'une énergie hydroélectrique à bon compte, en raison de la proximité des chutes Niagara, incite maintes industries lourdes, comme l'usine de pâtes et papiers représentie ici, à s'implanter dans la zone Thorold-St. Catharines, pour la plus grande prospérité de la région.

9-11 to 9-13: Gilbert A. Milne was born into a family of professional photographers. His family relocated from Alberta to Toronto when he was a young boy and Milne worked in the family studio before opening his own in 1945. During the late 1940s and 1950s, he ran a national photographic service for Canadian Press. Among some of his professional accomplishments were the creation of the Canadian Press national-picture network and the introduction of photographic innovations such as the mobile darkroom. Eventually, Milne gave up his Canadian Press contract and focused on his commercial studio.

The nine hundred Milne negatives acquired by the Archives in 1971 document Toronto's post-war urban expansion as well as members of its arts, academic, and broadcasting communities. In addition to formal studio portraits, Milne enjoyed taking more informal photographs of his subjects in their homes or workplaces. These settings provided important contextual information and likely made the subject feel more at ease.

9-11 à 9-13 : Gilbert A. Milne était issu d'une famille de photographes professionnels. Sa famille, originaire de l'Alberta, s'établit à Toronto alors qu'il est encore enfant, et Milne travaille au studio familial avant d'ouvrir le sien, en 1945. À la fin des années 1940 et pendant les années 1950, il dirige un service photographique national pour le compte de la Presse canadienne. Parmi ses réalisations, on relève la création du réseau photographique national de la Presse canadienne et l'introduction de nouveautés telles que le camion laboratoire. Par la suite, Milne met fin à sa collaboration avec la Presse canadienne pour se consacrer à son studio commercial.

Les neuf cents négatifs de Milne dont les Archives ont fait l'acquisition en 1971 documentent l'expansion urbaine d'après-guerre à Toronto, de même que certains personnages de ses milieux artistique, universitaire et médiatique. Parallèlement aux portraits formels en studio, Milne se plaisait à représenter ses sujets de façon plus détendue, dans leur milieu de travail ou dans leur foyer. Ces décors sont riches en information contextuelle et devaient certainement mettre les sujets plus à l'aise.

9-11

9-12

9-13

9-14 to 9-16: [9-14] When Hurricane Hazel struck Toronto in October 1954, more than fifteen centimetres of rain fell in less than twenty-four hours. As a result, creeks and rivers overflowed their banks, killing eighty-one people, washing away homes and roads, and wreaking millions of dollars of damage. Following the flood, the remaining homes and buildings were moved from the floodplains and replaced by what are now popular recreational sites and parkland.

[9-15 & 9-16] The 1950's marked a period of change and prosperity in Ontario. The return of the Korean war veterans meant a respite from participation in the war and global strife. Ontarians also saw significant growth and development in its major cities as reflected in this image of a changing Yonge Street.

LES ANNÉES 1950

9-14 à 9-16 : [9-14] Lorsque l'ouragan Hazel frappe Toronto en octobre 1954, on enregistre plus de quinze centimètres de pluie en moins de vingt-quatre heures. Une crue exceptionnelle des ruisseaux et rivières fait quatre-vingt-une victimes, emportant sur son passage maisons et routes et entraînant des millions de dollars en dommages. Après l'inondation, les maisons et immeubles épargnés sont déplacés, et l'on aménage dans les plaines d'inondation des parcs et terrains de jeux, aujourd'hui très fréquentés.

[9-15 et 9-16] Pour les Ontariens, les années 1950 ont été une période de changements et de prospérité. Le retour des vétérans de la guerre de Corée marquait un répit dans la participation canadienne aux conflits mondiaux. Les grandes villes ont vécu une croissance et un développement illustrées par cette photographie de la rue Yonge (Toronto) en pleine évolution.

9-14

9-15

9-16

9-17 & 9-18: Peace demonstrations were quite common in 1960s Toronto. Queen's Park and City Hall saw their share of them.

LES ANNÉES 1960

9-17 et 9-18 : Pendant les années 1960, les manifestations pacifistes étaient courantes à Toronto. Queen's Park et l'hôtel de ville en ont vu défiler un bon nombre.

9-17

9-18

9-19 to 9-21: Julien LeBourdais began his professional career as a freelance photographer in 1965. Among his clients were the Toronto *Daily Star*, United Press International, *Toronto Life*, and assorted medical associations. While continuing his freelance work, LeBourdais became a contract photographer for United Press International in 1969, a position he held until 1978. During this period he covered many sports and news stories.

In 1978 LeBourdais was made news-pictures bureau manager at United Press Canada, where he remained until 1985. Since 1988, he has operated his own photography business. He has also taught photojournalism courses on a part-time basis at Oakville Sheridan College since 1991, and he is a founding member, past president, and honorary life member of the Eastern Canadian News Photographers Association. LeBourdais continues to reside in the Toronto area.

In 1997, the Archives acquired more than 100,000 of LeBourdais's images. Representing much of his work from the early 1960s through the 1970s, these photographs depict public figures, various corporate clients and activities, the education and health sectors, and popular culture and entertainment.

[9-21] Martin Luther King's death touched many Canadians, including those shown here at a memorial ceremony held at Nathan Phillips Square shortly after his death.

9-19 à 9-21 : Julien LeBourdais amorce sa carrière de photographe indépendant en 1965. Parmi ses clients, on relève le *Daily Star* de Toronto, United Press International, *Toronto Life* et diverses associations médicales. Tout en poursuivant son travail à titre autonome, LeBourdais signe un contrat avec United Press International en 1969, affectation qu'il conserve jusqu'en 1978. Pendant cette période, il couvre une multitude d'actualités et d'événements sportifs.

En 1978, LeBourdais est nommé directeur du bureau des actualités en images à United Press Canada, où il demeure jusqu'en 1985. Depuis 1988, il dirige sa propre entreprise de photographie. Il enseigne également le photojournalisme à temps partiel, au Collège Sheridan d'Oakville depuis 1991, et il est membre fondateur, ancien président et membre honoraire à vie de la Eastern Canadian News Photographers Association. LeBourdais réside toujours dans la région de Toronto.

En 1997, les Archives acquéraient plus de 100 000 des images de LeBourdais. Ces photographies, qui représentent une grande partie de son travail du début des années 1960 jusqu'à la fin des années 1970, ont pour sujets des personnalités publiques, des entreprises et leurs activités, des thèmes liés aux secteurs de la santé et de l'éducation ainsi que du divertissement et de la culture populaire.

[9-21] La mort de Martin Luther King a bouleversé un grand nombre de Canadiens, dont ceux que l'on voit ici lors d'une cérémonie commémorative, tenue place Nathan Phillips, peu après l'événement.

9-19

9-20

9-21

9-1: People lining up outside the Scott Mission, Toronto [ca. 1949], Gilbert A. Milne (Gilbert Milne fonds, C 3, 9508-11800.2. I0004585)

9-2: Iroquois *Post* newspaper, 1941, Herb Nott (Herb Nott fonds, C 109-2, 18-5-145 H. I0008838

9-3: New Commercial Hotel, 1941, Herb Nott (Herb Nott fonds, C 109-2, 18-5-165 H. I0008819)

9-4: Main Street, 1941, Herb Nott (Herb Nott fonds, C 109-2, 18-5-144 H. I0008841)

9-5: Woman talking to shipbuilding workers about Victory Bonds, Toronto [ca. 1945], Gordon Powley (Gordon Powley fonds, C 5-1-0-102-10. I0002726)

9-6: Women doing war work in Marelco factory [ca. 1940], Gordon Powley (Gordon Powley fonds, C 5-1-0-129-3. I0002764)

9-7: Bombs for Hitler [ca. 1940], Herb Nott (Herb Nott fonds, C 109-5-0-41-15)

9-8: Family around table reading letter from the front [ca. 1940], Herb Nott (Herb Nott fonds, C 109-5-0-41-6)

9-9: Parade to mark United Nations Day, Hamilton, October 1947, Gordon Powley (Gordon Powley fonds, C 5-1-84-2)

9-10: Man working with pulp-and-paper machinery, January 1946, Gilbert Milne (Gilbert Milne fonds, C 3 9508-4290-3. I0004511)

9-11: Artist Jack Bush, March 1946, Gilbert Milne (Gilbert Milne fonds, C 3 9508-4684-4. I0004520)

9-12: Glenn Gould as a child, at his piano [ca. 1940], Gordon Powley (Gordon Powley fonds, C 5-1-0-133-2. I0002768)

9-13: Dr Charles Best, 20 May 1948, Gilbert Milne (Gilbert Milne fonds, C 3 9508-11098.1. I0004573)

9-14: Damage from Hurricane Hazel, 1954, Gordon Powley (Gordon Powley fonds, C 5-2-2-33-2. I0002914)

9-15: Korean veteran and family at Union Station, 1953 Gordon Powley (Gordon Powley fonds, C 5-1-0-180-5. I0002815)

9-16: Yonge Street during the construction of the subway, 24 June 1950, Gilbert Milne (Gilbert Milne fonds, C 3-9508-15510-5)

9-17: Air-raid shelter, Queen's Park Crescent and College St, Toronto, 1 July 1960, Gordon Powley (Gordon Powley fonds, C 5-2-2-47-3. I0002924)

9-18: Committee of 100 at City Hall, Toronto (anti-nuclear demonstration), 10 February 1962, Gordon Powley (Gordon Powley fonds, C 5-2-2-56-6. I0002923)

9-19: Pierre Trudeau speaking at Scarborough rally, 1968, Julien LeBourdais (Julien LeBourdais fonds, C 193-2, 417-9)

9-20: Fire at a Gerrard Street store, Toronto, January 17, 1971 (Julien LeBourdais fonds, C 193-3-0-213, neg. 33)

9-21: Martin Luther King memorial, 1968, Julien LeBourdais (Julien LeBourdais fonds, C 193-2, 749-17a)

9-1 : Des gens font la queue à la mission Scott, à Toronto [vers 1949], Gilbert A. Milne (Fonds Gilbert Milne, C 3, 9508-11800.2. I0004585)

9-2 : Le Post, journal d' Iroquois, 1941, Herb Nott (Fonds Herb Nott, C 109-2, 18-5-145 H. I0008838)

9-3 : Le New Commercial Hotel, 1941, Herb Nott (Fonds Herb Nott, C 109-2, 18-5-165 H. I0008819)

9-4 : Rue principale, 1941, Herb Nott (Fonds Herb Nott, C 109-2, 18-5-144 H. I0008841)

9-5 : Une femme fait de la réclame pour les obligations de la Victoire auprès des ouvriers d'un chantier naval, Toronto [vers 1945], Gordon Powley (Fonds Gordon Powley, C 5-1-0-102-10. I0002726)

9-6 : Travailleuses de guerre dans une usine Marelco [vers 1940], Gordon Powley (Fonds Gordon Powley, C 5-1-0-129-3. I0002764)

9-7 : Des bombes pour Hitler [vers 1940], Herb Nott (Fonds Herb Nott, C 109-5-0-41-15)

9-8 : Famille attablée, lisant une lettre du front [vers 1940], Herb Nott (Fonds Herb Nott, C 109-5-0-41-6)

9-9 : Défilé de la Fête des Nations Unies, Hamilton, octobre 1947, Gordon Powley (Fonds Gordon Powley, C 5-1-84-2)

9-10 : Opérateur de machine dans une usine de papier, janvier 1946, Gilbert Milne (Fonds Gilbert Milne, C 3 9508-4290-3. I0004511)

9-11 : Le peintre Jack Bush, mars 1946, Gilbert Milne (Fonds Gilbert Milne, C 3 9508-4684-4. I0004520)

9-12 : Glenn Gould enfant, à son piano [vers 1940], Gordon Powley (Fonds Gordon Powley, C 5-1-0-133-2. I0002768)

9-13 : Le Dr Charles Best, 20 mai 1948, Gilbert Milne (Fonds Gilbert Milne, C 3 9508-11098.1. I0004573)

9-14 : Après le passage de l'ouragan Hazel, 1954, Gordon Powley (Fonds Gordon Powley, C 5-2-2-33-2. I0002914)

9-15 : Ancien combattant de la guerre de Corée et sa famille, à la gare Union, 1953, Gordon Powley (Fonds Gordon Powley, C 5-1-0-180-5. I0002815)

9-16 : La rue Yonge pendant la construction du métro, 24 juin 1950, Gilbert Milne (Fonds Gilbert Milne, C 3-9508-15510-5)

9-17 : Abri antiaérien, à l'angle de Queen's Park Crescent et de la rue College, à Toronto, 1er juillet 1960, Gordon Powley (Fonds Gordon Powley, C 5-2-2-47-3. I0002924)

9-18 : Le comité des 100, à l'hôtel de ville de Toronto (manifestation antinucléaire), 10 février 1962, Gordon Powley (Fonds Gordon Powley, C 5-2-2-56-6. I0002923)

9-19 : Pierre Trudeau s'adresse à une assemblée publique à Scarborough, 1968, Julien LeBourdais (Fonds Julien LeBourdais, C 193-2, 417-9)

9-20 : Incendie dans un magasin de la rue Gerrard, à Toronto, 17 janvier 1971 (Fonds Julien LeBourdais, C 193-3-0-213, nég. 33)

9-21 : Cérémonie à la mémoire de Martin Luther King, 1968, Julien LeBourdais (Fonds Julien LeBourdais, C 193-2, 749-17a)

PART III

IMPORTANT EVENTS IN ONTARIO HISTORY

LES GRANDS ÉVÉNEMENTS DE L'HISTOIRE DE L'ONTARIO

Report of Resolutions adopted at A Conference of Delegates from the Provinces of Canada Nova Scotia and New Brunswick and the Colonies of Newfoundland and Prince Edward Island held at the City of Quebec tenth day of October one thousand eight hundred and sixty four as the Basis of a proposed Confederation of these Provinces and Colonies.

Certain key factors have influenced and shaped the history of Ontario. The physical environment, which includes a wide range of topographies, a system of connected waterways, and a climate that often reaches extremes, has surely played its part. So have aboriginal people, who managed to develop ways and means of coping with the physical environment that Europeans were quick to adopt. These aspects of Ontario's early history – that period of time before the advent of written records – are the realm not of historians and archivists but of archaeologists, anthropologists, and geographers.

Once the floodgates were opened, however, there was no stopping the tide of documents produced in Ontario, including letters, proclamations, legal papers, sketches, handbills, minutes, tax bills, account ledgers, and photographs. The people who jotted down notes about the weather in their diaries, kept scrapbooks, or took family photographs likely had no idea that they were making history, but they were. The records they left behind, many of which are found at the Archives of Ontario, assist in the re-creation of the past. And what of the major events in Ontario's history? The clash of British and American interests that drew the young colony of Upper Canada into the War of 1812, the struggle for representative government, the rush of immigrants fleeing persecution and poverty, the participation of Ontario in two world wars – these events and many others are also chronicled in records available at the Archives.

The illustrations included in the following pages document some of the most important moments in Ontario history. From anti-slavery legislation to the investigation into the Walkerton water tragedy, and from parchment paper with wax seals to electronic databases, the Archives of Ontario has a rich store of resources which captures that history and helps us to understand it.

Certains facteurs de base ont marqué l'histoire de l'Ontario et l'ont façonnée. L'environnement physique, avec un relief des plus variés, tout un réseau de voies navigables et un climat aux températures souvent extrêmes, y a indéniablement joué un rôle. Il en va de même pour les peuples autochtones, qui avaient réussi à se donner des moyens de composer avec le milieu naturel que les Européens n'ont pas tardé à adopter. Ces dimensions présentes au début de l'histoire de l'Ontario – à une époque qui précède les documents écrits – sont du ressort non pas des historiens et archivistes, mais des géographes, archéologues et anthropologues.

Cependant, une fois le mouvement enclenché, il n'y a pas eu de limites à la profusion des documents produits en Ontario : lettres, proclamations, actes juridiques, croquis, prospectus, procès-verbaux, comptes de taxes, registres comptables, photographies. Les particuliers qui tenaient un journal en y notant les températures, ajoutaient à leur spicilège ou croquaient leur famille en photos faisaient, bien à leur insu, œuvre d'historiens. Les documents qu'ils nous ont laissés, dont les Archives publiques de l'Ontario conservent un certain nombre, nous aident à reconstituer le passé. Et que dire des grands événements qui ont marqué l'histoire de la province? Les conflits entre intérêts britanniques et américains qui ont entraîné la jeune colonie du Haut-Canada dans la guerre de 1812, la lutte pour obtenir un gouvernement responsable, les vagues successives d'immigrants fuyant la misère et la persécution, la participation de l'Ontario aux deux guerres mondiales – ces événements et combien d'autres se retrouvent dans les documents des Archives.

Les illustrations des pages qui suivent font mieux connaître certains épisodes mémorables de l'histoire de l'Ontario. De la loi anti-esclavagiste à l'enquête sur la tragédie de l'eau à Walkerton, depuis les parchemins à sceau de cire jusqu'aux bases de données électroniques, les Archives publiques de l'Ontario possèdent un riche dépôt de ressources, qui éclairent l'histoire et nous aident à en comprendre le sens.

10

FROM COLONY TO PROVINCE

DE COLONIE À PROVINCE

This chapter focuses on some of the most important and symbolic moments in the history of Ontario from its official founding as a province in 1792 until its entry into Confederation in 1867. The subject matter is broad, including portraits of people, reproductions of private letters, government documents, and artifacts.

The story begins with the arrival of John Graves Simcoe as first lieutenant-governor of the new colony of Upper Canada in 1792, a colony that had recently become the home of Loyalist refugees from the American Revolution. Simcoe and his immediate successors endeavoured to turn Upper Canada into a conservative bastion of the British Empire, and while this vision was seriously tested in the War of 1812, it survived and indeed became entrenched. There were critics, of course, notably William Lyon Mackenzie, and their opposition to the colony's ruling oligarchy and the ideas it espoused led to the Rebellion of 1837.

Following the suppression of the Rebellion, and a similar series of events in the neighbouring colony of Lower Canada, the British government accepted Lord Durham's recommendation that the two Canadas be merged into a single colony. Implemented by the Act of Union of 1840, the new Province of Canada witnessed in its first decade an ultimately successful campaign for more representative government, a campaign led by Robert Baldwin of Canada West and Louis-Hippolyte LaFontaine of Canada East, as the old colonies of Upper and Lower Canada were then known. In its second decade, the challenge became one of political deadlock, and the inability of rival political forces in the Province of Canada to bring about stable government ultimately paved the way for the Confederation agreement of 1867.

The illustrations in the following pages touch upon these and other major events in Ontario history, and the people associated with them. Taken together, they help to explain the province's distinct identity.

Ce chapitre traite de certains moments emblématiques parmi les plus notables de l'histoire de l'Ontario, depuis sa fondation officielle en qualité de province, en 1791, jusqu'à son entrée dans la Confédération, en 1867. Le matériel est abondant et comprend, outre une foule d'artefacts, des portraits, des reproductions de lettres personnelles et des documents gouvernementaux.

L'histoire commence en 1791, avec l'arrivée de John Graves Simcoe, premier lieutenant-gouverneur de la nouvelle colonie du Haut-Canada, laquelle vient d'accueillir des Loyalistes chassés par la révolution américaine. Simcoe et ses successeurs immédiats s'efforcent de transformer le Haut-Canada en un bastion de l'Empire britannique, et il faut reconnaître que, même si cette vocation est mise à rude épreuve par la guerre de 1812, elle persiste et finira par s'ancrer fermement. Cette situation n'est bien entendu pas sans critiques, dont en particulier William Lyon Mackenzie, et c'est leur opposition à l'oligarchie régnant dans la colonie et à ses opinions qui entraîne la rébellion de 1837.

Après la répression de la rébellion et d'une série de troubles analogues dans la colonie avoisinante du Bas-Canada, le gouvernement britannique se résout à accepter la recommandation de Lord Durham, soit la fusion des deux Canadas en une seule colonie. Créée en vertu de l'Acte d'Union de 1840, la nouvelle Province du Canada assiste, au cours d'une première décennie, à une campagne qui aboutira éventuellement à l'obtention d'un gouvernement plus représentatif. Cette campagne est dirigée par Robert Baldwin, du Canada-Ouest, et Louis-Hippolyte Lafontaine, du Canada-Est, ainsi que les anciennes colonies du Haut et du Bas-Canada sont alors connues. Au cours de la deuxième décennie d'existence de la Province du Canada, ce qui avait été défi devient impasse; en rivalité constante, les forces politiques sont incapables d'instaurer un gouvernement stable, ce qui ouvrira la voie à la Confédération, en 1867.

Les illustrations des pages suivantes se rapportent à ces événements et à d'autres qui ont été marquants pour l'histoire de l'Ontario, de même qu'aux personnages qui y ont tenu un rôle. Dans leur ensemble, elles éclairent les sources de l'identité distincte de la province.

JOHN GRAVES SIMCOE

10-1: John Graves Simcoe (1752-1806) was appointed the first lieutenant-governor of Upper Canada, and, although he was only in Canada from 1792 until 1796, his tenure had a profound effect on the province's early development. He believed that American settlers would foster growth in the region and so he promoted the policy of granting land to settlers from the United States. These immigrants, added to the Loyalists who had arrived during and after the American Revolution, were to be followed by further waves of immigrants from Britain and the United States during the nineteenth century, all of whom together laid the foundations of early Ontario.

Simcoe founded York as the capital of Upper Canada and began the province's system of roads by constructing Dundas and Yonge streets. He also introduced the Court of King's Bench and pledged to abolish slavery in Upper Canada. Solidly British and elitist, Simcoe resisted attempts at republicanism and sought to invest the Church of England as Upper Canada's official church. He left a legacy of preferential treatment for Church of England supporters that pleased the provincial elites but chaffed on others less well placed, eventually leading to discontent and even rebellion in the 1830s.

JOHN GRAVES SIMCOE

10-1 : John Graves Simcoe (1752-1806) a été le premier lieutenant-gouverneur du Haut-Canada et, bien qu'il n'y soit demeuré que de 1792 à 1796, son mandat a profondément marqué les débuts de la province. Persuadé que l'établissement de colons américains dans la région en favoriserait le développement, il préconise une politique de cession de terres à ceux qui arrivent des États-Unis. Ces émigrants viennent grossir les rangs des Loyalistes venus pendant et après la révolution américaine et seront suivis, au dix-neuvième siècle, d'autres contingents en provenance de Grande-Bretagne et des États-Unis, contribuant ainsi à jeter les bases de l'Ontario naissant.

Simcoe fonde York, dont il fait la capitale du Haut-Canada. Il pose les rudiments d'un réseau routier, par l'aménagement des rues Dundas et Yonge. Il institue également la cour du banc du roi et s'engage à abolir l'esclavage dans le Haut-Canada. Loyal sujet britannique et pétri d'élitisme, Simcoe tient tête aux velléités républicaines et prend des dispositions pour faire de l'Église anglicane l'église officielle du Haut-Canada. Il instaure un régime de faveur pour les membres de l'église anglicane, mesure qui ne manque pas de plaire aux membres de la haute société, mais aussi d'indisposer les moins privilégiés. Il s'ensuit un climat d'insatisfaction qui débouche, pendant les années 1830, sur la rébellion.

10-1

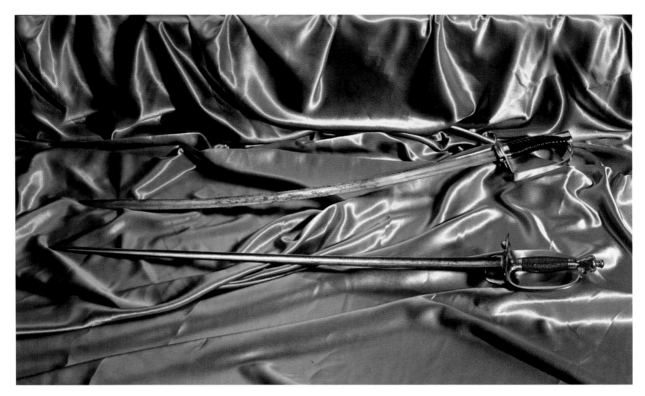

10-2

10-2: Simcoe was no stranger to North America when he took office in 1792, having served with the British army in North America during the American Revolution. Following the Battle of the Brandywine in 1777, he was promoted to the command of a militia formation known as the Queen's Rangers and subsequently led them for the remainder of the war. Simcoe revived this formation in Canada during his lieutenant-governorship.

The Archives acquired the sword and sabre pictured here from Simcoe's descendants in 1993. It is reported that Simcoe carried this sabre during his service in America, while the sword is reputed to be the one that he wore on state occasions as lieutenant-governor. The sword may have belonged to Simcoe's son, Francis, who also served in the British army and died at the siege of Badajoz in Spain in 1812.

10-2 : L'Amérique du Nord n'est pas territoire inconnu pour Simcoe lors de son entrée en fonction en 1792; en effet, au cours de la révolution américaine, il avait servi dans les rangs de l'armée britannique en Amérique du Nord. À la suite de la bataille de Brandywine, en 1777, il avait été promu au commandement d'une formation de milice, les Queen's Rangers, et était demeuré à sa tête durant le reste de la guerre. Simcoe fera revivre cette formation pendant son mandat de lieutenant-gouverneur au Canada.

Les Archives ont obtenu l'épée et le sabre qui apparaissent ici des descendants de Simcoe, en 1993. Il semble que Simcoe aurait porté le sabre pendant son service aux États-Unis, et qu'il aurait réservé l'épée aux réceptions officielles, dans son rôle de lieutenant-gouverneur. L'épée a peut-être appartenu au fils de Simcoe, Francis, qui a lui aussi été officier dans l'armée britannique et devait succomber en 1812, lors du siège de Badajoz, en Espagne.

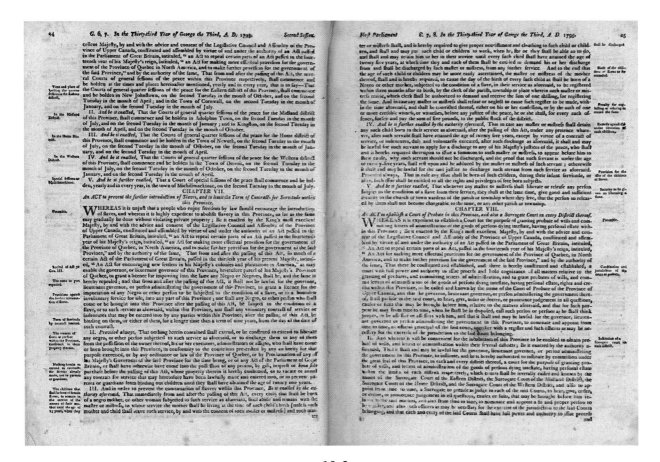

10-3

10-3: When the Loyalists moved to Canada during and after the American Revolution, many of them brought their slaves; by 1800, there were some five hundred slaves in Upper Canada. However, in 1793 Simcoe introduced anti-slave legislation, which was not universally popular since some members of the Legislative Council owned slaves themselves. Nevertheless, An Act to Prevent the Further Introduction of Slaves and to Limit the Term of Contracts for Servitudes within this Province, as the measure was called, was passed on 9 July 1793.

10-3 : Lorsque les Loyalistes viennent s'installer au pays, pendant et après la révolution américaine, beaucoup d'entre eux sont accompagnés de leurs esclaves – si bien que, en 1800, on dénombre cinq cents esclaves dans le Haut-Canada. Mais, en 1793, Simcoe avait introduit une loi anti-esclavagiste, ce qui n'avait pas eu l'heur de plaire à tout le monde, puisque certains membres du conseil législatif étaient visés. Néanmoins, la loi pour empêcher l'entrée d'autres esclaves et pour limiter la durée des contrats de servitude dans la province est adoptée le 9 juillet 1793.

10-4 & 10-5: Simcoe's legislation did not actually abolish the slavery that already existed in Upper Canada, as evidenced by this 1801 correspondence between Peter Russell (Upper Canada's first receiver-general and auditor-general, as well as the province's administrator after Simcoe's departure) and Captain M. Elliott. In a rather shocking exchange, they coolly discuss the sale of Russell's slave, Peggy, to Elliott and are most concerned about a missing bill of sale. Only with the British Emancipation Act of 1833 would slavery be abolished in all parts of the British Empire. Nevertheless, Simcoe's act was groundbreaking - Upper Canada was the first British jurisdiction in the New World to pass laws against slavery.

[Transcription of 10-4, which is on the following page.]

Captain Elliott at Sandwich
York 19 September 1801

Dear Sir,
My Slave Peggy, whom you were so good to promise to assist me in getting rid of, has remained in Prison [?] you left here (in expectation of your sending for her) as an Expense of above Ten pounds Halifax, which I was obliged to pay to the Gaoler - and release her last week by order of the Chief Justice. She is now at large, being not permitted by my Sister to enter this House, and shows a disposition at times to be very troublesome, which may perhaps compel me to commit her again to Prison. I shall therefore be glad that you would either taker [take her?] away immediately, or return to me the Bill of Sale I gave you to enable you to do so. For tho I have received no money from you for her, my property in her is gone from me while you hold the Bill of Sale, and I cannot consequently give a valid Title to any other who may be inclined to take her off my hands.
I beg to hear from you soon, & am very truly your most obedient humble servant,

Peter Russell
Dear Sir - sent through Mr. Dickson

[Transcription of 10-5, which is on the following page]

Peter Russell, Esquire
Malden 7 October 1801

Dear Sir,
I was a good deal surprised on receiving your letter of the 19th September to find that Captain Brant, with whom on my way home left the Bill of Sale of Peggy, had not sent to take her away as he promised me to send for her positively the next day. I have however wrote to him to lose no time in taking her away or return to you the Bill of Sale and am with my best compliments to Mrs. Russell.
Dear Sir, Your most obedient, Humble Servant,

M. Elliott

Ontario was to follow Simcoe's lead in its concern for human rights. The Racial Discrimination Act of 1944 was a pioneering piece of legislation since it represented the first time that a legislature explicitly declared that racial and religious discrimination would not be tolerated. In 1961 Ontario established the first Human Rights Commission in Canada, with the responsibility of administering a comprehensive provincial human rights code. The Ontario Human Rights Commission continues to work to protect and uphold the rights of all individuals.

10-4 et 10-5 : Concrètement, la loi promulguée par Simcoe n'abolit pas la situation de fait dans le Haut-Canada – à témoin les lettres suivantes, échangées par le capitaine M. Elliott et Peter Russell (premier receveur général et vérificateur général du Haut-Canada, de même qu'administrateur de la province après le départ de Simcoe). Sur un ton plutôt odieux, il y est froidement question de la vente à Elliott de l'esclave de Russell, Peggy, et les correspondants semblent se soucier avant tout de cet acte de vente égaré. Ce n'est qu'en 1833, avec l'adoption de la loi britannique sur l'émancipation, que l'esclavage sera aboli dans l'ensemble de l'empire britannique. Notons toutefois que Simcoe a fait œuvre de pionnier en promulguant cette loi – le Haut-Canada a été le premier territoire britannique du Nouveau Monde à se donner une loi contre l'esclavage.

[Transcription de la lettre 10-4, reproduite à la page suivante.]

Au capitaine Elliott, à Sandwich
York, le 19 septembre 1801

Monsieur,
Mon esclave Peggy, dont vous m'aviez aimablement promis de me défaire, est demeurée en prison [?] après votre départ (en attendant que vous la fassiez venir) entraînant des frais de plus de dix livres d'Halifax, que j'ai été forcé de payer au gardien – et elle a été relâchée la semaine dernière, sur l'ordre du juge en chef. Elle est maintenant en liberté, mais ma sœur lui a interdit de remettre les pieds à la maison et elle menace parfois de nous causer des ennuis, ce qui pourrait m'obliger à la faire de nouveau incarcérer. Je vous serais donc obligé soit de venir la chercher immédiatement, soit de me renvoyer l'acte de vente que je vous avais remis pour vous autoriser à l'emmener. En effet, vous ne m'avez pas remis d'argent, je n'ai plus aucun droit de propriété sur elle tant que vous conservez l'acte de vente, et je ne peux donc en conséquence transmettre un titre valide à quiconque serait disposé à m'en débarrasser.
Je vous prie de donner bientôt suite à cette affaire et demeure votre très humble et obéissant serviteur,

Peter Russell
Envoyée par les soins de M. Dickson

[Transcription de la lettre 10-5, reproduite à la page suivante.]

À M. Peter Russell
Malden, le 7 octobre 1801

Monsieur,
J'ai été grandement étonné d'apprendre, par votre lettre du 19 septembre, que le capitaine Brant, à qui j'avais en chemin remis l'acte de vente relatif à Peggy, n'avait pas fait venir celle-ci, car il m'avait fermement promis de s'en occuper le lendemain. Je lui ai aussitôt écrit de bien vouloir aller la chercher sur-le-champ ou, à défaut, de vous renvoyer l'acte de vente. Tous mes compliments à Mme Russell.
Je demeure, monsieur, votre très obéissant et humble serviteur,

M. Elliott

L'Ontario devait suivre la voie tracée par Simcoe au chapitre des droits de la personne. La loi interdisant la discrimination raciale de 1944 était avant-gardiste : c'était la première fois qu'un corps législatif déclarait expressément que la discrimination, raciale ou religieuse, ne serait plus tolérée. En 1961 était instaurée la première commission des droits de la personne au Canada, laquelle était chargée d'appliquer dans la province un code exhaustif en la matière. La Commission ontarienne des droits de la personne continue à œuvrer dans le sens de la protection et de l'affirmation des droits de tous les citoyens.

Dear Sir   York 19: September 1807

My Slave Peggy, whom you were so good to promise to assist me in getting rid of, has remained in Prison ever since you left this (in expectation of your sending for her) at an Expence of above Ten pounds Halifax, which I was obliged to pay to the Goaler — and release her last Week by order of the Chief Justice. She is now at large, being not permitted by my Sister to enter this House, and shows a disposition at Times to be very troublesome, which may perhaps compel me to commit her again to Prison. I shall therefore be glad that you would either take her away immediately, or re-turn to me the Bill of Sale I gave you to enable you to do so. For tho' I have received no money from you for her, my property in her is gone from me while you hold the Bill of Sale; and I cannot consequently give a valid Title to any other who may be inclined to take her off my hands. I beg to hear from you Soon, & am very truly

Dear Sir
Your most obedient humble serv.t

Mathd.
Capt. Elliott   Ins Ken Mr. Dickson   Peter Russell
+
Sandwich

10-4

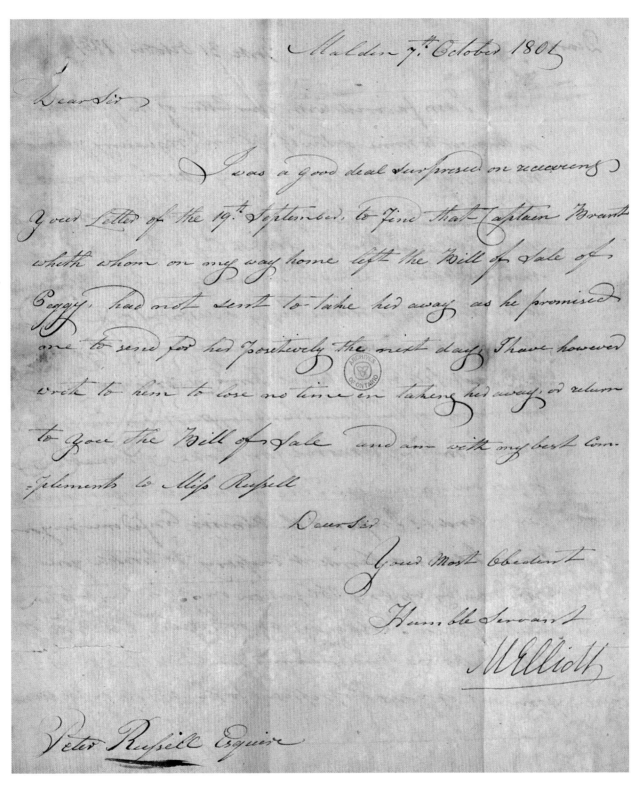

Malden 7th October 1801

Dear Sir

I was a good deal surprised on receiving your Letter of the 19th September, to find that Captain Brant with whom on my way home left the Bill of Sale of Peggy, had not sent to take her away as he promised me to send for her positively the next day. I have however writ to him to lose no time in taking her away, or return to you the Bill of Sale and am with my best Compliments to Miss Russell

Dear Sir
Your Most Obedient
Humble Servant
M Elliott

Peter Russell Esquire

10-5

10-6 to 10-8: On 18 June 1812 the United States declared war on Great Britain and, as a British colony, Canada was inevitably drawn into the conflict. The Americans were confident that capturing Canada would be easy since U.S. forces far outnumbered the British and Canadians. In addition, political and military leaders in the United States assumed that the many Americans in the colony would gladly welcome the chance to free themselves from British rule. However, this was a serious miscalculation, because most Loyalists and later American arrivals were happy with their new life, complete with free land and low taxes, and wished to be left alone.

The British troops, supplemented by Upper Canadians and Native fighters, rallied under the leadership of Major-General Isaac Brock and surprised the Americans by winning battles at Detroit and Queenston Heights. Fighting together successfully and having a common enemy helped the populace forge a sense of identity as 'Upper Canadians.' As well, the eventual outcome of the war and peace negotiations defined the colony's borders and solidified a sense of 'us and them.' The legislature of Upper Canada passed an act that underlined this concept of nationalism by declaring that those Upper Canadian landholders who had fought with the Americans were now aliens and could no longer own land in the province.

10-6 à 10-8: Le 18 juin 1812, les États-Unis déclarent la guerre à la Grande-Bretagne; à titre de colonie britannique, le Canada est inévitablement entraîné dans le conflit. Les Américains ne doutaient pas que la conquête du Canada serait facile, puisque leurs forces étaient de beaucoup supérieures à celles des Britanniques et des Canadiens. En outre, les dirigeants politiques et militaires des États-Unis étaient persuadés que les nombreux Américains de la colonie accueilleraient avec joie l'occasion de secouer le joug britannique. Or, c'était là un bien mauvais calcul, puisque la plupart des Loyalistes et arrivants américains ultérieurs étaient on ne peut plus satisfaits de leur nouvelle vie, sur des terres qui leur avaient été cédées gratuitement et moyennant une taxation minime, et ils ne demandaient qu'à être laissés en paix.

Les troupes britanniques, augmentées de recrues haut-canadiennes et autochtones, se rassemblent donc sous le commandement du major-général Isaac Brock et déroutent les Américains par leurs victoires de Détroit et de Queenston Heights. Le fait d'affronter un ennemi commun et de le combattre côte à côte avec succès contribue à forger, chez les habitants, un sentiment de leur identité comme « citoyens du Haut-Canada ». De plus, à l'issue de la guerre et des pourparlers sur les conditions de paix, les frontières de la colonie allaient être définies et cristalliser la distinction entre « eux et nous ». La Chambre d'assemblée du Haut-Canada finit par adopter une loi enchâssant ce concept de nationalisme, en édictant que ceux des propriétaires fonciers du Haut-Canada qui ont combattu aux côtés des Américains sont désormais des « étrangers », lesquels ne sont plus autorisés à posséder des terres dans la province.

10-6

10-7

10-8

intituled, " an Act to repeal certain parts of an Act passed in the fourteenth year of His Majesty's Reign, intituled, " an Act for making more effectual provision for the Government of the Province of Quebec, in North America, and to make further provision for the Government of the said Province." And by the authority of the same, That the said Act of Parliament of this Province passed in the fifty third year of His Majesty's Reign shall be, and the same is hereby continued. *Act passed in the* 53ᵈ Geo. 3, *to prohibit the Distillation of Grain, &c. continued.*

II. *And be it further enacted by the authority aforesaid,* That nothing herein contained shall extend to or be construed to extend to prevent the Governor, Lieutenant Governor, or person administering the Government to Licence any person or persons to work stills for making Spirituous Liquors from Rye for the use of His Majesty in this Province. Provided always, that if any person or persons so licenced as aforesaid, shall vend any Spirituous Liquors, so made by him or them, otherwise than for the use of His Majesty, such person or persons upon being convicted thereof, by confession, or by the oath of one Credible witness before any of His Majesty's Justices of the Peace, shall forfeit and pay for every Gallon of Sprituous Liquors, so sold contrary to the provision of this act, the sum of ten pounds, and a proportionate sum for any greater or less quantity, to be levied by distress and sale of the offender's Goods and Chattels, one half of which sum shall be given to the informer, and the other half to be paid into the hands of His Majesty's Receiver General to and for the uses of this Province, to be accounted for to His Majesty through the Lords Commissioners of His Majesty's Treasury for the time being in such manner and form as His Majesty shall direct. *Governor, &c. may licence any person or persons to distil from Rye for the use of Government. Penalty for persons so licenced selling Liquors distilled, otherwise than for the use of Government. How the Penalty levied, and applied.*

III. *And be it further enacted by the authority aforesaid,* That the fourth clause of the said act be, and the same is hereby repealed. *4th clause of the said act of 53 Geo. 3 repealed.*

IV. *And be it further enacted by the authority aforesaid,* That in case any prohibition for the distillation of Wheat, Corn, or other Grain, Flour or Meal by virtue of any Proclamation from the Governor, Lieutenant Governor, or person administering the Government, it shall and may be lawful for the Inspector in each and every District of this Province—and he is hereby required on application being made to him by any person or persons who may have paid money for a Licence to distill for the present year, to return to such applicant the whole amount of such Licence money *In case of prohibition inforced the Inspector to return the whole amount of money paid by any person for a licence to distill this year.*

V. *And be it further enacted by the authority aforesaid,* That this act shall be, and continue in force from the passing thereof to the end of the next Session of Parliament and no longer. *Continuance of this Act.*

CHAP. IX.

An Act to declare certain Persons, therein described, Aliens, and to vest their Estates in His Majesty.

[*Passed the 14th March,* 1814.]

WHEREAS many persons, inhabitants of the United States of America, claiming to be Subjects of His Majesty, and renewing their allegiance as such by oath, did solicit and receive grants of Lands from His Majesty, or became seized of Lands by inheritance or otherwise, within this Province, which persons since the declaration of War by the said United States of America, against His Majesty and his Subjects of the United Kingdom of Great Britain and Ireland, have voluntarily with- *Preamble. Persons who having come from the U. S. of America and received grants of land in this Pro-*

K

10-9a

10-9: [Extract]

'That all such persons … who having received grants of land … shall have voluntarily withdrawn themselves from this Province into the United States of America, since the first day of July, One Thousand eight hundred and twelve, or who may hereafter during the present war, withdrawn themselves … shall be taken and considered to be Aliens born and incapable of holding Lands within this Province.'

10-9 : [Extrait] [traduction]

« Toutes les personnes qui, ayant reçu des concessions de terres, ont volontairement quitté la province pour se rendre aux États-Unis d'Amérique depuis le premier jour de juillet mil huit cent douze ou qui en partiront au cours de la présente guerre seront fait prisonniers, considérés comme étant étrangers de naissance et inaptes à posséder des terres dans la province. »

GORDON DRUMMOND, ESQUIRE, PRESIDENT.

vince, representing themselves to be British subjects, & having taken the oath of allegiance, who after 1st July, 1812, shall have voluntarily left this Province and gone into the U. S. of America without licence, or may hereafter go thither during the present war with America without such licence shall be deemed Aliens, and incapable of holding lands in this Province.

drawn themselves from their said allegiance, and the defence of the said Province : Be it therefore enacted by the King's Most Excellent Majesty, by and with the advice and consent of the Legislative Council and assembly of the Province of Upper Canada, constituted and assembled by virtue of and under the authority of an Act passed in the Parliament of Great Britain, intituled, " an Act to repeal certain parts of an Act passed in the Fourteenth year of His Majesty's Reign, intituled, " an Act for making more effectual provision for the Government of the Province of Quebec, in North America, and to make further provision for the Government of the said Province," and by the authority of the same, That all such persons as aforesaid, who having received grants of Land or may have become seized of Lands within this Province, by inheritance or otherwise as shall have voluntarily withdrawn themselves from this Province into the United States of America, since the first day of July, one thousand eight hundred and twelve, or who may hereafter during the present war, voluntarily withdraw themselves from this Province into the said United States, without licence granted under the authority of the Governor, Lieutenant Governor or person administering the Government of this Province, shall be taken and considered to be Aliens born and incapable of holding Lands within this Province.

Governor, &c. may authorise by commission under the Seal of the Province, any Sheriff, Coroner, or other person in the several Districts of this Province, to inquire of such persons by a Jury, and also what lands they were seized of, and after such inquisition such lands shall revert to his Majesty.

II. *And be it further enacted by the authority aforesaid,* That it shall and may be lawful for the Governor, Lieutenant Governor, or person administering the Government, by Commission under the Great Seal of this Province to authorise any Sheriff, Coroner or other person or persons in the several Districts of this Province, to enquire by the oath of twelve good and lawful men of their respective Districts, and by inquisition indented under the hands and Seals of the said Jurors, and of the said Commissioner or Commissioners to return to His Majesty's Court of King's Bench all such persons as aforesaid, who seized of Land in the respective Districts, shall have Voluntarily withdrawn from the Province into the United States of America since the first day of July, and before the conclusion of the existing war with those States, without Licence granted under the authority of the Governor, Lieutenant Governor, or person administering the Government, and from and after the said finding by such inquisition, His Majesty shall become seized of the Lands so found to have been in the Seisin of such person on the said first day of July. Provided always that nothing in this Act contained, shall be construed to prevent any persons interested in the said Lands from traversing any inquisition or office respecting the same at any time within one year after the Peace shall be established between His Majesty and the United States of America, or within one year after the finding of such inquisition.

Persons interested in the said lands may traverse such inquisition within one year after peace with America, or after finding of the said inquisition.

This act not to affect the claim of any bona fide creditor, or defeat any just lien or claim on such lands.

III. Provided always, That nothing in this Act shall extend or be construed to extend to affect the claim of any bona fide creditor, or to defeat any just lien or security of, or upon any Lands, Tenements or Hereditaments whatsoever.

CHAP. X.

An Act to grant to His Majesty an additional duty on Shop and Tavern Licences.

MOST GRACIOUS SOVEREIGN, [*Passed the 14th March,* 1814.]

Preamble. WHEREAS it is necessary that the revenues of this Province should be increased to meet in some measure the expenditures occasioned by the present War—

10-9b

WILLIAM LYON MACKENZIE AND THE REBELLION OF 1837

10-10 & 10-11: In the 1820s and 1830s, discontent began to brew among settlers who objected to the domination of the 'family compact' in the granting of land and to the favouritism shown towards members of the Church of England. This discontent led to the formation of the Reform party, which was successful in winning control of the House of Assembly in 1828 and again in 1834. After Lieutenant-Governor Sir Francis Bond Head engineered a Tory victory at the polls in 1836, extremists on the opposition side began to mobilize under the leadership of William Lyon Mackenzie.

Taking advantage of the fact that Bond Head had sent all his troops to Lower Canada to help suppress the rebellion there, Mackenzie tried to take control of the government by force. On the 5 December 1837 he led his rebels in a raid on Toronto that was utterly doomed. Forced to flee to the United States, Mackenzie became an embittered man. Nevertheless, the Rebellion of 1837 did have positive results in the long term. Lord Durham was made governor-in-chief of British North America and charged with investigating the causes of the uprisings in both Upper and Lower Canada. His subsequent report recommended the unification of the Canadas and introduced the notion of responsible government, which was eventually achieved in 1849.

WILLIAM LYON MACKENZIE ET LA RÉBELLION DE 1837

10-10 et 10-11 : Au cours des années 1820 et 1830, le mécontentement grandit chez les colons, outrés de la mainmise du « family compact » sur la concession des terres et du favoritisme dont jouissent les adeptes de l'Église anglicane. Ce mécontentement mène à la fondation du parti réformiste, qui réussit à dominer la Chambre d'assemblée en 1828, puis, de nouveau, en 1834. Après l'orchestration, par le lieutenant-gouverneur Sir Francis Bond Head, d'une victoire Tory lors du scrutin de 1836, des extrémistes du parti adversaire commencent à se mobiliser, sous la direction de William Lyon Mackenzie.

Bond Head ayant dépêché le gros de ses troupes dans le Bas-Canada pour aider à étouffer la rébellion qui y gronde, Mackenzie en profite pour tenter de renverser le gouvernement par la force. Le 5 décembre 1837, il marche sur Toronto avec ses rebelles, raid voué à l'échec. Contraint de se réfugier aux États-Unis, Mackenzie en conçoit une grande amertume. Cependant, la rébellion de 1837 aura des résultats positifs à longue échéance. En effet, Lord Durham est nommé gouverneur en chef de l'Amérique du Nord britannique, avec le mandat d'enquêter sur les causes des soulèvements, tant dans le Haut que dans le Bas-Canada. Son rapport préconise l'unification des deux entités et définit la notion de gouvernement responsable, laquelle finira par s'imposer en 1849.

10-10

10-11

THE REBELLION BANNER

10-12 & 10-13: This banner was recovered from Montgomery's Tavern after the dispersal of the rebels on 7 December 1837 and is almost three metres long. It is a relic of a turning point in Ontario history – the beginning of the fight for responsible government. The Head family in Britain held it for more than one hundred years, until Sir Francis's descendants restored it to Ontario in 1962. The powder burns on the banner are clearly visible.

The proclamation issued on 7 December by Lieutenant-Governor Bond Head provides an intriguing contrast to the banner. There is no doubting the message in the proclamation, whereas the meaning of the slogans on the banner has been subject of some debate.

LA BANNIÈRE DE LA RÉBELLION

10-12 et 10-13 : Cette bannière a été retrouvée à la Montgomery's Tavern après la dispersion des rebelles, le 7 décembre 1837; elle mesure près de trois mètres de long. C'est le vestige d'un tournant fatidique dans l'histoire ontarienne, où s'amorce la lutte pour l'obtention d'un gouvernement responsable. L'objet a été conservé pendant plus de cent ans dans la famille Head en Grande-Bretagne, jusqu'à ce que les descendants de Sir Francis le remettent à l'Ontario, en 1862. On y distingue encore clairement des traces de poudre.

La proclamation du lieutenant-gouverneur Bond Head, le 7 décembre, fait contraste avec les inscriptions de la bannière, ce qui ne manque pas d'intriguer. On ne peut contester le sens de la proclamation, tandis que celui des devises inscrites sur la bannière ne fait pas l'unanimité.

10-12

PROCLAMATION.

BY His Excellency SIR FRANCIS BOND HEAD, Baronet, Lieutenant Governor of Upper Canada, &c. &c.

To the Queen's Faithful Subjects in Upper Canada.

In a time of profound peace, while every one was quietly following his occupations, feeling secure under the protection of our Laws, a band of Rebels, instigated by a few malignant and disloyal men, has had the wickedness and audacity to assemble with Arms, and to attack and Murder the Queen's Subjects on the Highway—to Burn and Destroy their Property—to Rob the Public Mails—and to threaten to Plunder the Banks—and to Fire the City of Toronto.

Brave and Loyal People of Upper Canada, we have been long suffering from the acts and endeavours of concealed Traitors, but this is the first time that Rebellion has dared to shew itself openly in the land, in the absence of Invasion by any Foreign Enemy.

Let every man do his duty now, and it will be the last time that we or our children shall see our lives or properties endangered, or the Authority of our Gracious Queen insulted by such treacherous and ungrateful men. MILITIA-MEN OF UPPER CANADA, no Country has ever shewn a finer example of Loyalty and Spirit than YOU have given upon this sudden call of Duty. Young and old of all ranks, are flocking to the Standard of their Country. What has taken place will enable our Queen to know Her Friends from Her Enemies—a public enemy is never so dangerous as a concealed Traitor—and now my friends let us complete well what is begun—let us not return to our rest till Treason and Traitors are revealed to the light of day, and rendered harmless throughout the land.

Be vigilant, patient and active—leave punishment to the Laws—our first object is, to arrest and secure all those who have been guilty of Rebellion, Murder and Robbery.—And to aid us in this, a Reward is hereby offered of

One Thousand Pounds,

to any one who will apprehend, and deliver up to Justice, WILLIAM LYON MACKENZE; and FIVE HUNDRED POUNDS to any one who will apprehend, and deliver up to Justice, DAVID GIBSON—or SAMUEL LOUNT—or JESSE LLOYD—or SILAS FLETCHER—and the same reward and a free pardon will be given to any of their accomplices who will render this public service, except he or they shall have committed, in his own person, the crime of Murder or Arson.

And all, but the Leaders above-named, who have been seduced to join in this unnatural Rebellion, are hereby called to return to their duty to their Sovereign—to obey the Laws—and to live henceforward as good and faithful Subjects—and they will find the Government of their Queen as indulgent as it is just.

GOD SAVE THE QUEEN.

Thursday, 3 o'clock, P. M. 7th Dec.

☞ The Party of Rebels, under their Chief Leaders, is wholly dispersed, and flying before the Loyal Militia. The only thing that remains to be done, is to find them, and arrest them.

R. STANTON, Printer to the QUEEN'S Most Excellent Majesty.

10-13

10-14 & 10-15: This letter on the right, from Marshall Bidwell, the same Bidwell named on the banner, is dated the day after the banner was captured. In it, Bidwell asserts his innocence of any treasonous acts while at the same time accepting exile. Below is a letter from a Mrs Bridgman, believed to be a governess to the children of Sir Francis Bond Head and Lady Julia, to a friend, Fanny, in England, describing the events of 7 December. She comments that George Gurnett, Toronto's mayor, 'brought the rebels flag, which he presented to Lady Head, he told us that the victory was complete, that the rebels were flying in all directions, and that Sir Francis had pardoned many who were brought up prisoners.' The letter is 'cross-written' to save paper and postage.

10-14 et 10-15 : La lettre à droite de Marshall Bidwell, celui même dont le nom figure sur la bannière, date du lendemain de la prise de l'étendard. Dans sa lettre, Bidwell affirme être innocent de tout acte de trahison, tout en se résignant à l'exil. À côté, on voit une lettre de Mme Bridgman (qui aurait été gouvernante des enfants de Sir Francis Bond Head et Lady Julia) adressée à une amie anglaise, Fanny, décrivant les événements du 7 décembre. Selon le commentaire de la lettre, le maire de Toronto, George Gurnett, [traduction] « était porteur du drapeau des rebelles, qu'il a présenté à Lady Head; il nous a raconté que la victoire était totale, que les rebelles fuyaient dans toutes les directions et que Sir Francis avait fait libérer un bon nombre de ceux qui avaient été constitués prisonniers ». L'auteure de la lettre a écrit sur les deux côtés de la feuille, pour économiser le papier et les frais de port.

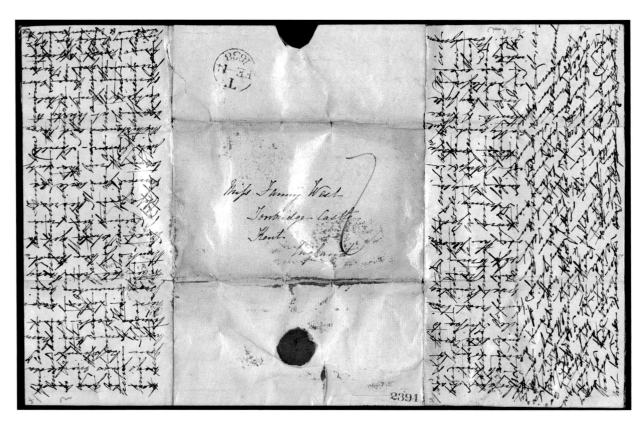

10-14

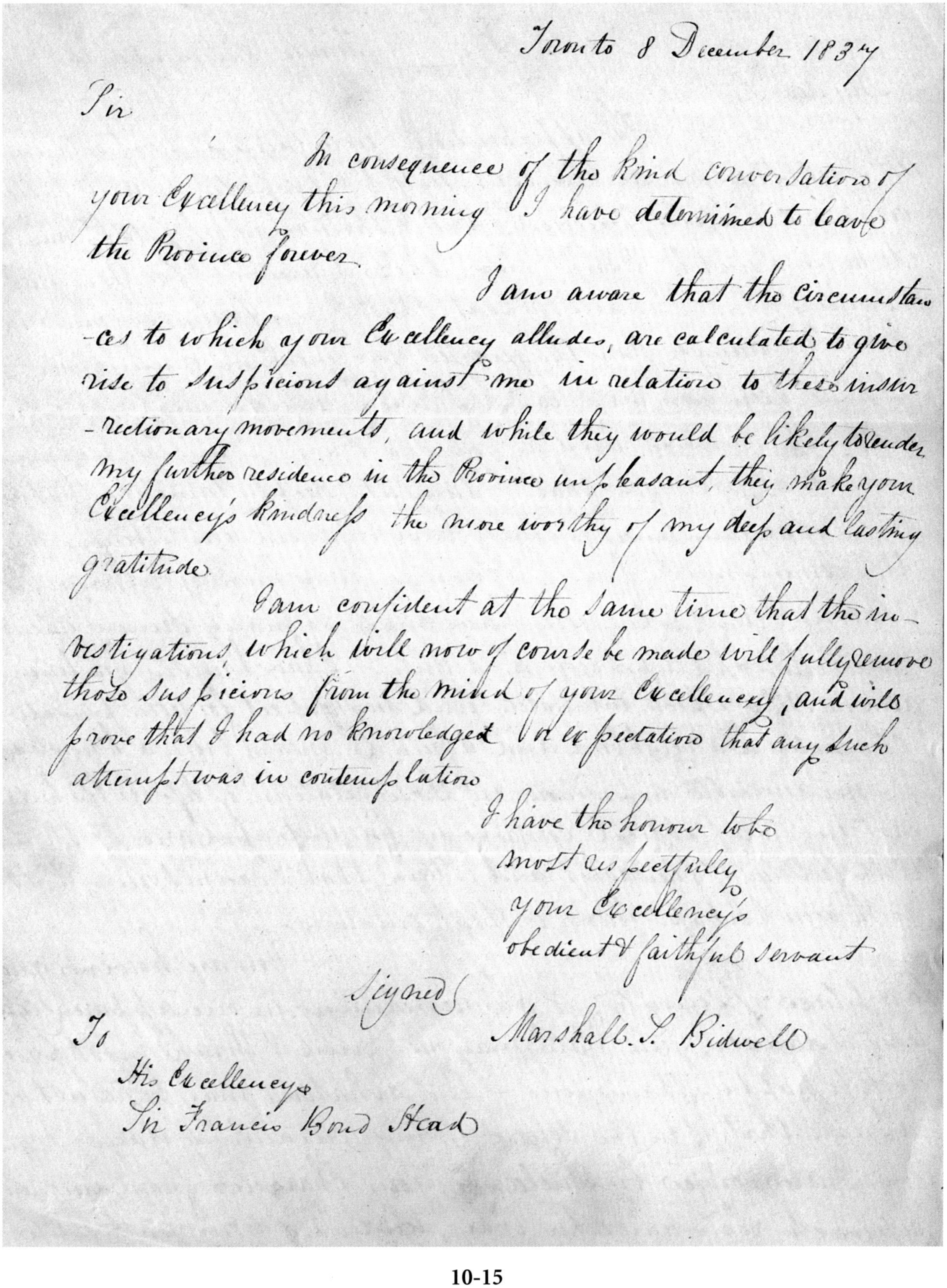

Toronto 8 December 1837

Sir

In consequence of the kind conversation of
your Excellency this morning I have determined to leave
the Province forever.

I am aware that the circumstan-
ces to which your Excellency alludes, are calculated to give
rise to suspicions against me in relation to these insur-
rectionary movements, and while they would be likely to render
my further residence in the Province unpleasant, they make your
Excellency's kindness the more worthy of my deep and lasting
gratitude.

I am confident at the same time that the investigations which will now of course be made will fully remove
those suspicions from the mind of your Excellency, and will
prove that I had no knowledge or expectations that any such
attempt was in contemplation

I have the honour to be
most respectfully
your Excellency's
obedient & faithful servant

Signed

Marshall. S. Bidwell

To
His Excellency
Sir Francis Bond Head

10-15

10-16 & 10-17: This letter, written by W.L. Mackenzie in 1850, twelve years after the failed rebellion, gives us some sense of his continued obsession with the disastrous uprising and also of his penchant for the dramatic - perhaps honed during his years as a newspaper editor.

[Notation on original: 'Transcription of an account of events on Friday, 8 December 1837, at William Comfort's farm. The original is in William Lyon Mackenzie's handwriting and on paper which bears, on its reverse side, evidence that Mackenzie wrote it about January 1850 when in Washington. Presumably Allan Wilcox was the narrator. The woollen factory was known as Sutton and Comfort.']

[Transcription of 10-16, which is on the following page.]

Mr William Comfort - Kenilworth, 9 miles from London, C.W. He is partner in a woollen factory. Address him, 'Kenilworth via London.'

William Lyon Mackenzie came to his house - 3/4 mile below Streetsville a few miles past it - with Allan Wilcox - Mr. Comfort had just done dinner. Wilcox came in first and said, 'Are you of the same mind in politics as me?' 'Just the same.' - 'Mackenzie is here.'- We went out. Mackenzie was coming on with Thomas Granville, blacksmith, Streetsville (since deceased) - he was before me. - He gave me a hint he knew Mackenzie. - Comfort took Mackenzie to the entry on the ground floor - and shut the door - and Granville, Charles Crawford (there yet - same spot) - Ray a cabinet maker (swore that he did afterwards) - was then a great radical - he was a witness on Comfort's indictment against him, through old Barnhart - Mrs. Comfort had no fear - she made tea and dinner - Mackenzie's first remark was - 'I must get round to Niagara - we can do nothing without artillery.' - Mackenzie then asked [for?] his waggon - Comfort felt he should recommend no course as Mackenzie's life was at stake but willingly gave the waggon - while Mackenzie sat at table Comfort took out his old pocket book stuffed with bank bills and laid it on the table asking Mackenzie to take a supply. [B]ut he said, 'I have plenty of that.' - A young Irishman, a catholic, harnessed up 2 horses - and off we 3 started to Springfield - Comfort (unknown to Mackenzie) started after them, and was 1/2 a mile behind Mackenzie when he left the waggon. - Comfort was on horseback, and remarked to his wife, 'Good bye, wife - perhaps I may never see you again' - some more followed - I never saw her more - she was then nearly 35 - When Comfort rode up, several men with guns were keeping sentry - he asked why they did so? - They said that Mackenzie was near in a waggon and horses and that [?] and another had [?] towards the woods - this was near where I left. W. Chisholm was true and good - did all the good he could for both parties - Comfort tells he would not have taken Mackenzie if he could.

At Chalmer's place (16 Hollow) the news was that Mackenzie was in the woods, was surrounded, and would be taken prisoner that night or next morning - people were running out and in. Women were screaming and sorry.

10-16 et 10-17 : Cette autre lettre est de la main de W. L. Mackenzie et remonte à 1850, soit douze ans après l'échec de la rébellion. On y retrouve la marque de son obsession persistante à l'égard du désastreux soulèvement et aussi de son penchant pour le drame, qu'avaient peut-être accentué ses années à la direction d'un journal.

[Annotation de l'original : [traduction] « Transcription d'un récit des événements survenus le vendredi 8 décembre 1837, à la ferme de William Comfort. L'original est de la main de William Lyon Mackenzie, des indices au verso portant à croire que Mackenzie l'aurait rédigé vers janvier 1850, à Washington. On suppose que le narrateur est Allan Wilcox. La fabrique de laine était connue sous le nom de "Sutton and Comfort" ».]

[Transcription du document 10-16, reproduite à la page suivante.]

M. William Comfort – Kenilworth, à neuf milles de London, en C.-O. Il est associé dans une fabrique de laine. Lui adresser à « Kenilworth via London ».

William Lyon Mackenzie est arrivé chez lui [Comfort] – à 3/4 de mille au sud de Streetsville, à quelques milles plus loin – avec Allan Wilcox – M. Comfort venait de souper. Wilcox est entré le premier et a demandé : « Avez-vous les mêmes opinions politiques que moi? » « Précisément. » – « Mackenzie est arrivé. » – Nous sommes sortis. Mackenzie se rapprochait en compagnie de Thomas Granville, forgeron de Streetsville (décédé depuis) – il était devant moi. – Il m'a laissé entendre qu'il connaissait Mackenzie. – Comfort a conduit Mackenzie jusque dans l'entrée du rez-de-chaussée – et a refermé la porte – et Granville, Charles Crawford (là encore – même endroit) – Ray l'ébéniste (a juré par la suite qu'il l'avait vu) – était alors un grand radical – il a servi de témoin à charge lors de la mise en accusation de Comfort par l'entremise du vieux Barnhart – Mme Comfort n'avait aucune crainte – elle a fait du thé et préparé le dîner – la première chose que Mackenzie a dite a été – « Je dois me rendre à Niagara – nous ne pouvons rien sans artillerie. » – Mackenzie a ensuite demandé qu'on lui amène [?] son chariot – Comfort ne croyait pas devoir exprimer de recommandations, car la vie de Mackenzie était en jeu, mais lui a volontiers passé le chariot – pendant que Mackenzie était assis à table, Comfort a sorti son vieux portefeuille, débordant de billets de banque, et l'a posé sur la table en disant à Mackenzie de se servir. Mais celui-ci a répondu « J'ai tout ce qu'il me faut. » – Un jeune Irlandais, un catholique, a attelé deux chevaux – et nous sommes partis tous les trois pour Springfield – Comfort (à l'insu de Mackenzie) est parti à leur suite, et il était encore à un 1/2 mille derrière Mackenzie lorsque celui-ci est descendu du chariot. – Comfort était à cheval et a lancé à sa femme : « Adieu – je ne te reverrai peut-être jamais » – et autre chose – Je ne l'ai jamais revue – Elle avait alors près de 35 ans – Lorsque Comfort s'est rapproché, il a vu plusieurs hommes armés qui montaient la garde – il leur a demandé pourquoi – Ils ont répondu que Mackenzie était tout près, dans un chariot tiré par des chevaux, et que [?] et qu'un autre avait [?] avancé vers les bois – c'est près de cet endroit que je suis parti. W. Chisholm était loyal et sincère – il a fait tout ce qu'il a pu pour les deux parties – Comfort déclare qu'il n'aurait pas capturé Mackenzie s'il avait eu le choix.

Chez Chalmer (16 Hollow), on disait que Mackenzie se trouvait dans les bois, qu'il était cerné et qu'il serait fait prisonnier cette nuit-là ou le lendemain matin – des gens entraient et sortaient continuellement. Les femmes étaient en larmes et poussaient des cris.

Mr Wm Comfort — Kilworth, 9 m's fm London, CW

He is partner in a woollen factory. Address him, "Kilworth via London"

W. L. M. came to his house — ¼ m. below street width a farm of 1 — with A. Wilcox — Mr Comfort had just done dinner. Wilcox came in 1st & sd "are you of the same mind in politics as ever?" "Just the same." — "McKenzie's here." — [illegible] McK. was coming on, with Tho. Granville, blacksmith, [illegible] [illegible] — he was before me. — He gave me a hint he knew McK. — [struck out] Comfort took McK. to the entry on the gr. floor — & shut the door — & Granville, [illegible] Crawford [thought — same thing] — Ray a cabinet mr. (swore that he did apl.) — was then a good radical — he was a witness on [illegible] indictment agst him, thro' old Barnhart — Mrs Comfort had no fear — she made tea & dinner — McK.'s 1st remk was — "I must get up to Niagara — we can do nothing with the artillery." — McK. then asked his waggon — Comfort felt as if he [illegible] second. no conn. as his life was at stake, but unwilling gave the waggon — while McK. sat at table Comfort took out his old pocket bk stuffed with Bk bills & laid it on the table ask'd McK. to take a receipt, but he sd "I have plenty of that." — [illegible] Irishman, a catholic, [illegible] [illegible], 2 horses — and off we 3 started to [illegible] P. — Comfort [illegible] [illegible] to McK) started after them, & was ½ a mile behd. McK when he left the waggon. — Comfort was on horseback, & reached to his wife, [struck out] "good bye, Wife — Perhaps I may never see you again." — some more folk. — never saw her more — she was then near 35 — [illegible] When Comfort rode up, sev. men with guns were keeping sentry. he asked why they did so. — they said that Mr Kenzie was near in a waggon & horses, & that [illegible] head was near in a — in across town the woods — this was nr where I left them — [illegible] parties — Comfort tells he [illegible] (16 Hollow) at Chalmers' place, the news was that McK. was in the woods, was surrounded, & had been prisoner that or next morng — people were running about & in. Women were screaming & sorry.

10-17

10-18: Among all the consequences of the Rebellion, one cannot neglect the impact that it had upon the general population, many of whom were just trying to get on with their lives. Consider the story of one beleaguered tax collector caught up in a swirl of events not of his making and out of his control.

In December 1837 Leonard Misener was the tax collector of Wainfleet Township, west of Port Colborne. In addition to the local farmers not exactly welcoming his arrival just before Christmas, Misener had other problems.

The first was making his rounds. The Rebellion of 1837 made the Niagara peninsula a busy place. The newspapers were filled with articles about political agitation and pitched battles in Lower Canada and of the exchange of gunfire between rebels and Toronto militia at Montgomery's Tavern. Meanwhile, Colonel Allan MacNab's troops were riding around the countryside looking for rebels. Their leader, William Lyon Mackenzie, after fleeing from Toronto to Buffalo, made his way to Navy Island, where he proclaimed a provisional government and prepared to lead a small band of American 'Patriots' in an invasion of Upper Canada. The rebels' ship, *Caroline*, had been burnt by Upper Canadian militiamen and broke up above Niagara Falls. In the midst of all this, Misener was slogging through snowdrifts collecting taxes.

Misener's second problem was the money he collected. The Agricultural Bank of Upper Canada had printed some of the banknotes and, by the time he got them, the bank had failed. As Misener trudged towards the warmth of his kitchen, George Truscott the banker was fleeing to Europe while his partners headed for Buffalo. Attorney General Christopher Hagerman wrote his American counterparts requesting the arrest of the bank's directors, and Upper Canada went into economic paralysis. Goods, lands, and houses lost half their value. Thousands of settlers liquidated what assets they could and left for Michigan. The construction of public works was halted. The government verged on bankruptcy. And, on his spring trip into town, tax collector Leonard Misener found himself holding worthless banknotes and had to pay the taxes himself.

Next June in St Catharines, Misener stood before the imposing justices of the Niagara District Court of General Quarter Sessions of the Peace. Misener's petition blamed the delay between his collecting the notes and their submission to the treasurer on the thirty-two-mile trip required and on 'the disaffected state of that part of our country, many thinking that they would get clear of paying tax until they could pay to support a republican government.' That comment may have pleased the justices' political sensibilities. They granted Misener's petition for reimbursement, and the court clerk tossed the now-worthless bills into his files.

10-18 : Au nombre des conséquences de la rébellion, il faut signaler l'impact qu'elle a eu sur la population civile, qui, en général, ne demandait qu'à s'occuper tranquillement de ses affaires. Prenons par exemple les déboires d'un certain préposé au fisc, qui a tout à coup été happé par un tourbillon d'événements auxquels il était étranger et qui lui échappaient complètement.

En décembre 1837, Leonard Misener était percepteur d'impôt pour le canton de Wainfleet, à l'ouest de Port Colborne. À la veille de Noël, on devine que les fermiers de l'endroit ne se réjouissaient pas de le voir arriver – sans compter que Misener avait bien d'autres tracas.

Tout d'abord, il lui fallait trouver le moyen d'effectuer sa tournée, ce qui n'était pas chose simple. La rébellion de 1837 avait fait de la péninsule de Niagara une région chaotique, en plein tumulte. Dans les journaux, il n'était plus question que de l'agitation politique omniprésente, des batailles rangées qu'on se livrait dans le Bas-Canada, des échanges de coups de feu à la Montgomery's Tavern entre les rebelles et les miliciens de Toronto. Entre-temps, les troupes du colonel Allan MacNab parcouraient les campagnes, traquant les rebelles. Le chef de ces derniers, William Lyon Mackenzie, après avoir fui de Toronto à Buffalo, s'était rendu dans l'île Navy, où il avait proclamé la constitution d'un gouvernement provisoire et d'où il s'apprêtait à envahir le Haut-Canada, à la tête d'un petit groupe de « patriotes » américains. Le navire des rebelles, le *Caroline*, brûlé par des miliciens du Haut-Canada, avait coulé juste au-dessus des chutes Niagara. C'est au milieu de pareille confusion qu'on peut s'imaginer Misener, se frayant péniblement un passage entre les bancs de neige, d'un contribuable à un autre.

Un deuxième problème allait accabler Misener et tenait à la valeur du numéraire perçu. L'Agricultural Bank of Upper Canada avait bien émis des billets de banque, mais, au moment où les espèces tombaient dans la sacoche du percepteur, l'établissement était déjà en faillite. À l'heure où Misener cheminait avec peine vers la chaleur de sa cuisine, le banquier George Truscott se réfugiait en Europe, et ses associés à Buffalo. Le procureur général Christopher Hagerman avait prié son homologue américain de mettre les administrateurs de la banque sous écrou, tandis que le Haut-Canada était en état de stagnation, économiquement paralysé. Biens, terres et maisons, tout avait perdu la moitié de sa valeur. Des milliers de colons liquidaient ce qu'ils pouvaient et partaient pour le Michigan. Les travaux publics avaient été suspendus, le gouvernement était au bord de la banqueroute. Tant et si bien que, se rendant en ville le printemps venu,

l'infortuné représentant du fisc n'avait plus en sa possession qu'un monceau de coupures dépourvues de toute valeur, avec l'obligation outrageante de s'acquitter personnellement de ces mêmes impôts.

Au mois de juin suivant, Misener comparaissait à St. Catharines devant les imposants juges de la cour des sessions générales de la paix du district de Niagara. Dans sa supplique, Misener se disculpe : le laps de temps écoulé entre la perception des billets et leur remise au trésorier s'explique par le trajet de trente-deux milles qu'il a dû parcourir, mais aussi par [traduction] « l'état de dissidence de cette partie de notre pays, de nombreux administrés croyant pouvoir s'exempter de payer des taxes qu'ils préféreraient verser à un gouvernement républicain. » L'orthodoxie du commentaire devait rejoindre les opinions politiques des juges, qui ont favorablement accueilli la requête du percepteur et l'ont exonéré. Le greffier a dû se contenter de consigner aux oubliettes les comptes rendus caducs.

10-18a

10-18c

10-18b

10-18d

ROBERT BALDWIN AND RESPONSIBLE GOVERNMENT

10-19 & 10-20: Robert Baldwin (1804-58), a lawyer who lived in York, was elected to the House of Assembly in 1829 as a Reformer but defeated the following year. He re-entered political life early in 1836, but that March he and the other members of the Executive Council resigned over Lieutenant-Governor Francis Bond Head's refusal to consult with them. Baldwin took no part in the uprising that occurred in late December 1837. In 1838 he met with the governor-in-chief, Lord Durham, and two months after this meeting he presented Durham with a memorandum on the principle of responsible government. This memo certainly influenced Durham's 1838 report regarding the future government of Upper and Lower Canada that was presented to the new British monarch, Queen Victoria.

A key recommendation of Durham's report was implemented with the unification of the provinces of Upper and Lower Canada. Thus, under the Act of Union in 1840, the province of Canada was formed, with an administrative divide between Canada West (Ontario) and Canada East (Quebec). However, Lord Durham's report did not result in immediate political changes. Conflict continued in the new province over fundamental issues of ministerial responsibility and patronage.

ROBERT BALDWIN ET L'AVÈNEMENT DU GOUVERNMENT RESPONSABLE

10-19 et 10-20 : En 1829, Robert Baldwin (1804-1858), avocat à York, est élu à la Chambre d'assemblée sous l'étendard réformiste, pour être défait l'année suivante. Il revient en politique au début de 1836, mais au mois de mars, lui-même et les autres membres du conseil exécutif doivent démissionner, le lieutenant-gouverneur Francis Bond Head ayant refusé de les consulter. Baldwin ne joue aucun rôle dans le soulèvement qui a lieu à la fin de décembre 1837. En 1838, il rencontre le gouverneur en chef, Lord Durham, et, deux mois après, lui remet un mémoire sur le principe du gouvernement responsable. Ce document influe très certainement sur le rapport de 1838 relatif au futur gouvernement du Haut et du Bas-Canada que Durham présente à la reine Victoria, peu après son accession au trône.

Une recommandation clé du rapport Durham est mise en œuvre lors de l'unification des provinces du Haut et du Bas-Canada. C'est ainsi que l'Acte d'Union de 1840 institue la Province du Canada, partagée en deux entités administratives : le Canada-Ouest (l'Ontario) et le Canada-Est (le Québec). Cependant, le rapport de Lord Durham n'aboutit pas à des changements politiques immédiats. La nouvelle Province voit le conflit se prolonger, en raison des enjeux fondamentaux de la responsabilité ministérielle et du favoritisme.

10-19

10-20

UNION OF THE CANADAS AND CONFEDERATION

10-21: Despite difficulties in the new parliament, Baldwin forged an alliance with his Quebec counterpart, Louis-Hippolyte LaFontaine, and the two of them worked steadily to achieve reform. They governed as co-premiers in two ministries, in 1842-3 and 1848-51, and, particularly in the latter period, had great accomplishments to their credit. The second ministry saw the formal adoption of responsible government and two important pieces of legislation were passed, the Rebellion Losses Bill and the Amnesty Act for those who had participated in the rebellions. These successes and his strong advocacy of cooperation between English and French Canadians have secured Baldwin's place in Ontario history.

The achievement of responsible government in 1849 was followed by the breakdown of alliances and a period of political instability. Basic differences relating to language, religion, and land ownership came to the fore and made political progress difficult.

A decisive step forward occurred when the Province of Canada participated in the Quebec Conference of 1864. The aim of this conference was to further the plan for a united British North America. The other delegates at the conference included those from the Maritime provinces and two observers from Newfoundland. They worked on a detailed plan for union and their conclusions were embodied in the Quebec Resolutions. Later, these resolutions would be the foundation of the British North American Act and the Confederation of Canada.

L'UNION DES CANADAS ET LA CONFÉDÉRATION

10-21 : Malgré les embûches qui ne manquent pas au nouveau parlement, Baldwin réussit à forger une alliance avec son homologue du Québec, Louis-Hippolyte Lafontaine; tous deux vont travailler sans relâche en vue de la réforme. Ensemble, ils gouvernent dans le cadre de deux ministères de coalition, en 1842-1843 et en 1848-1851; plus particulièrement pendant la deuxième de ces périodes, des réalisations notables sont à leur actif. Le second ministère assiste à la sanction officielle d'un gouvernement responsable et à l'adoption de deux lois importantes, la loi d'indemnisation des pertes subies lors des rébellions et la loi sur l'amnistie à l'égard de ceux qui avaient participé aux rébellions. Ces réussites et son vigoureux plaidoyer en faveur de la coopération entre Canadiens anglais et français ont taillé à Baldwin une place d'honneur dans l'histoire de l'Ontario.

L'avènement du gouvernement responsable, en 1849, est suivi de l'éclatement des alliances et d'une période d'instabilité politique. Des perspectives fondamentalement différentes sur la langue, la religion et le territoire prennent le pas et entravent les progrès d'ordre politique.

Une étape décisive est franchie lorsque la Province du Canada participe à la Conférence de Québec, en 1864. Le but de cette conférence est de faire avancer le projet d'unification de l'Amérique du Nord britannique. Les autres délégués à la Conférence représentent les provinces maritimes, et deux observateurs de Terre-Neuve sont aussi présents. On y travaille à définir un plan d'union détaillé, dont les conclusions prendront la forme des Résolutions de Québec. Plus tard, ces Résolutions constitueront l'assise de l'Acte de l'Amérique du Nord britannique et de la Confédération canadienne.

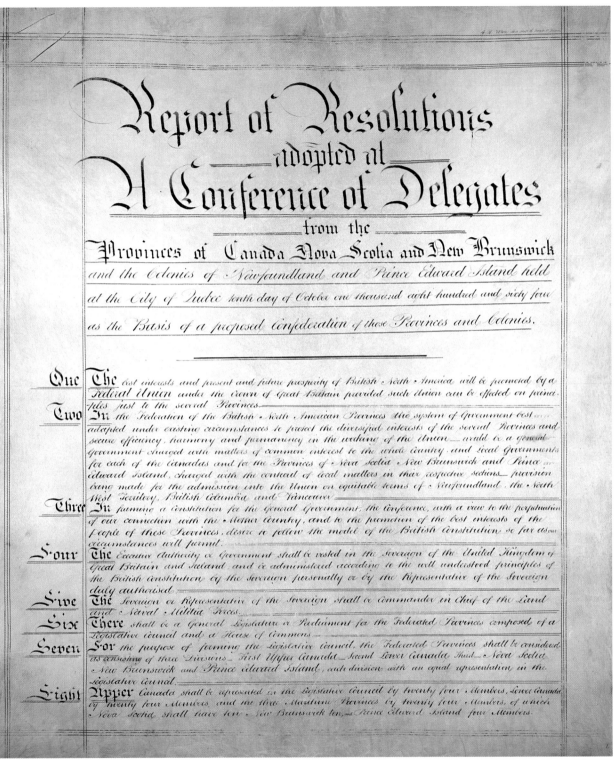

Report of Resolutions
adopted at
A Conference of Delegates
from the
Provinces of Canada Nova Scotia and New Brunswick
and the Colonies of Newfoundland and Prince Edward Island held
at the City of Quebec tenth day of October one thousand eight hundred and sixty four
as the Basis of a proposed Confederation of these Provinces and Colonies.

One — The best interests and present and future prosperity of British North America will be promoted by a Federal Union under the crown of Great Britain provided such Union can be effected on principles just to the several Provinces.

Two — In the Federation of the British North American Provinces the system of Government best adapted under existing circumstances to protect the diversified interests of the several Provinces and secure efficiency, harmony and permanency in the working of the Union — would be a general Government charged with matters of common interest to the whole country, and local Governments for each of the Canadas and for the Provinces of Nova Scotia New Brunswick and Prince Edward Island, charged with the control of local matters in their respective sections — provision being made for the admission into the Union on equitable terms of Newfoundland, the North West Territory, British Columbia and Vancouver

Three — In framing a Constitution for the General Government, the Conference, with a view to the perpetuation of our connection with the Mother Country, and to the promotion of the best interests of the people of these Provinces, desire to follow the model of the British Constitution so far as our circumstances will permit.

Four — The Executive Authority or Government shall be vested in the Sovereign of the United Kingdom of Great Britain and Ireland and be administered according to the well understood principles of the British Constitution by the Sovereign personally or by the Representative of the Sovereign duly authorised.

Five — The Sovereign or Representative of the Sovereign shall be Commander in Chief of the Land and Naval Militia Forces.

Six — There shall be a General Legislature or Parliament for the Federated Provinces composed of a Legislative Council and a House of Commons.

Seven — For the purpose of forming the Legislative Council, the Federated Provinces shall be considered as consisting of three Divisions. First Upper Canada. Second Lower Canada. Third Nova Scotia New Brunswick and Prince Edward Island, each division with an equal representation in the Legislative Council.

Eight — Upper Canada shall be represented in the Legislative Council by twenty four Members, Lower Canada by twenty four Members, and the three Maritime Provinces by twenty four Members, of which Nova Scotia shall have ten New Brunswick ten, and Prince Edward Island four Members.

10-21

10-1: Colonel John Graves Simcoe [ca. 1881], George Theodore Berthon (1806-92) (Government of Ontario Art Collection, 694156, Thomas Moore Photography, Toronto)

10-2: Simcoe sword and sabre [ca. 1800] (Simcoe Family fonds, F 47, AO 6028)

10-3: An Act to Prevent the Further Introduction of Slaves, and to Limit the Term of Contracts for Servitude with This Province, *Statutes of Upper Canada*, 33 George III, Chapter VII (1793)

10-4: Letter, Peter Russell to Capt. Elliott, Sandwich, 19 Sept. 1801 (Peter Russell fonds, F 46)

10-5: Letter, Capt. Elliott to Peter Russell, 7 October 1801 (Peter Russell fonds, F 46)

10-6: Portrait bust of Laura Secord, 1902, Mildred Peel (1856-1920) (Government of Ontario Art Collection, 619701, Thomas Moore Photography, Toronto)

10-7: Portrait bust of Tecumseh, 1896, Hamilton Plantagenet MacCarthy (1847-1939) (Government of Ontario Art Collection, 619883, Thomas Moore Photography, Toronto)

10-8: Portrait bust of Major-General Sir Isaac Brock, 1896, Hamilton Plantagenet MacCarthy (1847-1939) (Government of Ontario Art Collection, 619882, Thomas Moore Photography, Toronto)

10-9a-b: An Act to Declare Certain Persons, Therein Described, Aliens, and to Vest Their Estates in His Majesty, *Statutes of Upper Canada*, 54 George III, Chapter IX (14 March 1814)

10-10: William Lyon Mackenzie [ca. 1903], John Wycliffe Lowes Forster (1850-1938) (Government of Ontario Art Collection, 606898, Thomas Moore Photography, Toronto)

10-11: Portrait of Sir Francis Bond Head, Bart, KCH [ca. 1883], George Theodore Berthon (1806-92) (Government of Ontario Art Collection, 606899, Thomas Moore Photography, Toronto)

10-12a-b: The Rebellion Banner (front and back), 1837 (Mackenzie-Lindsey fonds, F 37, AO 4565)

10-13: Proclamation by Sir Francis Bond Head, 1837 (Mackenzie-Lindsey fonds, F 37, Poster 4, AO 4241)

10-14: Mrs F.L. Bridgman to Fanny West, 15 December 1837 (Miscellaneous Collection, F 775, 1837-10)

10-15: Marshall Bidwell to Sir Francis Bond Head, 8 December 1837 (Marshall Spring Bidwell Family fonds, F 19)

10-16: Letter [January 1850] (Mackenzie-Lindsey fonds, F 37)

10-17: *The March of the Rebels upon Toronto in December 1837* [ca. 1921], Charles William Jefferys (1869-1951) (Government of Ontario Art Collection, 621229)

10-18a-d: Exhibits in the case of Leonard Misener (Lincoln County Court of General Sessions of the Peace, RG 22-372, box 32, 'Orders - June Sessions 1838')

10-19: The Honourable Robert Baldwin [ca. 1840], after Theophile Hamel (1817-70) (Documentary Art Collection, C 281-0-0-0-144. I0003075)

10-20: Lord Durham [ca. 1800], engraver unknown (Ontario Legislative Library print collection, RG 49-33-0-0-18. I0009121)

10-21: Excerpt from the Quebec Resolutions, 1864 (Miscellaneous Collection, F 775, 1864-7, AO 5989)

10-1 : Le colonel John Graves Simcoe [vers 1881], George Theodore Berthon (1806-1892) (Collection d'œuvres d'art du gouvernement de l'Ontario, 694156, Thomas Moore Photography, Toronto)

10-2 : L'épée et le sabre de Simcoe [vers 1800] (Fonds Famille Simcoe, F 47, AO 6028)

10-3 : Loi pour empêcher l'entrée d'autres esclaves et pour limiter la durée des contrats de servitude dans la province, Lois du Haut-Canada, 33 George III, Chapitre VII (1793)

10-4 : Lettre de Peter Russell au capitaine Elliott, Sandwich, 19 sept. 1801 (Fonds Peter Russell, F 46)

10-5 : Lettre du capitaine Elliott à Peter Russell, 7 oct. 1801 (Fonds Peter Russell, F 46)

10-6 : Portrait en buste de Laura Secord, 1902, Mildred Peel (1856-1920) (Collection d'œuvres d'art du gouvernement de l'Ontario, 619701, Thomas Moore Photography, Toronto)

10-7 : Portrait en buste de Tecumseh, 1896, Hamilton Plantagenet MacCarthy (1847-1939) (Collection d'œuvres d'art du gouvernement de l'Ontario, 619883, Thomas Moore Photography, Toronto)

10-8 : Portrait en buste du major-général Sir Isaac Brock, 1896, Hamilton Plantagenet MacCarthy (1847-1939) (Collection d'œuvres d'art du gouvernement de l'Ontario, 619882, Thomas Moore Photography, Toronto)

10-9 a-b : Loi visant à déclarer étrangères certaines personnes ci-après décrites et à restituer leurs biens à Sa Majesté, Lois du Haut-Canada, 54 George III, Chapitre IX (14 mars 1814)

10-10 : William Lyon Mackenzie [vers 1903], John Wycliffe Lowes Forster (1850-1938) (Collection d'œuvres d'art du gouvernement de l'Ontario, 606898, Thomas Moore Photography, Toronto)

10-11 : Portrait de Sir Francis Bond Head, Bart, KCH [vers 1883], George Theodore Berthon (1806-1892) (Collection d'œuvres d'art du gouvernement de l'Ontario, 606899, Thomas Moore Photography, Toronto)

10-12 a-b : Bannière de la rébellion (endroit et envers), 1837 (Fonds Mackenzie-Lindsey, F 37, AO 4565)

10-13 : Proclamation de Sir Francis Bond Head, 1837 (Fonds Mackenzie-Lindsey, F 37, affiche 4, AO 4241)

10-14 : Lettre de Mme F. L. Bridgman à Fanny West, 15 décembre. 1837 (Collection mixte, F 775, 1837-10)

10-15 : Lettre de Marshall Bidwell à Sir Francis Bond Head, 8 décembre. 1837 (Fonds Famille Marshall Spring Bidwell, F 19)

10-16 : Lettre [janvier 1850] (Fonds Mackenzie-Lindsey, F 37)

10-17 : *The March of the Rebels upon Toronto in December 1837* [vers 1921], Charles William Jefferys (1869-1951) (Collection d'œuvres d'art du gouvernement de l'Ontario, 621229)

10-18a-d : Pièces soumises dans l'affaire Leonard Misener (Cour du comté de Lincoln, sessions générales de la paix, RG 22-372, boîte 32, 'Orders - June Sessions 1838')

10-19 : L'honorable Robert Baldwin [vers 1840], d'après Théophile Hamel (1817-1870) (Collection d'art documentaire, C 281-0-0-0-144. I0003075)

10-20 : Lord Durham [vers 1800], graveur inconnu (Collection de gravures de la Bibliothèque de l'Assemblée législative de l'Ontario, RG 49-33-0-0-18. I0009121)

10-21 : Extrait des Résolutions de Québec, 1864 (Collection mixte, F 775, 1864-7, AO 5989)

11

THE DEVELOPING PROVINCE

L'ESSOR DE LA PROVINCE

11-1

As a province, Ontario is rich with natural resources: there is an abundance of fine agricultural land, large stores of mineral resources, and plentiful water in the Great Lakes and in the rivers that can be used for hydro-electric power. Under the British North America Act of 1867, the Ontario government gained a greater degree of control over the development of these resources, and it quickly set about using its new powers and responsibilities to encourage the economic development of the province.

And develop Ontario certainly did. Beginning in the late nineteenth century, what was once a mainly rural, agricultural society evolved into an increasingly urbanized and industrialized one. This transformation, fuelled in large part by the province's resource-based economy, further accelerated in the twentieth century. Following the Second World War, the Ontario economy continued to grow, and society began to change along with it. Immigration from Europe, the Caribbean, and Asia, among other places, made Ontario increasingly multicultural – and culturally richer. The diverse, vibrant Ontario of the present day is rooted as much in these changing immigration patterns as in the economic changes of the second half of the twentieth century.

The Archives of Ontario has numerous records that trace the rapidly developing province that took shape from the late nineteenth century on. It also has a rich collection of records revealing a parallel phenomenon, the growth of government. As Ontario grew, particularly after the Second World War, so did the range of government activities and the size of government itself. Its expanding size and reach has affected many aspects of our daily lives – and generated records. Some of these records document important events while others are representative of the many services provided by government on a daily basis. Those records that have enduring historical value are preserved and made available by the Archives of Ontario.

This chapter provides examples of the kinds of records held by the Archives Ontario that reflect the development both of the province and of its government over the last century and a half. These records are huge in volume, diverse in type, and far-reaching in scope, relating to subjects such as immigration, war, municipal life, and royal commissions. Most are in the form of paper, but, more and more, they are also electronic.

Managing an ever growing amount of paper has problems of its own, but the challenges of dealing with computer records are not inconsiderable either. As the Archives of Ontario moves into its second century, it will continue to develop the archival infrastructure required to deal with new types of records and, more generally, to meet the demands of an increasingly technological society.

La province de l'Ontario est riche en ressources naturelles : une abondance de terres agricoles fertiles, d'immenses gisements de ressources minérales et les généreuses réserves d'eau des Grands Lacs et des rivières, qui peuvent servir à la génération d'énergie hydroélectrique. En 1867, aux termes de l'Acte de l'Amérique du Nord britannique, le gouvernement de l'Ontario acquérait une plus grande mesure d'autonomie dans le développement de ses ressources, et il est prompt à se servir de ses nouveaux pouvoirs et responsabilités pour stimuler la mise en valeur économique du territoire.

On peut certes parler de développement pour

l'Ontario d'alors. À compter de la fin du dix-neu-vième siècle, cette société, surtout rurale et agricole, devient de plus en plus industrielle et urbaine. Cette transformation, alimentée en grande partie par une économie fondée sur les ressources, s'accélère au vingtième siècle. Après la Deuxième Guerre mondiale, l'économie onta-rienne poursuit sa croissance, et la société va changer en conséquence. L'immigration, en provenance notamment de l'Europe, des Caraïbes et de l'Asie, forge un Ontario de plus en plus mul-ticulturel, toujours plus riche au plan culturel. Le dynamisme et la diversité de l'Ontario contempo-rain tiennent au moins autant à cette mutation des schèmes d'immigration qu'aux changements économiques survenus pendant la seconde moitié du vingtième siècle.

Les Archives publiques de l'Ontario possèdent d'innombrables documents qui retracent l'essor de la province, laquelle prend une forme plus définie à compter de la fin du dix-neuvième siècle. On y retrouve également une imposante collection de documents qui révèlent un phénomène con-comitant, la croissance du secteur public. Au fur et à mesure du développement de l'Ontario, en par-ticulier après la Deuxième Guerre mondiale, l'éventail des activités gouvernementales et le gou-vernement proprement dit prennent de l'ampleur. L'envergure et l'emprise grandissantes des pou-voirs publics se manifestent dans maints secteurs de notre vie quotidienne – tout en générant une traînée de documents. Certains de ces documents rappellent des événements importants, tandis que d'autres sont représentatifs de la gamme des services dispensés par l'État sur une base journa-lière. Les documents à valeur historique durable sont déposés aux Archives publiques de l'Ontario, où ils peuvent être consultés.

Ce chapitre présente donc des spécimens de divers types de documents conservés par les Archives qui reflètent le développement tant de la province que de son gouvernement depuis un siècle et demi. Ces documents, qui constituent une masse énorme, sont de natures extrêmement diverses et d'une portée remarquable, puisqu'ils se rapportent à des sujets tels que l'immigration, la guerre, la vie municipale et les commissions royales. La plupart sont sur papier, mais ils appa-raissent de plus en plus sur support électronique.

La gestion d'une quantité de papier en cons-tante prolifération comporte ses problèmes, mais les défis que pose la conservation des documents informatisés ne sont pas non plus négligeables. À l'orée d'un second siècle d'existence, les Archives publiques de l'Ontario entendent poursuivre le développement d'une infrastructure archivistique correspondant à des types nouveaux de docu-ments et, de façon plus générale, aux exigences d'une société à caractère de plus en plus tech-nologique.

11-2 to 11-4: Immigration to Upper Canada did not begin in earnest until the arrival of the Loyalists. Fleeing the American Revolution, these settlers came to a wild and difficult land where they suffered many hardships. However, they were not without assistance from the government, which offered them land grants and supplies. After the Loyalists, most of the immigrants came from Britain and Europe. They were also escaping, either from famine or war, and Upper Canada offered a promised land of opportunity. The Ontario government continued to make efforts to attract new settlers and in 1869 formed the Immigration Branch of the Department of Agriculture and Public Works. These posters from 1869 and 1878 show how free land was used as an incentive.

L'IMMIGRATION

11-2 à 11-4 : Dans le Haut-Canada, l'immigration ne commence véritablement qu'avec l'arrivée des Loyalistes. Fuyant la révolution américaine, ces colons abordaient une contrée sauvage, hérissée d'obstacles, où ils devraient affronter des épreuves sans nombre. Ils pouvaient cependant compter sur l'aide du gouvernement, qui leur offrait des concessions de terres, des fournitures et des provisions. Après la vague loyaliste, la plupart des immigrants sont venus de Grande-Bretagne et d'autres pays européens. Eux aussi fuyaient la guerre ou la famine, et le Haut-Canada leur présentait une terre promise, riche d'avenir. Le gouvernement de l'Ontario a poursuivi ses efforts pour attirer de nouveaux colons, et, en 1869, a constitué une direction de l'Immigration au ministère de l'Agriculture et des Travaux publics. Ces affiches de 1869 et 1878 montrent comment les concessions de terres – qui étaient gratuites – servaient de mesures incitatives.

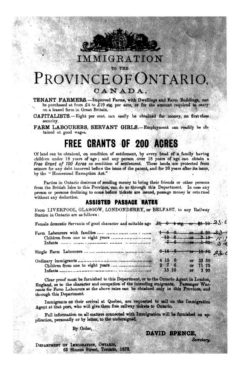

11-2

11-3

11-4

11-5 & 11-6: This 1874 letter from John Thorrington to the Immigration Department shows how farmers were eager to pay for the passage warrants for poor families in Britain. It was much to his advantage to pay for the import of two impoverished families with numerous children, on the understanding that they would work on his farm at Tiverton. Hard as this must have been for the immigrating families, they likely held on to the promise of a better life for their grandchildren, if not their children.

11-5 et 11-6 : Cette lettre de 1874, adressée par John Thorrington au ministère de l'Immigration, atteste que les fermiers sont tout à fait disposés à payer le certificat de transport de familles pauvres qui partent de Grande-Bretagne. En effet, il est extrêmement avantageux pour ce fermier d'assumer les frais de transport de deux familles indigentes, chargées d'enfants, dont les membres vont ensuite travailler pour lui, dans sa ferme de Tiverton. Ces conditions devaient être très dures pour les familles immigrantes, qui étaient par ailleurs motivées par la perspective d'une vie meilleure pour leurs petits-enfants, sinon pour leurs enfants.

11-5

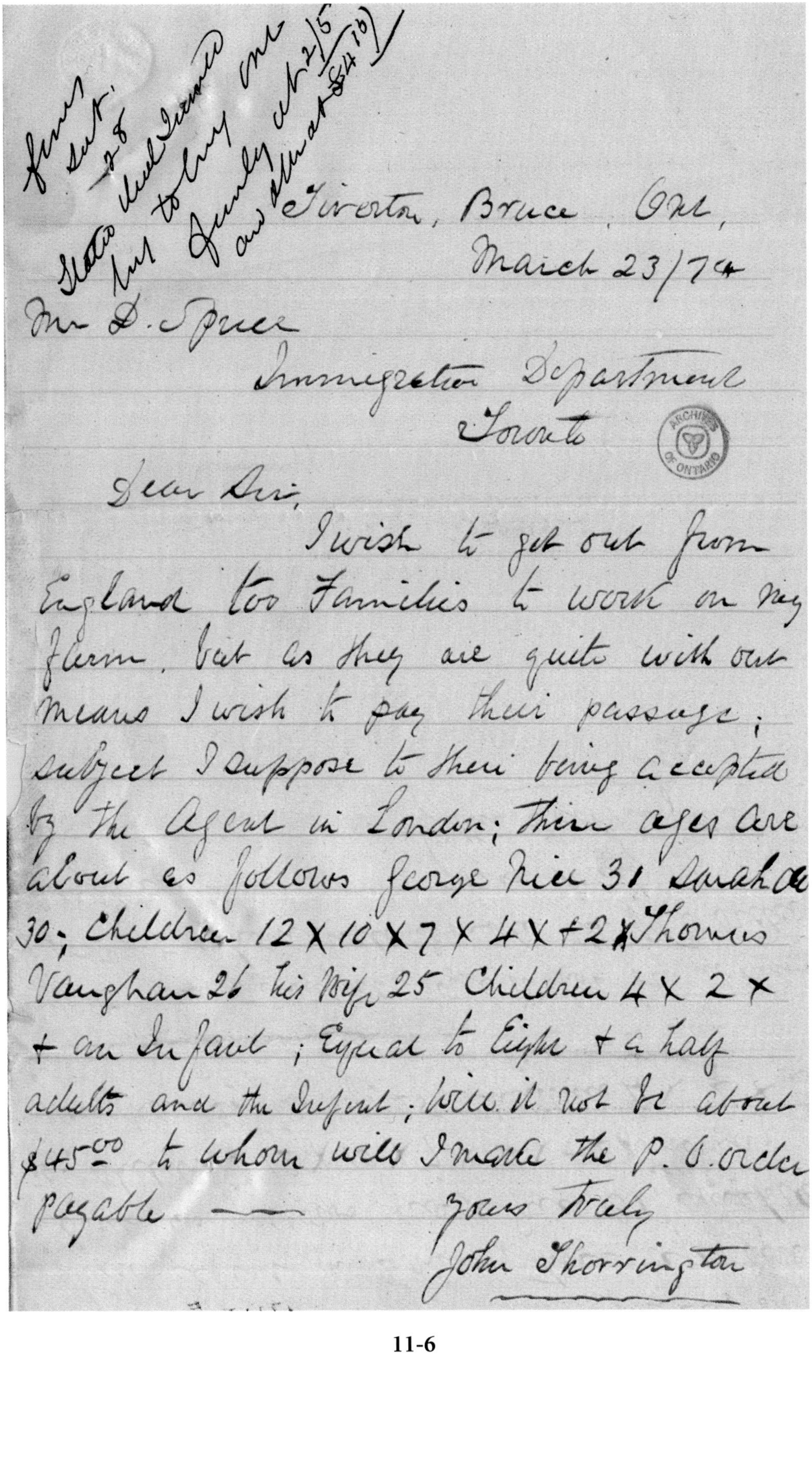

Tiverton, Bruce, Ont,
March 23/74

Mr D. Spence
Immigration Department
Toronto

Dear Sir,

I wish to get out from England too Families to work on my farm, but as they are quite with out means I wish to pay their passage; subject I suppose to their being accepted by the Agent in London; their ages are about as follows George Nice 31 Sarah do 30; Children 12 X 10 X 7 X 4 X + 2 X Thomas Vaughan 26 his Wife 25 Children 4 X 2 X + an Infant; Equal to Eight + a half adults and the Infant; will it not be about $45.00 to whom will I make the P. O. order payable ——

Yours Truly
John Thorrington

11-6

11-7 to 11-9: Further assistance for immigrants came in the form of bonus certificates, which aided in the payment of ocean passage to the New World. The newcomers found ready work on farms such as these in southwestern and northern Ontario.

11-7 à 11-9 : Le gouvernement offrait également des primes, sous forme de certificats, afin d'aider les immigrants à défrayer le coût de leur traversée vers le Nouveau Monde. Les nouveaux arrivants trouvaient du travail sur des fermes comme celles-ci, dans le sud-ouest et le nord de l'Ontario.

11-7

11-8

11-9

11-10   11-11

11-10 & 11-11: Between 1944 and 1949, approximately 81,000 people immigrated to Ontario from the British Isles. The demand for travel to Ontario far exceeded available accommodation on passenger ships, so the Ontario government assisted by sponsoring a program to transport approximately 7,000 successful applicants from the British Isles by air. The program was promoted widely through Ontario House in London, England, and was intended to attract young British workers for the agricultural, forestry, and mining sectors as well as other industries. Many immigrants, including war brides and their children, continued to travel by passenger ship.

11-10 et 11-11 : De 1944 à 1949, la province reçoit 81 000 immigrants des îles Britanniques. En matière de transport pour l'Ontario, la demande dépasse de loin le nombre des places disponibles à bord des paquebots, de sorte que le gouvernement provincial parraine un programme de transport aérien à l'intention des quelque 7 000 postulants britanniques qui répondent aux critères. Ce programme, dont l'annonce est largement diffusée par les soins de la Maison de l'Ontario à Londres, vise le recrutement de jeunes travailleurs britanniques pour les secteurs de l'agriculture, de la foresterie et des mines, aussi bien que d'autres champs d'activités. Un très grand nombre d'immigrants, dont des épouses de guerre et leurs enfants, ont continué d'arriver par bateau.

11-12

11-13

11-12 & 11-13: Immigrants now come to Ontario from all corners of the globe. Toronto is home to one of the largest Chinatown's in North America and to Caribana, the largest Carribean festival in North America.

11-12 et 11-13 : De nos jours, les immigrants arrivent en Ontario de tous les coins du globe. À Toronto, le quartier chinois compte parmi les plus considérables d'Amérique du Nord, tandis que le festival antillais Caribana est d'une envergure sans pareille sur le continent.

WORLD WAR I

11-14 to 11-16: On 4 August 1914, Britain declared war on Germany and Canada was automatically drawn into the conflict. By October, some 32,000 volunteers were sailing to England and Canada's war effort was under way. Many of these volunteers were like Charlie and Wally Gray, recent immigrants to Canada from Britain. The brothers signed up in 1915 and, before they knew it, were part of the Canadian unit fighting at Ypres. Charlie was killed by shrapnel and, in this touching letter home, his brother Wally tells his family the story.

LA PREMIÈRE GUERRE MONDIALE

11-14 à 11-16 : Le 4 août 1914, la Grande-Bretagne déclare la guerre à l'Allemagne, entraînant le Canada dans le conflit. En octobre, quelque 32 000 volontaires s'embarquent pour l'Angleterre, et l'effort de guerre canadien se met en branle. Beaucoup de ces volontaires sont dans la situation de Charlie et Wally Gray, immigrants britanniques récemment arrivés au Canada. Les deux frères s'engagent en 1915, et, du jour au lendemain, sont intégrés à l'unité canadienne envoyée sur le front d'Ypres. Charlie devait être tué par un obus, et, dans cette lettre émouvante, Wally fait le récit de l'événement à sa famille.

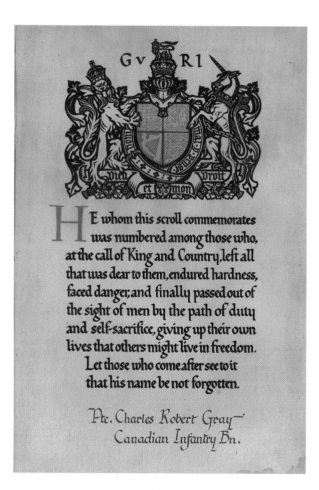

11-14

11-15

Pte W H Gray
N° 03 Ward
3 Western General Hospital
Lansdown Rd
Canton Cardiff
July 10 - 1916

Dear Mother & Father

Just a few lines hoping to find you in the best of health as I am pleased to say I am feeling much better myself. the wounded itself it quite better now but my foot is just as bad as ever but I expect to go under another operation soon as the Docter thinks there is something touching my nerves under the knee if so it will mean quite a time yet before I can get up but I am getting used to that now getting on into the six week's. Well Dear Mother & Father Beat & Annie came & saw me last week from Tuesday to Thursday so I got all the news from them, but they got there at a rottern time as there lots of wounded coming in from the big battle so that made it a bit awkward for them but it was managed alright. & I was so pleased to see them, they told me you had got the news of poor old Charlie it was nearly three week's befor I knew. they would not tell me at first but I got the news

I am going to have a good leg yet so go and try my leg will always be weak that will do my

11-16a

by a lady writing to the Record office, a & had
an idea something had happened to him by
the way the stretcher bearers spoke to me
they said he was alright they had been speaking
to him but I thought different as no sooner had
the shell exploded those who was not hit run for
safety so they never had the chance to speak to
him but I would have like to have said goodbye. but cheer
up we know he died for his King & Country. which
every man out there is prepared to do or die. It
was an aufull place where we were. It was on
the night of the 3rd & the battle was going like
fury & the Canadians were going to attack at dawn
& our Batt was going up to supports in case we
should be wanted & we were on the Ypres road
just before we got to the canal bridge a shell
came over & either killed or wounded 12 to 15 of us
you ask how much my leg is wounded well a
piece of sharpnell hit me above the knee cap &
as it went through it cut the artery so as soon
as I got to the clearing station they operated on
it & tied it together again they could not trust
me for 24 hrs as it have proved fatal to my
leg it may have had to lose it if they had but
I had got over that now so dont worry. Beat told

11-16b

me about poor old Erne Cox getting it too, I guess that will upset his people too, poor old kid will miss us now as we were always together at any time we could & Charlie Goddard who as luck happened hurt his foot one day so he had a job on the cook waggon & never had to go up with us. I guess some one will have the parcel they need it though & they are welcome to it I hope you will get all Charlie personal property from them & know they are very particular about sending it & it is collected & sealed up it front of his officer Well Dear Mother & Father I have received your letter & thanking you for the money sorry to hear you all are not feeling grand you will be like it for a time but I hope you feel better the next time I hear. You can tell Lucy that her Brother George has been in to see me he is only a short till distance about half & hrs walk he is looking fine & did not know him for a time when he walked in but after a few minutes I had a little Idea but he knew me as soon as he got a full look at my face he wishes to be remembered to all. Will old May & Herbert have soon moved & next door that good. Well Dear Mother & Father I think this is all this time so Remember me to all & with love From Your Loving Son Hoping to see you soon Wally x x x . x x x x x

11-16c

11-17 to 11-21: The war placed an extreme burden on the finances of Canada, already suffering from a poor economy. By 1915, expenditures were so great that authorities had to turn to the people of Canada to lend money to their own government. The 1915 victory bond campaign raised $400 million and was followed by a similar effort in 1917. In total, nearly two billion dollars were raised between 1917 and 1919. In order to encourage Canadians to buy the bonds, the government used all means at its disposal to whip up patriotism, including portraying the enemy in the worst possible light. These First World War posters, which depict both fresh-faced Canadian lads doing their patriotic duty and the effects of cruel enemy action, were part of the campaign to pay for the war effort.

11-17 à 11-21 : La guerre représente un fardeau financier énorme pour le pays, déjà aux prises avec une économie mal en point. En 1915, les dépenses atteignent des proportions telles que les autorités doivent se tourner vers les citoyens et leur demander de prêter à leur gouvernement. La campagne des obligations de la Victoire de 1915 réunit 400 millions de dollars, et elle est suivie d'une autre semblable en 1917. Au total, de 1917 à 1919, on a ainsi pu recueillir près de deux milliards de dollars. Pour inciter les Canadiens à se procurer des obligations, le gouvernement exploite tous les moyens concevables de faire vibrer la corde patriotique, y compris une représentation de l'ennemi sous le plus mauvais jour possible. Ces affiches de la Première Guerre font partie d'une campagne destinée au soutien de l'effort de guerre; elles dépeignent de jeunes Canadiens dans leur prime jeunesse s'acquittant de leur devoir de patriotes et les cruels effets de l'action ennemie.

11-17

11-18

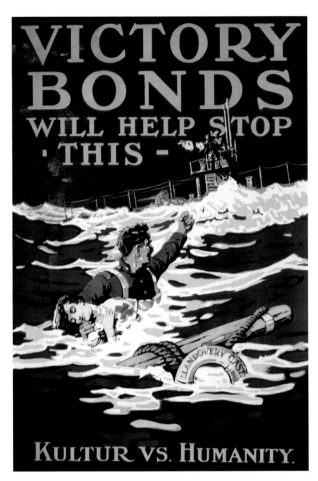

11-19

11-20

11-21

PEACE, ORDER AND GOOD GOVERNMENT

11-22 to 11-27: One of the important roles of our elected officials is to provide safeguards for society by regulating business, industry, and agriculture. An example of such safeguards is the Dairy Standards Act, which was passed to set criteria for the proper and unpolluted production of milk products. In this order-in-council from 1922, the regulations of the Dairy Standards Act are updated, primarily to include higher standards for pasteurization and testing. The desire for pure foods was and is a priority for Ontario residents and the twentieth century saw much technological and scientific progress towards that end. We now enjoy safe foods in an abundance and variety that would have seemed unimaginable one hundred years ago.

LA PAIX, L'ORDRE ET UN BON GOUVERNEMENT

11-22 à 11-27 : Un des rôles les plus importants de nos élus consiste à instaurer des mesures de protection pour la population, en réglementant le commerce, l'industrie et l'agriculture. Un exemple de ces mesures est la loi sur les normes dans l'industrie laitière, qui édictait les critères de salubrité relatifs à cette production. Dans ce décret de 1922, les règlements de ladite loi sont mis à jour, principalement pour intégrer des normes plus strictes de pasteurisation et de contrôle. La salubrité des aliments était et demeure une priorité pour les Ontariens, et le vingtième siècle a assisté à la réalisation en ce sens de nombreux progrès scientifiques et technologiques. Nous avons maintenant à notre disposition des aliments sûrs, d'une abondance et d'une variété qui aurait semblé inimaginable il y a un siècle.

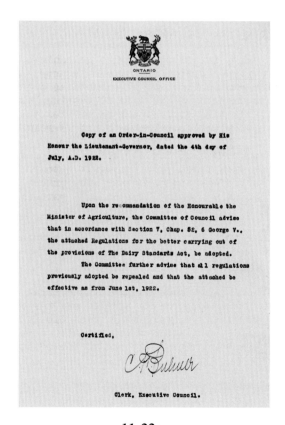

11-22a

REGULATIONS UNDER THE DAIRY STANDARDS ACT.

---

1.   "Pasteurization" under Section 6 of the Act, shall mean that the whey shall be heated to 155 degrees F. for at least 30 minutes, and other by-products shall be heated to 170 degrees F. for ten minutes.

2.   In order that pasteurization may be made effective, where the whey is returned to the farms in the milk cans, it will be necessary for each patron to remove his share of whey regularly.

3.   Each factory coming under the provisions of this Act shall provide:

   (a)   Two sets of glass bottles, each bottle to hold not less than one pint (pint milk bottles with close fitting stoppers may be used) in which to keep composite samples of milk.

   (b)   An approved preservative, such as standard corrosive sublimate tablets, or a mixture of three parts of powdered potassium bicromate with one part of corrosive sublimate, (sufficient preservative must be used to properly preserve the samples) for keeping the composite milk samples.

   (c)   Babcock sulphuric acid of a correct specific gravity (1.82 to 1.83) to be used in making the test.

   (d)   A small tank, preferably made of galvanized iron, 30" long, 12" wide, by 8" deep, inside measurements, to hold 24 pint composite sample bottles, to be used as a tempering bath for the composite samples at the time of testing, and also as a water bath, in which to place the test bottles to insure a uniform temperature when the percent of fat is read.

4.   All cheese factories desiring the services of the dairy instructors to do the milk testing once each month will be required to provide a 24 bottle steam turbine Babcock tester with the necessary Government stamped glassware, except in the case of factories having less than 24 patrons, when a hand Babcock machine may be provided.

5.   The composite sample bottles, in which the samples of milk delivered by each patron are kept, shall be plainly labelled with the name or number of the patron.

6.   Not less than one half ounce sample of the mixed milk of each delivery shall be taken for the composite sample, and the bottle containing composite sample shall be given a rotary shake each time a fresh sample is added. The composite sample bottles in which the milk samples are collected from each delivery must be kept tightly stoppered and protected from extremes of temperature.

11-22b

LIFT LOCK
BRAND
Creamery Butter

The delicate taste of this butter can be best preserved by keeping it away from vegetables or other articles likely to impart undesirable flavors.

CANADA PACKERS LIMITED
PETERBOROUGH · ▲ ONTARIO

11-23

FARM SERVICE REPORT
Proper Methods and Equipment on Farms Protect Milk and Cream Quality.

Producer_____ Address *RR 1 Ayr*

Plant *Roselawn Dairy* Address *Toronto*

REASON FOR SERVICE CALL: Sediment____; Acidity____; Flavour;

Re DB 139. Bacteria____; Milk fat test____; Other____.

with Driver Jack

	Satisfactory	
	Yes	No
MILKING COWS		
1. Clean flanks____Udders____Teats____	✓	1
MILKING BARN ✓ **or PARLOR**____		
2. No housing of poultry____swine____	✓	2
3. Bull Pens and calf pens clean____	✓	3
4. Clean floors____Gutters____	✓	4
5. Sufficient bedding in loafing barn____	✓	5
6. Walls and ceiling clean____Painted____ or white washed____ ✓	✓	6
7. Sufficient light____and ventilation____	✓	7
COW YARD		
8. Clean____Drained____Dry____	✓	8
WATER SUPPLY		
9. Sufficient____Potable____Cold____Hot____	✓	9
COOLING OF MILK OR CREAM		
*10. Adequate facilities____Proper methods____ Bulk tank____ ✓	✓	10
*11. Milk House____used only for milk, cream and utensils____	✓	11
MILK UTENSILS		
*12. Pails and strainer: Proper construction____ good repair____	✓	12
*13. Utensils clean: Pails____Strainer____other____	✓	13
14. Brush used daily for cleaning utensils____	✓	14
15. Soapless dairy cleanser used____	✓	15
16. Utensils chemically sterilized before use____	✓	16
*17. Utensils properly stored____	✓	17
*18. Single service strainer used exclusively____	✓	18
*19. Milking machine head____claw____tubes____clean____	✓	19
*20. Milk pipeline good condition____clean____	—	20
*21. Separator: location____pan____bowl, discs, spouts____ clean____	—	21

REMARKS: *Milking barn and milk House and utensils clean and tidy*

11-24

11-25

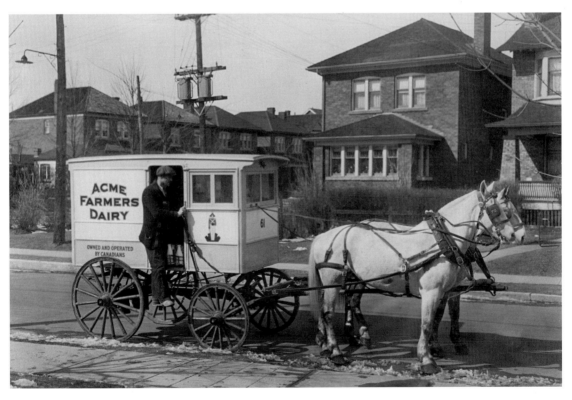

11-26

11-27

11-27: The discovery of gold and other valuable mineral resources in the Porcupine region in the early 1900s saw the rapid expansion of the mining industry. Steady employment and the promise of high wages attracted many European immigrants to the mines of northern Ontario.

11-27 : Au début des années 1900, la découverte de gisements d'or et d'autres minerais précieux dans la région de Porcupine déclenche une expansion rapide de l'industrie minière. La perspective d'emplois stables et de salaires élevés attire de nombreux immigrants européens dans les régions minières du nord de l'Ontario.

11-28

11-28: The lumber industry was the first large-scale manufacturing industry in Upper Canada. It continues to provide direct employment to many people and supports tens of thousands of indirect jobs. The economies of more than forty communities in Ontario currently rely on the forest industry.

11-28 : La première industrie manufacturière à grande échelle du Haut-Canada a été celle du bois de sciage. L'industrie continue d'ailleurs à assurer des emplois directs à une foule de travailleurs et elle crée des dizaines de milliers d'emplois indirects. L'économie de plus de quarante collectivités ontariennes repose actuellement sur l'industrie forestière.

11-29: By the early 1900s, a source for cheap and plentiful electricity was required to replace the nearly exhausted supply of wood used for fuel and expensive coal. Under the direction of Sir Adam Beck, the publicly owned Ontario Hydro Electric Power Commission built the Queenston-Chippawa Power station at Niagara Falls, capitalizing on the single largest source of hydro-electric power in Ontario. Built over a four-year period, the Powerhouse was completed in 1921 and was 181 metres in length, 41.5 metres wide, and 18 stories in height. It consisted of ten generators and cost $76 million dollars to build. In 1950, on the twenty-fifth anniversary of his death, the facility was renamed the Sir Adam Beck – Niagara Generating Station.

11-29 : Au début des années 1900, il fallait trouver une source d'électricité, durable et à bon compte, pour remplacer les combustibles dont on s'était alimenté jusque là – le charbon désormais trop coûteux et le bois dont les réserves s'épuisaient. Sous la direction de Sir Adam Beck, un organisme public, l'Ontario Hydro Electric Power Commission, aménage la centrale électrique Queenston-Chippawa à Niagara Falls, pour la mise en valeur de l'unique source importante d'énergie hydroélectrique de la province. En chantier pendant quatre ans, la centrale a été achevée en 1921. Elle avait 181 mètres de long, 41,5 mètres de large et 18 étages de haut, abritait dix générateurs, et sa construction avait coûté 76 millions de dollars. En 1950, au vingt-cinquième anniversaire de son promoteur, l'installation est rebaptisée Sir Adam Beck - Niagara Generating Station.

11-29

ONTARIO MUNICIPAL BOARD

11-30 & 11-31: The Ontario Municipal Board (OMB) is the oldest quasi-judicial body operating in Ontario today. Originally established in 1906 as the Ontario Railway and Municipal Board, it has been responsible for the review of many aspects of local government and administration. The board has considered issues ranging from the approval of electrical-rail systems to the examination of urban-redevelopment plans, from disputes over land severances to balancing development versus preservation of natural areas like the Niagara Escarpment. Its decisions have had a major impact on the lives of Ontario residents. The document presented here is the title page of the 1953 OMB decision regarding the various proposals submitted to the board for the reorganization of municipal government in the Toronto area.

In 1949, there were thirteen municipalities within the area and the provision of such services such as transit and water across municipal boundaries was inefficient. Three different applications setting out plans for amalgamation and joint-services commissions were submitted to the OMB. The board examined the submissions, held hearings on the general issues, and in 1953 issued a decision that rejected all the pending applications in favour of a scheme for limited amalgamations and the creation of a metropolitan system for the Toronto area. The provincial government supported this approach and within the year, the Metropolitan Toronto Act incorporated most of the OMB's recommendations in the structure of the new municipal body, whose first chairman was Frederick G. Gardiner.

LA COMMISSION DES AFFAIRES MUNICIPALES DE L'ONTARIO

11-30 et 11-31 : La Commission des affaires municipales de l'Ontario (CAMO), qui existe toujours, est l'organisme quasi-judiciaire le plus ancien de la province. Instituée en 1906 sous l'appellation Ontario Railway and Municipal Board, elle se penche sur de nombreux aspects de l'administration municipale. La Commission doit trancher les questions les plus diverses – depuis l'approbation de systèmes ferroviaires électriques à celle de plans de rénovation urbaine, en passant par les différends liés au démembrement des terres et au juste équilibre entre développement et préservation d'aires naturelles telles que l'escarpement du Niagara Ses décisions ont toujours un impact marqué sur la vie des Ontariens. Le document présenté ici est la page de titre de la décision rendue par la CAMO en 1953, touchant les différentes propositions qui lui avaient été soumises en vue de la réorganisation de

l'administration municipale dans la région de Toronto.

En 1949, la région comptait treize municipalités, et les limites municipales faisaient que la fourniture de services tels que le transport et l'eau était inefficiente. Après l'examen de trois projets distincts, énonçant des plans de fusion et d'une commission de services communs, et la tenue d'audiences sur des questions d'ordre général, la CAMO a, en 1953, rendu sa décision : elle rejetait toutes les propositions présentées, en faveur d'un projet visant des fusions restreintes et la mise sur pied d'un régime métropolitain pour la région de Toronto. Le gouvernement provincial a appuyé cette solution et, au cours de l'année qui a suivi, la Loi sur la municipalité de la communauté urbaine de Toronto incorporait la plupart des recommandations de la CAMO à la structure du nouvel organisme municipal, dont le premier président a été Frederick G. Gardiner.

ONTARIO

THE ONTARIO MUNICIPAL BOARD

In the Matter of Sections 20 and 22 of *"The Municipal Act,"*
(R.S.O., 1950, Chapter 243)

The Corporations of

The City of Toronto and The Town of Mimico,

Applicants

— and —

The Corporations of

The County of York,

The Towns of Leaside, New Toronto and Weston,

The Villages of Forest Hill, Long Branch and Swansea

and

The Townships of Etobicoke, York, North York,

East York and Scarborough,

Respondents

DECISIONS AND RECOMMENDATIONS
OF THE BOARD

Dated January 20, 1953

TORONTO
Printed and published by Baptist Johnston, Printer to the Queen's Most Excellent Majesty

11-30

11-31

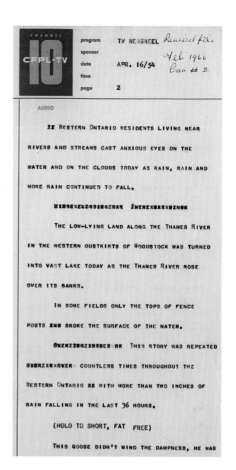

11-32a

11-32b

THE PEOPLE OF ONTARIO ARE WATCHING

11-32: Ontarians got their first taste of television by tuning in to American border stations. In 1952, however, CBC Television went on the air and in 1953 the first private television broadcasters followed. CFPL-TV hit the airwaves in London on 28 November 1953. Watching local and national television news eventually became part of daily life.

The CFPL-TV collection of televison news, comprising some 2700 reels of film, was recently donated to the Archives by CHUM. This scene shows the return of Canadian soldiers from the Korean War on 16 April 1954.

LES ONTARIENS À L'ÉCOUTE

11-32 : Les Ontariens avaient eu un avant-goût de la télévision, en syntonisant les postes américains des zones frontalières. En 1952, toutefois, Radio-Canada inaugurait son poste de télévision et, en 1953, un premier poste privé était en ondes. Le lancement des émissions de CFPL-TV a eu lieu à London, le 28 novembre 1953. L'écoute des actualités à la télévision nationale ou régionale devait s'intégrer graduellement au quotidien.

La collection CFPL-TV comprend quelque 2700 bobines de film; le réseau CHUM en a don aux Archives recemment. On voit ici des soldats canadiens à leur retour de la guerre de Corée, le 16 avril 1954.

11-33

11-33: In recognition that the Ontario public was accustomed to watching the news on television, there was a move to broadcast the debates in the Legislative Assembly. The first broadcast of live debates went out to the people of Ontario via local cable channels in October 1986. This opened up the legislature and its elected members to public scrutiny in an immediate way. It also gave the television media quick access to sound bites for the daily news. The legislature recom- mended from the start that these broadcast records be preserved in the Archives.

One of the major bills on the new Liberal govern- ment's agenda in 1986 was the Pay Equity Act (equal pay for work of equal value). Premier David Peterson, whose government introduced television into the legis- lature, is shown here in one of the skirmishes with the opposition over the bill.

11-33 : Reconnaissant que la population ontarienne a l'habitude de regarder les actualités à la télévision, on envisage de téléviser les débats de l'Assemblée législa- tive. C'est en octobre 1986 que le public ontarien a pu regarder les premières séances, transmises en direct par câblodistribution. Voilà qui soumettait de façon immé- diate l'Assemblée et ses membres élus aux regards des citoyens. Également, cette mesure donnait aux journa- listes un accès rapide aux trames sonores nécessaires à leurs reportages quotidiens. Dès le début l'Assemblée législative a recommandé le dépôt de ces enregistrements télédiffusés aux Archives.

En 1986, l'un des principaux projets de loi au programme du nouveau gouvernement libéral touchait la Loi sur l'équité salariale (salaire égal à travail de valeur égale). Le premier ministre David Peterson, dont le gouvernement a introduit la télévision à l'Assemblée législative, est représenté ici au cours d'une escar- mouche avec l'opposition à propos du projet de loi.

11-34 & 11-35: In 1958, the Ontario government acquired its first computer. In those days, computers were used primarily to do complex calculations or to produce reports. Today, the government has tens of thousands of computers and more and more government services are supported by computers. In fact, it is a goal of the Ontario government to become a world leader in delivering government services online.

In 2002, the Walkerton Commission transferred its records to the Archives. Many of these records were in electronic format and were critical to the commission's ability to determine what caused hundreds of people in the Walkerton area to become ill, and some to die, in May and June 2000. Preserving records such as these poses new challenges for the Archives.

A paper record has a tangible existence, but the same is not true of electronic records. These require computer hardware and software to be legible and such products quickly become obsolete. Moreover, archivists cannot easily tell if electronic records are complete, unmodified, or even sometimes if they are still where they are supposed to be. All these are difficult problems that go far beyond the range of issues suggested by the selection of electronic-storage media pictured here.

However, electronic technology also offers exciting new possibilities for the Archives to serve researchers. Descriptions of most of our holdings are already available on our website and digital images of some of the Archives records are accessible worldwide to anyone with a computer.

À L'HEURE CONTEMPORAINE – L'AVÈNEMENT DES DOCUMENTS ÉLECTRONIQUES

11-34 et 11-35 : En 1958, le gouvernement de l'Ontario faisait l'acquisition de son premier ordinateur. À l'époque, on recourait à l'ordinateur principalement pour des calculs complexes et la production de rapports. Aujourd'hui, le gouvernement possède des dizaines de milliers d'ordinateurs, et un nombre croissant de services gouvernementaux sont informatisés. En fait, le gouvernement de l'Ontario s'est donné pour objectif de devenir un chef de file mondial en matière de prestation en direct des services gouvernementaux.

En 2002, la Commission d'enquête sur Walkerton a versé ses dossiers aux Archives. Un bon nombre de ces documents sont sur support électronique et ont été d'une importance critique lorsque la Commission a cherché à déterminer les causes et circonstances de l'épidémie (en mai et juin 2000, plusieurs centaines de personnes de la région de Walkerton étaient tombées malades et certaines étaient décédées). Or, la conservation de ce genre de documents pose de nouveaux défis aux Archives.

Contrairement aux documents sur papier, les documents électroniques n'ont pas d'existence tangible. Pour en prendre connaissance, il faut passer par un matériel et des logiciels informatiques, qui sont vite dépassés. De plus, il est difficile pour les archivistes de savoir si les documents électroniques sont complets, s'ils ont ou non subi des modifications, ou même parfois s'ils se trouvent bien à l'endroit désigné. Ce sont là des questions épineuses, qui dépassent de loin l'éventail des problèmes associés aux quelques médias de stockage électronique qu'on voit ici.

Par ailleurs, la technologie électronique fait entrevoir des ressources inédites et exaltantes, qui permettront aux Archives d'améliorer leurs services aux chercheurs. Notre site Web affiche déjà la description de la plupart de nos fonds et collections, et des images numériques d'une partie de nos documents sont accessibles à quiconque dispose d'un ordinateur, où que ce soit dans le monde.

11-34

11-35

11-1: Opening ceremonies of the Ontario legislature [Queen's Park], 1949 (Premier Leslie M. Frost Photographs, RG 3-38-2-5. I0005365)

11-2: *Dominion of Canada! Emigration to the Province of Ontario*, Department of Immigration, October 1869 (Archives of Ontario Poster Collection, C 233-1-5-1938. AO 5454)

11-3: *Immigration to the Province of Ontario*, Canada, Department of Immigration, 1878 (Archives of Ontario Poster Collection, C 233-1-5-2073. AO 413)

11-4: *The Pioneer* [ca. 1921], Charles William Jefferys (1869-1951) (Government of Ontario Art Collection, 623327, Thomas Moore Photography, Toronto)

11-5 & 11-6: Letter, 23 March 1874 (Department of Immigration numbered correspondence files, RG 11-8-1, item 2444)

11-7: Emigrant six-dollar bonus certificate, 1875 (Department of Immigration, RG 11-24, item 435)

11-8 & 11-9: Top: Seed onions, Essex County [ca. 1910] (Department of Agriculture, Agricultural Representative Photograph Albums, RG 16-274, Album 3, 60). Bottom: Loading Hay, Thunder Bay District, 1928 (Department of Agriculture, Agricultural Representative Photograph Albums, RG 16-274, Album 3, 53)

11-10: Potential immigrants viewing poster for air immigration program, 1947 (Ontario House photographs, RG 9-7-4-1-1. I0002993)

11-11: British immigrants coming to Canada aboard the S.S. *Aquitania* (Ontario House photographs, RG 9-7-4-4-40. I0003008)

11-12: Caribana Parade, ca. 1985 (Ministry of Transportation photographs, RG 14-151). I0013626)

11-13: Chinatown, Dundas Street, Toronto, ca. 1985 (Ministry of Transportation photographs, RG 14-151-3-157. I0013627)

11-14 to 11-16: Photo: Charles R. Gray (standing) and Walter Gray (seated) [ca. 1915] (Gray Family fonds, F 4383-1-0-0-30). Scroll: Scroll presented posthumously to Charlie by the Canadian government commemorating his service to his country during the First World War (Gray Family fonds, F 4383-0-0-32). Letter: Letter from Wally to his parents, 10 July 1916 (Gray Family fonds, F 4383-1-0-0-27).

11-17 to 11-21: *Back Him Up! Buy Victory Bonds*, 1917-18 (Archives of Ontario Poster Collection, C 233-2-1-11. AO 2341). *For Industrial Expansion, Buy Victory Bonds*, 1917-18 (Archives of Ontario Poster Collection, C 233-2-1-14. AO 5633). *Victory Bonds Will Help Stop This - Kultur vs. Humanity*, 1917-18 (Archives of Ontario Poster Collection, C 233-2-1-19. AO 5639). *Bring Him Home with the Victory Loan*, 1917-18 (Archives of Ontario Poster Collection, C 233-2-1-299. AO 5656). *Pave the Way to Victory. Buy Victory Bonds*, 1917-18 (Archives of Ontario Poster Collection, C 233-2-1-26. AO 5656).

11-22a-b: Cover and first page of Ontario order-in-council 121/120, 4 July 1922 (Executive Council - Orders-in-Council, RG 75-57)

11-23: Colour advertisement for Lift Lock Brand Creamery Butter [ca. 1935] (Department of Agriculture, Chief Creamery Instructor correspondence files, RG 16-177, box 1)

11-24: Form used by an inspector to record conditions at milk producing farms, 25 November 1960 (Department of Education, Milk Industry Board of Ontario correspondence and subject files, RG 16-167, box 1)

11-25: Milk cans being sterilized [ca. 1920] (Department of Education, Photographs of the Audio-Visual Education Branch, RG 2-71-SHC-31. I0004247)

11-26: Acme Farmers Dairy milk-delivery wagons [ca. 1920] (Department of Education, photographs of the Audio-Visual Education Branch, RG 2-71-SHC-66)

11-27: Finnish miners in South Porcupine, 1928 (Multicultural Historical Society of Ontario fonds, F 1405-15-109)

11-28: Hardwood Logs at McCalls Mills, Norfolk, ca. 1910 (Ministry of Natural Resources, RG 1-448-1-351)

11-29: Construction of the Sir Adam Beck - Niagara Generating Station, 1921 (John Boyd fonds, C 7-3, 17076)

11-30: Title page of Ontario Municipal Board file C2978, 20 January 1953 (Ontario Municipal Board, Record on hearings into Toronto amalgamation, Application and Appeal files, RG 37-6-2)

11-31: Photo of F.G. Gardiner [ca. 1953] (Archives of Ontario Library, Pamphlet 1953, no. 3)

11-32 a&b: Segment of news film and script, 16 April 1954 (CFPL fonds, F 4396-1-1-14)

11-33: Image from a videotape of the Ontario legislature, 28 October 1986 (Televised Proceedings of the Ontario Legislature, RG 49-9, AO 6031 and 6032)

11-34: Cover of the *Report of the Walkerton Inquiry* (Royal Commissions, RG 18-210)

11-35: Selection of obsolete electronic-storage media in the collection of the Archives of Ontario (AO 6030)

LÉGENDES

11-1 : Cérémonies d'ouverture de la législature de l'Ontario [Queen's Park], 1949 (Photographies du premier ministre Leslie M. Frost, RG 3-38-2-5. I0005365)

11-2 : *Dominion of Canada! Emigration to the Province of Ontario*, Ministère de l'Immigration, octobre 1869 (Collection d'affiches des Archives publiques de l'Ontario, C 233-1-5-1938. AO 5454)

11-3 : *Immigration to the Province of Ontario*, Canada, Ministère de l'Immigration, 1878 (Collection d'affiches des Archives publiques de l'Ontario, C 233-1-5-2073. AO 413)

11-4 : *The Pioneer* [vers 1921], Charles William Jefferys (1869-1951) (Collection d'œuvres d'art du gouvernement de l'Ontario, 623327, Thomas Moore Photography, Toronto)

11-5 et 11-6 : Lettre, 23 mars 1874 (Dossiers de correspondance numérotés du ministère de l'Immigration, RG 11-8-1, article 2444)

11-7 : Certificat de la prime à l'émigrant de six dollars, 1875 (Ministère de l'Immigration, RG 11-24, pièce 435)

11-8 et 11-9 : En haut: Oignons à semis, comté d'Essex [vers 1910] (Albums de photos de représentants agricoles, ministère de l'Agriculture, RG 16-274, album 3, 60).En bas: Transport du foin, district de Thunder Bay, 1928 (Albums de photos de représentants agricoles, ministère de l'Agriculture, RG 16-274, album 3, 53)

11-10 : Immigrants éventuels devant une affiche du programme d'immigration par voie aérienne, 1947 (Photographies de la Maison de l'Ontario) (RG 9-7-4-1-1. I0002993)

11-11 : Immigrants britanniques en route pour le Canada, à bord du S.S. *Aquitania* (Photographies de la Maison de l'Ontario) (RG 9-7-4-4-40. I0003008)

11-12 : Défilé du festival Caribana, vers 1985 (Photographies du Ministère des Transports, RG 14-151, I0013626)

11-13 : Le quartier chinois, rue Dundas, à Toronto, vers 1985 (Photographies du Ministère des Transports, RG 14-151-3-157, I0013267)

11-14 à 11-16 : Photo: Charles R. Gray (debout) et Walter Gray (assis) [vers 1915] (Fonds Famille Gray, F 4383-1-0-0-30). Parchemin: document présenté à titre posthume à Charlie par le gouvernement canadien, en mémoire des services rendus à son pays pendant la Première Guerre mondiale (Fonds Famille Gray, F 4383-0-0-32). Lettre: lettre de Wally à ses parents, 10 juillet 1916 (Fonds Famille Gray, F 4383-1-0-0-27).

11-17 à 11-21 : *Back Him Up! Buy Victory Bonds*, 1917-1918 (Collection d'affiches des Archives publiques de l'Ontario, C 233-2-1-11. AO 2341). *For Industrial Expansion, Buy Victory Bonds*, 1917-1918 (Collection d'affiches des Archives publiques de l'Ontario, C 233-2-1-14. AO 5633). *Victory Bonds Will Help Stop This - Kultur vs. Humanity*, 1917-18 (Collection d'affiches des Archives publiques de l'Ontario, C 233-2-1-19. AO 5639). *Pave the Way to Victory. Buy Victory Bonds*, 1917-1918 (Collection d'affiches des Archives publiques de l'Ontario, C 233-2-1-26. AO 5656). *Bring Him Home with the Victory Loan*, 1917-1918 (Collection d'affiches des Archives publiques de l'Ontario, C 233-2-1-299. AO 5656)

11-22a-b : Couverture et première page du décret 121/120 de l'Ontario, 4 juillet 1922 (Conseil exécutif - décrets, RG 75-57)

11-23 : Annonce en couleurs du beurre de fabrique de marque Lift Lock [vers 1935] (Ministère de l'Agriculture, dossiers de correspondance de l'instructeur-chef du secteur laitier, RG 16-177, boite 1)

11-24 : Formule de rapport des inspecteurs de la production laitière dans les fermes, 25 nov. 1960 (Ministère de l'Éducation, dossiers de correspondance et autres de la commission de l'industrie laitière de l'Ontario, RG 16-167, boîte 1)

11-25 : Stérilisation de bidons à lait [vers 1920] (Ministère de l'Éducation, photographies de la Direction des moyens audiovisuels, RG 2-71-SHC-31. I0004247)

11-26 : Voiture de la laiterie Acme Farmers qui fait sa tournée de livraison [vers 1920] (Ministère de l'Éducation, photographies de la Direction des moyens audiovisuels, RG 2-71-SHC-66)

11-27 : Mineurs finnois à South Porcupine, 1928 (Fonds Multicultural Historical Society of Ontario, F 1405-15-109)

11-28 : Grumes de bois dur à la scierie McCalls de Norfolk, vers 1910 (Ministère des Richesses naturelles, RG 1-448-1-351)

11-29 : Construction de la centrale électrique Sir Adam Beck-Niagara, 1921 (Fonds John Boyd, C 7-3, 17076)

11-30 : Page de titre du dossier C2978 de la Commission des affaires municipales de l'Ontario, 20 janv. 1953 (document sur les audiences relatives aux fusions à Toronto, dossiers des requêtes et appels, RG 37-6-2)

11-31 : Photo de F. G. Gardiner [vers 1953] (Bibliothèque des Archives publiques de l'Ontario, brochure 1953, no 3)

11-32 a et b : Segment d'un film d'actualités et texte correspondant, 16 avril 1954 (Fonds CFPL, F 4396-1-1-14)

11-33 : Image d'une vidéo tournée à l'Assemblée législative de l'Ontario, 28 octobre 1986 (Débats télévisés de l'Assemblée législative de l'Ontario, RG 49-9, AO 6031 et 6032)

11-34 : Couverture du *Rapport de la Commission d'enquête sur Walkerton* (Commissions, RG 18-210)

11-35 : Choix de médias de stockage électronique périmés de la collection des Archives publiques de l'Ontario (AO 6030)